NICHOLAS MANSERGH ON IRELAND

Volume 2

THE GOVERNMENT OF
NORTHERN IRELAND

THE GOVERNMENT OF NORTHERN IRELAND

A Study in Devolution

NICHOLAS MANSERGH

Routledge
Taylor & Francis Group

LONDON AND NEW YORK

First published in 1936 by George Allen & Unwin Ltd.

This edition first published in 2023
by Routledge
4 Park Square, Milton Park, Abingdon, Oxon OX14 4RN

and by Routledge
605 Third Avenue, New York, NY 10158

Routledge is an imprint of the Taylor & Francis Group, an informa business

British Library Cataloguing in Publication Data
A catalogue record for this book is available from the British Library

ISBN: 978-1-032-35650-1 (Set)
ISBN: 978-1-032-35249-7 (Volume 2) (hbk)
ISBN: 978-1-032-35252-7 (Volume 2) (pbk)
ISBN: 978-1-003-32606-9 (Volume 2) (ebk)

DOI: 10.4324/9781003326069

Publisher's Note
The publisher has gone to great lengths to ensure the quality of this reprint but points out that some imperfections in the original copies may be apparent.

Disclaimer
The publisher has made every effort to trace copyright holders and would welcome correspondence from those they have been unable to trace.

PARLIAMENTARY AND ADMINISTRATIVE BUILDING, STORMONT

Stewart Bale, Liverpool

THE GOVERNMENT OF NORTHERN IRELAND

A STUDY IN
DEVOLUTION

by

Nicholas Mansergh
M.A., B.Litt., D. Phil.

LONDON
GEORGE ALLEN & UNWIN LTD
MUSEUM STREET

FIRST PUBLISHED IN 1936

TO

MY MOTHER

PRINTED IN GREAT BRITAIN BY
UNWIN BROTHERS LTD., WOKING

PREFACE

THAT challenge to democracy, which the post-war generation in Europe viewed with an indifference born of disillusion, has in many countries dethroned those ideals of political liberty once held to be the only foundation of civilized society. It is difficult to find occasion for rejoicing in the fact that a large part of the people of Europe prefer despotic to free government. But regrets, however sincere, for a decline in the prestige of popular self-government are unavailing as a reply to the clamorous pretensions of the totalitarian State. For the survival of representative government must depend upon statesmanship; and under such a form of government the only basis of statesmanship is that public opinion should be statesmanlike. It is because of the failure of public opinion in certain nations to fulfil its responsibility that the challenge to democracy has not been successfully withstood. This failure may be due in part to war-neurosis, and in part to the growing complexity of the problems raised by social and economic organization in the modern state. But whatever the cause the consequence is plain for all to see. A critical examination of the varied developments of representative self-government in recent years assumes a new significance because of this crisis in the history of democracy. It is the purpose of this book to analyse the system of government established in Northern Ireland after the War. Though distinctive in character, this settlement of the Ulster Question typifies in many respects the normal response of democracy to a problem of this kind. Moreover, it reveals in a somewhat accentuated form deficiencies peculiar to democratic statesmanship.

The Irish Question confronted British democracy with a problem in politics susceptible of no democratic solution in keeping with its traditional conception of the fundamental unity of the British Isles. For this reason the political sovereignty of the people of the twenty-six counties now comprising the

Irish Free State was acknowledged only after an appeal to arms. But the British Government, though unable to retain the allegiance of the large majority of the Irish people, conceded the substance of the Unionist demand in North-East Ulster. As a result the settlement reached involved the partition of Ireland. The aim of this book is to examine the foundations and to analyse the operation of subordinate self-government in Northern Ireland.

Under the Government of Ireland Act, 1920, the six north-eastern counties of Ulster were granted a restricted measure of self-government, whilst remaining an integral part of the United Kingdom. This decentralization of government—in itself a constitutional reform of no little significance—has been admired as an example of that flexibility of outlook and of that spirit of compromise so proper a characteristic of democratic government. More than fifteen years' experience of self-government in Belfast enables one to decide how far such admiration is warranted.

A critical analysis of self-government in Northern Ireland involves consideration of two outstanding questions. How far has the settlement of 1920 proved a just and reasonable settlement of the Ulster Question? And how far is Devolution a desirable reform in a large democratic state? With regard to the former it is well to observe that the settlement of 1920—though it has proved more durable than was anticipated in some quarters—does not bear the imprint of finality. Consequently no little interest attaches to the direction of contemporary political thought in Northern Ireland. In respect of the latter, the grant of self-government to Northern Ireland originated the only practical trial of Devolution that has been witnessed in the British Isles. The problem was thereby transferred from the sphere of abstract speculation to that of experience. It is clear that Devolution must be judged on its merits as a constitutional reform quite independently of its value as a solution of the Ulster Question. It has, after all, been advocated on many occasions as a reform applicable to all the component parts of the British Isles. In addition a scheme suggesting a substantial Devolution of function from an all-Ireland Parliament to Northern Ireland does appear to offer the only means whereby the ideal of a united Ireland might be translated into a practical proposal likely, in a not too distant future, to appeal to political sentiment both in the North and in the South.

.   .   .   .   .

In writing an analysis of contemporary government, it is essential to ask many questions of those who control or influence, or are affected by, the functioning of that government. I would like to take this opportunity of thanking all those in Northern Ireland, members of the Government and of the Opposition, civil servants and private citizens, who with patience and unfailing courtesy answered my rather numerous questions I have to thank Mr. Frank Hardie for much valuable criticism, and my brother, Mr. C. O. Mansergh, for revising the proofs. Especially am I indebted to Mr. R. B. McCallum, Fellow of Pembroke College, Oxford, who read through the MS. of this book and made most helpful suggestions.

Needless to say, neither he nor anyone other than myself is responsible for any statement appearing in this book.

GREMANE HOUSE
TIPPERARY
September 1936

CONTENTS

PART I
The Demand for Devolution

PART II
The Ulster Question

PART IV

The Merits and Defects of Devolution in the Light of Experience in Northern Ireland

CHAPTER I

THE PRINCIPLES OF DEVOLUTION

THERE are but few observers of present-day political tendencies who have failed to comment upon the diminishing popularity of democratic self-government. Upon the fact they are agreed; as to its explanation they hold widely divergent views. Between the extreme individualist, regarding every accession of function to the State as a milestone on the road to political perdition, and the socialist, maintaining that by State control alone may the apotheosis of democratic government be attained, there lie many parties and persons each with its distinctive solution. This is not surprising; for in the last analysis it is evident that no final critérion, by which our democratic system may be judged, is available to this generation. For we, at least, must weigh alternatives and base our decisions upon calculation rather than absolute knowledge. The panaceas put forward to remedy the decline in prestige of representative government must be judged by a generation which does not possess material essential for forming a judgment. A leap in the dark is not a matter of policy; it is a necessity. Popular interest is concentrated upon proposals involving the most spectacular leap. Consequently it is possible that the scientific constitutionalist—the Maitland—of the future will detect weaknesses in the machinery of government which to-day pass unobserved. Three centuries ago John Selden wrote: "In troubled Water you can scarce see your face, or see it very little till the Water be quiet and stand still. So in troubled times you can see little Truth; when times are quiet and settled then Truth appears." And so we are tempted to write to-day. The dramatization of political issues relegates questions of the most profound—but not sensational —significance to the backwaters of Parliamentary Committees and academic research. And though, notoriously, still waters run deep, it is not a little aggravating that deep waters should run so consistently still. Yet such is the fate which has overtaken the problem of Devolution in the British Isles.

It is of first importance to inquire what precise meaning is to be attached to the word "Devolution." The answer is comparatively simple so long as one confines oneself to the fact, and disregards the problem which it raises. For the term itself is applied to a delegation of powers by a superior to an inferior authority. The clearest example in the British Isles of Devolution in a political sense is provided by the government set up in Northern Ireland as a result of the Government of Ireland Act, 1920. In terms of political sovereignty, Northern Ireland is not a sovereign State. It is, and remains, part and parcel of the United Kingdom, not merely in matters of external, but also of internal, policy. In the important field of Finance the Parliament at Stormont wields a control that is of very secondary importance. Hence it follows that no scheme of Devolution is likely to satisfy a demand for self-government prompted by national sentiment. The essential weakness of the later Home Rule Bills was that they attempted to solve a problem in political sovereignty by a proposal for better government. They provide an object lesson in confused political thinking.

Thus when we ask the larger question; what is the problem of Devolution? we must beware of supposing that it is a means of satisfying nationalist claims. It is not. It suggests only a means whereby better government may be secured within a single State. Its value disappears once the unity of the State is questioned. Since the intention of any scheme of Devolution is to establish an improved system of government, it follows that, broadly speaking, the interests most closely affected are, on the one hand the Central Government devolving certain powers, and on the other the area or authority upon which such powers are conferred. If any scheme of Devolution is to be given trial it should be quite clearly shown that it will prove favourable to the efficiency and well-being of both the interested parties.

The issues thus stated have provided the motive for the various proposals for Devolution in the British Isles which have been put forward in this century. The dual source of their inspiration may be subjected to a brief examination. First, from the point of view of the locality, a demand for Devolution is occasioned by a belief, either that the administration of local services is not related, to a sufficient extent, to local needs, or that the interests of the locality are continuously and of a set purpose placed second to the interests of the larger political and administrative unit of which it forms a part. However obscured by extraneous, and frequently totally irrelevant issues, the latter usually provides the basis of a local demand for Devolution. The justice of the claim depends rather upon an examination of particular conditions in industry, agriculture and local services than upon a general and rigid political principle. It is from this aspect that a consideration of the Scottish claims for Home Rule is required. The practical experiment carried out in Northern Ireland is not so valuable an illustration as might at first sight be expected, both because of the frozen conditions of its political life and because that particular form of government was not desired by the people of Ulster. As Sir James Craig[1] in a characteristic letter remarked, "as a final settlement and supreme sacrifice in the interest of a peace the Act of 1920 was accepted by Northern Ireland." But from another aspect the experience gained from the Ulster experiment is invaluable. A period of close on fifteen years of local self-government at Belfast has added very considerably to our knowledge, both theoretical and practical, of the issues involved in any grant of Devolution. It has illumined many of the problems discussed so fully, yet so inadequately, in the debates on Home Rule Bills and at the Conference on Devolution. We shall learn from this practical experiment how far it is desirable for the administration to be recruited and controlled by the local authority; we shall

[1] Letter from Sir J. Craig to the Prime Minister, November 11, 1921, Cmd. 1561.

discover to what extent it is necessary that the Central Government should delegate the power to impose direct and indirect taxation; we shall be able to examine the vexed question of double representation. For a discussion upon all these issues —administrative, financial, political—the government of Northern Ireland gives us a wealth of material which provides a very substantial basis upon which to frame a judgment upon the merits of Devolution in modern government.

In addition, apart from questions of policy and administration, the psychological factor is a force with which we must reckon. Here the normal reaction to a grant of self-government is in direct ratio to the extent of the powers conferred. The wider the authority of the local legislature the more likely is it to secure whole-hearted support. And without the full co-operation of the citizens most closely concerned no scheme of Devolution can function successfully. This dependence of the Government upon the people is increased by the recent extensions of the field of legislation and State control. For, whatever may be the ultimate outcome of the political movement of our time, it is apparent that in all economic systems planning and conscious direction are taking the place of the confusion of the free market. Advocates of economic planning in Great Britain, as Mr. Harold MacMillan is careful to emphasize,[1] intend that such planning should "preserve those liberties to which we have become so accustomed as hardly to remember their value" and not to pave the way for the foundation of a Corporate State. If one allows that the organizational structure indicated by the internal aspect of the Agricultural Marketing schemes [2] is in full accord with the true tradition of British development, then it is evident that any scheme of Devolution must aim at stimulating popular interest in the localities in the work of administration. Some years ago Mr. and Mrs. Webb wrote: "It is abundantly clear

---

[1] *Reconstruction*, pp. 126–7.
[2] E.g. in the Milk Marketing Scheme where the second and external part of Mr. Elliot's proposals are hardly apparent.

that what is wrong with the world to-day is not too much Democracy, but too little, not too many thoroughly democratic institutions, but too few."[1] Accepting for the moment a democratic interpretation of recent tendencies in English government, it will be seen that the number of democratic institutions may be increased by associating the producer and the distributor more closely with the administration of the industry with which he is directly concerned. This tendency, if it has been correctly interpreted, enlarges the scope and significance of a devolution of administrative power, very considerably beyond that envisaged by the framers of the 1920 Report. What was then a tendency is now a fact. Modern administration cannot be explained as the execution of duties already defined, but is in itself a creative act. This at once extends the field of governmental function to be devolved and enlarges the responsibility of the local authority. Moreover, as the working of the Milk and Pig Marketing Boards has shown, it strengthens the demand for Devolution by demonstrating that local knowledge and local experience are peculiarly necessary if such an integration of production is to be successfully administered.

The enlargement of the field of governmental function brings us back to the all-important issue of financial control. In the report of 1920 the Conference recommended certain minor powers of taxation should be devolved to meet the expenditure of the transferred services. The amount (at existing rates of taxation) which such taxes would yield was infinitesimal when contrasted with estimated expenditure. In the case of Scotland it amounted to between one and two million pounds. The balance was to be met by the transfer of the net yield of so many pence in the pound income tax as was necessary. At the outset such a proposal is open to attack from every quarter. It will give either too much or too little. It will either encourage extravagant expenditure or it will give excessive control to the Central Government. In either event the benefits of Devolution are destroyed, for the people have not those

[1] *A Socialist Commonwealth for Great Britain*, p. 89.

powers without which self-government is but an empty formula. Later we shall consider whether the case for a local budget, framed according to local taxable capacity, has been proved by the experience of Northern Ireland, or whether an inter-dependent co-operation with the central authority is necessary to preserve financial stability.

To turn now from a consideration of the interests of the localities in securing Devolution to that of the Central Government, we find that the most important evidence was collected and analysed by the Conference assembled in 1920. That Conference, it should be noted, approached the issue only from the one standpoint—namely, that of the Central Government. The creation of the Conference was proposed in a Resolution of the House of Commons[1] which stated:

"That with a view to enabling the Imperial Parliament to devote more attention to the general interests of the United Kingdom, and, in collaboration with the other Governments of the Empire, to matters of common Imperial concern, this House is of the opinion that the time has come for the creation of Subordinate Legislatures within the United Kingdom and to this end the Government, without prejudice to any proposals it may have to make with regard to Ireland, should forthwith appoint a Parliamentary body to consider and report:

"(1) Upon a measure of Federal Devolution . . ." Hence the Conference had a limited objective. The purpose of their appointment was *not* to secure a pronouncement for or against the principle of Devolution, but only to consider, if Devolution is accepted, what is the most practical way of putting it into operation.[2] Moreover, the intention of such a scheme of Devolution was solely to relieve the congestion of business in the Imperial Parliament. Owing to these somewhat limited aims the Conference produced a Report which does not carry conviction. To this we shall return. Here it is to be noted that the negative approach—that is an approach dictated by supposed ills in the central machinery of govern-

---

[1] June 4, 1919.   [2] Report, p. 3.

ment—is unlikely to produce valuable results. For it neglects
the most vital element involved—the reaction of the inhabitants
in the areas concerned to a devolution of function. It is their
co-operation, their enthusiasm, which will decide the fate of
any such experiment. It is for this reason that Devolution
to a Parliamentary Committee composed of members for the
area concerned has few attractions. The Scottish Standing
Committee to-day has not the confidence of the Scottish
people. Its meetings pass unnoticed, its decisions carry little
weight. And the same criticism would apply to Speaker
Lowther's scheme put forward in the 1920 Conference. It
rested upon a similar basis, and though more comprehensive
is open to similar objections.

The weaknesses of the Committee System suggest the
alternative of the Local Legislature. This system of government is in practice in many countries. In a federal system
it is customary (though not invariable) that political sovereignty
should lie with the component States. Or alternatively powers
are devolved upon the Central Government. A tendency towards
centralization, inevitable in a large State, has often meant,
as in the United States of America to-day, that while the
States may be *de jure* sovereign the Central Government is
the *de facto* sovereign. It is in times of emergency that
such a turn-over of political power becomes apparent. In
the British Isles Devolution would involve, in contrast
to the more normal process, a delegation of power by
the central to the local authority. The Conference of 1920
concluded that the areas must be the national areas of Wales,
Scotland, and England. With their conclusion it is scarcely
possible to disagree. But it gives rise to the further question
—What rôle is to be played by national sentiment in the con-
struction and the operation of local institutions? The statement
of the Scottish Nationalist demands makes the question per-
tinent. Any answer must at best be provisional. But it would
appear on the one hand that national sentiment would provide
that enthusiasm and motive power without which Devolution

would prove unworkable; on the other, should national feeling
be aroused not for good, but for national, government then
the day for Devolution has passed and that of national and
independent institutions has dawned. In theory, therefore,
it may appear that the basis upon which Devolution rests is
narrow; that it is no more than an isthmus dividing the tide
of centralized bureaucracy from the rising tide of nationalism;
and that as such it is at best a temporary expedient designed
to facilitate the transition to the federal State. The theoretic
appearance is, however, deceptive in that Devolution is
designed, whilst retaining the unity of the State, to solve
the problems raised by excessive centralization and at the
same time to remove those evils which may give rise to a
nationalist movement. But it must be emphasized that Devolution accompanied by numerous reservations and carefully
planned restrictions is unlikely to commend itself to national
areas. In addition it must be clear to electors, who in the
event of the creation of local legislatures would have double
duties to perform, that their votes would return members
competent to decide matters of first importance. Again exten-
sive powers alone are likely to draw to the local legislatures
men of talent and ability. It is instructive to observe that
even moderate Scottish Nationalists consider the powers
exercised by the Parliament of Northern Ireland as too
restricted to be acceptable to Scottish opinion.

The proposals for some form of Devolution which have been
elaborated from time to time have received but scanty attention.
This is partly because such schemes, as for example that
promulgated by the Conference of 1920, are in themselves
unconvincing; but more largely because it is widely felt that
an experiment of this kind runs directly counter to the political
movements of our time. It is held that in an age which has
seen in almost every nation a rapid concentration of political
power, it is paradoxical to put forward schemes involving no
insignificant measure of decentralization. In contemporary
Europe we are witnessing the heyday of the corporate

State, and it is certain that its creed will be closely studied in Great Britain. But its implications conflict with the underlying assumptions which prompt any scheme of Devolution. For a delegation of function depends essentially upon a democratic basis of government. Its strength is derived from local patriotism; its *raison d'être* is government from below. The demand for its creation is equivalent to the claim that government from above—that the authoritarian State—does not supply any final solution. And even when formal Democracy is retained as the system of government, it tends with the passage of time to create a governmental machine which becomes less and less in contact with the needs of areas distant from the capital. It is not so much a centralization of government that is the issue as a concentration of administrative power. The latter tendency is emphasized—as it is to-day—by a complex programme of reconstruction of reform in political and economic affairs. Moreover, a large democratic State is open to peculiar difficulties. To the Greeks it would have been a contradiction in terms, and later democratic thinkers—as Rousseau—have seen clearly the difficulties it must overcome. For in the democratic State, as Mr. Lionel Curtis[1] points out, "the task of making decisions is thrown as completely as possible on the citizens themselves. And those decisions reduced to law are the final authority in the State, an authority as binding on the citizens as the edicts of a Persian king on his subjects. But the laws are not unchangeable like those of the Medes and Persians. They are subject to revision in the light of experience; but the duty of reading the experience and making the change rests on the citizens themselves. Their faculty for doing these things is developed by exercise." In a city State these duties were by no means light; they are far more onerous in the nation State of to-day. And the larger the State, the more complex the problems to be decided by the citizens. Consequently there is a growth of apathy and indifference to political issues among the people. It is the

[1] *Civitas Dei*, p. 71.

purpose of Devolution to check this tendency by creating institutions deciding the affairs of localities whose interests are more readily understood by their inhabitants. It is its aim to associate the people more closely in the work of government by enabling them to secure a rapid and obvious decision upon matters of local importance. For if the Greeks were right in supposing that the State exists for the sake of goodness—that the highest form of character and intelligence can emerge only in a Society which demands of its members that they should exert their faculties in the public as well as in their private interest—then Devolution may be justified in principle by the claim that in clarifying the issues it renders this truth more evident to the citizen of the modern State. To quote Mr. Curtis[1] again, "it is the wise democrat who is ready to risk immediate order to a certain degree in order to cultivate in a larger number of citizens that loyalty and knowledge of public affairs upon which in the long run the structure of the State can alone rest in security."

[1] *Civitas Dei*, p. 72.

PART I

THE DEMAND FOR DEVOLUTION

"But it is not only the hypertrophy of business in the House of Commons and Cabinet that we have to complain of. The heterogeneity of the functions inconsiderately heaped upon the political institutions is itself a factor not only in the bewilderment of legislator, but also in the growing inefficiency of the institutions themselves."

A Constitution for the Socialist Commonwealth of Great Britain. SIDNEY AND BEATRICE WEBB.

"Sooner or later, this must end in a despotism or a republic. Perhaps both. The Orangemen are the true link between English Government and the Irish, and yet that link *must* be broken."

BULWER LYTTON in a letter to Disraeli from Ireland, 1834.

CHAPTER II

THE INFLUENCE OF POLITICAL THEORY

THE gradual evolution of British government is held to represent its most valuable quality. Its essence lies, not in the precision of constitutional formulae, but in the readiness of its response to changing conditions. A distinguished line of critics has endorsed the opinion of Walter Bagehot that:[1]

"We have made, or rather stumbled on, a constitution which—though full of every species of incidental defect, though of the worst *workmanship* in all out-of-the-way matters of any constitution in the world—yet has two capital merits: it contains a simple efficient part which on occasion, and when wanted, *can* work more simply and easily, and better, than any instrument of government that has yet been tried; and it contains likewise historical, complex, august, theatrical parts . . . which guide by an insensible but omnipotent influence the associations of its subjects."

The complacency of this analysis serves to indicate both the strength and weakness of English constitutional development. On the one hand the Constitution allows of easy amendment in detail, it is flexible and elastic; on the other its very structure debars a drastic change in principle. In both respects it is an accurate reflection of the predominant school of English political thought. In no country is the dependence of the Present upon the Past more openly championed as the rock upon which all political institutions must be built. Thus in 1770 Burke writes: "A restoration of the right of free election is a preliminary indispensable to every other reformation."[2] And half a century later Lord John Russell introduced the Great Reform Bill in the same conservative spirit. They were determined, he said, that the House of Commons "should not be

---

[1] *The English Constitution*, p. 10.
[2] *Thoughts on Present Discontents*, p. 69.

the representatives of a small or of a particular interest; but
form a body . . . representing the people, springing from the
people and sympathizing with the people." Such an innovation
quite certainly meant a very considerable break with the tradition
of aristocratic government by which England had been ruled
since the Glorious Revolution. But Lord John found its justification in the fact that it would revive popular rights as they
existed under the Lancastrian experiment.

SURVIVAL OF TRADITIONAL FORMS OF GOVERNMENT

This extreme appreciation of the value of tradition explains
how a remarkable change in the equilibrium of government
may take place almost unobserved. For that elasticity of constitutional form which this attitude creates involves as a corollary
a time-lag, frequently of considerable duration, between an
actual achievement in parliamentary government and its
expression in legal form. This transitional period is the chrysalis
of many of the conventions of the Constitution. By means of
it each need is enabled to call forth its own particular and
practical remedy. This very considerable advantage is none the
less entirely at a discount when a wide issue of political principle
is at stake. For the English form of evolutionary progress
in politics depends, in the last analysis, upon the reduction
of a political principle to a political detail.

The failure of the constitution to register institutional
changes at the moment of transition involves a certain mental
confusion. For the private citizen is uncertain of whether
or no any such alteration has occurred. And so the Truth
being obscure the majority, like Pilate of old, "stay not for
an answer." But among those who remained at the close of the
last century was Professor Gneist, who observed[1] that it was
"not by the forms of Parliamentary rule but by personal
activity in the daily work of the State" that "the greatness of
England had been created, as was once that of Republican

[1] *History of the English Parliament*, p. 415.

Rome." It was the decline of "personal activity" that filled this great conservative constitutionalist with apprehension. He knew that the stability of English society depended upon the existence of a democratic will, not merely indicated, but also executed, by the whole body of citizens. Today we know his fears were well-founded. Government from below tends to be eliminated by government from above. This predominance at the centre rests upon two foundations: (*a*) increase and consequent concentration of function and (*b*) elimination of competing authorities. Both these developments merit a brief examination.

EXTENSION OF THE FIELD OF GOVERNMENT

It is far from our purpose to embark on a discussion as to the original aims of parliamentary government. It is sufficient to suggest the manner in which the conception of its functions had changed in the course of history in order to show that its constitutional formation bears a somewhat tenuous relation to its present-day duties. No doubt the cleavage between original purpose and contemporary function is most marked in the "theatrical elements" of the Constitution. But such aspects of traditional influence upon the form of government are irrelevant to this inquiry. For it is our purpose to explain how it was that a machinery of government established to deal with a political problem of well-defined dimensions, came without fundamental alteration to deal with a political and administrative and economic problem of the greatest complexity.

The increase of the functions of government in recent years is a matter of everyday comment. Its principal features are summed up in the Macmillan Report:

"The most distinctive indication of the change of outlook of the government of this country in recent years has been its growing preoccupation, irrespective of party, with the management of the life of the people. A study of the Statute Book will show how profoundly the conception of the function of government has altered. Parliament finds itself increasingly engaged in legislation which has for its conscious aim the regulation of the day-to-day affairs of the community and now intervenes in matters formerly thought to be quite outside its scope."[1]

The extract not only summarizes a recent development in government, but also directs our attention to the contrast with the duties of Parliament in the last century—the epoch, be it remembered, which marked the peak point of parliamentary prestige. The most significant cause of the change in outlook towards political control has been the decline of *laissez-faire* thought.

THE INFLUENCE OF THE PHILOSOPHIC RADICALS

The growth of Philosophic Radicalism was peculiarly the product of contemporary political and social developments. Without the interplay of French thought its outlook would, as M. Halèvy has so convincingly shown,[2] have been more restricted; but for the problems raised by the Industrial Revolution its influence might well have been confined to an intellectual côterie. But the eventful combination of circumstance produced a political creed of enduring significance, from which the origins of the modern problem of Devolution are derived.

It was the intention of the Utilitarians that the State should exercise only negative functions. It was to safeguard economic conditions. It was not to control them. Legislation was to be directed to the reform of abuses; to the destruction of the older forms of interference. It was not within its sphere to construct a new social or economic order. The same principle that guided legislation was also displayed in administration. The negation of action was an end in itself. Administration was the passive execution of functions ordained by the legislature. It was not in itself creative. This attitude was prompted by governing principle of utility. "By the principle of utility,"

---

[1] *Report of Committee on Finance and Industry*, 1931, pp. 44-5.
[2] Cf. *Growth of Philosophic Radicalism.*

wrote Bentham,[1] "is meant that principle which approves or disapproves of every action whatsoever, according to the tendency which it appears to have to augment or diminish the happiness of the party whose interest is in question: or what is the same thing in other words, to promote or oppose that happiness. I say of every action whatsoever; and therefore not only of every action of a private individual, but of every measure of government." This test of a "felicific calculus" would not in itself demand a policy of *laissez-faire*. But when there is added to it a belief in the "natural identity of interests," then the case against control from above is complete. For actuated by motives of enlightened self-interest the individual is likely to prove a better judge of his own happiness than any corporate institution.

THE UTILITARIANS AND BURKE

The attitude of the Utilitarians towards political science was critical. Where John Stuart Mill deplored the lack of invention displayed by its theorists[2] many of the earlier Utilitarians had been sceptical as to its existence. While it is possible to proceed scientifically as regards economic and financial legislation, Adam Smith held that it was impossible to effect a compromise between "the science of the legislator, whose deliberations ought to be governed by general principles which are always the same," and "the skill of that insidious and crafty animal, vulgarly called a statesman or politician, whose counsels are directed by the momentary fluctuations of affairs."[3] And, as M. Halèvy points out, in matters of constitutional law, Bentham himself was also a sceptic.[4] This political scepticism provided a direct deterrent to all who placed their faith in the corporate State, or those who favoured a planned political and economic system. Moreover, the Philosophic Radicals disliked the existence of any parties or institutions within

[1] *Introduction to the Principles of Morals and Legislation*, edited Bowring, vol. i, p. 1.　　[2] *Representative Government*, chapter iv.
[3] *Wealth of Nations*, Book IV, chapter ii.　　[4] Op. cit., p. 142.

the State. This is an antipathy common to doctrinaires of all creeds. As M. Halèvy has said, "There is nothing more unintelligible to the man who devotes his whole life to proving that a certain political conception is true, and therefore should be realized, than the doctrine which says that it is good that there should subsist, as permanent institutions, differences of opinion and doctrine."[1] The general application of this statement is realized when one remembers that both Hobbes and Rousseau—the former in the interests of an irresponsible despot, the latter in the interest of the sovereign people—denied the right of association within the State.[2] This advocacy of the *tabula rasa* within the State paves the way for despotism.

In England the Philosophic Radicals were opposed by Burke, and the great influence of his thought prevented more than a partial adoption of the programme. Burke gloried in the existence of political parties. "Certain it is," he writes, "the best patriots in the greatest Commonwealths, have always commended and promoted such connexions."[3] This same divergence in outlook is illustrated also in the conflict between Burke on the one hand and Paine, Mackintosh and Godwin on the other as to the respective merits of complex and simple laws. The doctrinaire democrats held that simplicity in legislation was of supreme importance; Burke that simple laws were suited to despotic States; that we must rather aim at uniting "into a consistent whole the various anomalies and contending principles that are found in the mind and affairs of men. From hence arises not an excellence in simplicity but one far superior, an excellence in composition."[4] The development of this controversy is of first importance to our subject. For the champion of Devolution must necessarily be opposed to the "simplicity" of legislation inspired by centralized government without regard to variations in local needs.

[1] Op. cit., p. 146.
[2] Cf. *Leviathan*, chapter xviii, and *Contrat Social*.
[3] *Thoughts on Present Discontents*, p. 79.
[4] *Reflections on the French Revolution: Works*, vol. v, p. 304.

THE REFORM BILLS

The historical events, under whose aegis Philosophic Radicalism attained the zenith of its influence, played no insignificant rôle in determining the attitude of its disciples towards political affairs. The first third of the nineteenth century coincided with the long era of Tory supremacy. The Philosophic Radicals might endeavour to make use of that government, but they had no respect for their governors. If the government acted, it would almost inevitably act unwisely. In these circumstances the doctrine of *laissez-faire* had distinct, if ephemeral, merits. By means of it an intellectual protest against the anachronisms of Tory government was elevated to the status of an immutable dogma. From this aspect the strength of the protest was relative to the weakness of the Old Tory Régime, and so long as the graver abuses of that system of government remained, *laissez-faire* was assured of a wide intellectual support. But, with the passage of the Great Reform Bill, changes in its application as the principle of all legislation become inevitable. Political power was transferred to the middle classes who provided the backbone of this school of thought. And consequently one of the causes of a mistrust of all creative legislation was destroyed. At the same time, as Bertrand Russell[1] remarks:

"Although the principle of free competition was increasingly limited in practice—by Factory Acts, Trade Unions, protective tariffs and trusts—it remained an ideal to which business men appealed whenever there was any proposal to interfere with their activities." In addition the middle classes in Great Britain having acquired political power in 1832 were divided by the conflict between humanitarian sentiment and the orthodox principles of utilitarian legislation. This struggle is well-known from the writings of Dickens. For in all Dickens's work there is, as Mr. Young[2] suggests, a confusion of mind which reflects

---

[1] *Freedom and Organization*, p. 166 (George Allen & Unwin Ltd.).
[2] *Early Victorian England*, 1830–65, vol. ii, p. 456.

"the perplexity of his time, equally ready to denounce on the grounds of humanity all who left things alone; and on the grounds of liberty all who tried to make them better." As we now know the heyday of utilitarian and *laissez-faire* supremacy was brief; so brief indeed that its most distinguished disciple— J. S. Mill—learned before the end of his life that he had been "sucked in a creed outworn."[1]

The general conclusion to be drawn from the passage of the Reform Bills is that a more representative House of Commons, commanding a wider confidence, automatically draws to itself an ever-increasing burden of function. This rather evident consequence appears to have escaped the attention of contemporaries. Its effect was emphasized by the progress of the Utilitarians towards a *tabula rasa*. The removal of restraints and a rationalization of the powers of certain independent authorities within the State renders practicable those "simple" laws which Montesquieu held to be the essence of despotism. The Education Act of 1870 provides the accepted turning-point in the development of State control. Thenceforward the increase of government activity has proved continuous, supported as it was by the growth or rather the revival of a State philosophy. The immediate consequence of this outlook was the widening of the scope of legislation. This extension of the duties of the State has proceeded so rapidly during the last half-century that now it has invaded that stronghold of individualism—Agriculture. These new functions of government constitute one cause of the demand for Devolution— namely the inability of the machinery of government to perform, with adequate efficiency, all its new duties.

STATE CONTROL AND ITS CONSEQUENCES

In writing of the increase of the functions of government it is necessary to make certain reservations, principally with regard to the output of legislation. Since the middle years of

[1] Cf. J. S. Mill, *Autobiography*.

the nineteenth century there has, in fact, been no increase in
the number of statutes passed by Parliament. On the contrary,
such change as there has been has tended toward a lessening
of the numerical output. The actual figures are of sufficient
importance to be quoted.

Year	Public General Acts passed.	Year	Public General Acts passed
1866	122	1920	82
1867	146	1921	67
1869	117	1923	42
1871	117	1924	41
1873	91	1925	91
1875	96	1926	63
1904	36	1928	45
1905	20	1929	39
1911	58	1931	52
		1934	58

At first sight this decline appears very remarkable.[1] But we
must remind ourselves that these figures are thoroughly
misleading if they suggest that parliamentary legislation is
more confined in scope. In fact, the mere number of statutes
is no criterion of their importance. An act involving legislation
on some major question of principle is quantitatively, though
most certainly not qualitatively, the equivalent of an act
adjusting some minor detail.

The enlargement of parliamentary duties is more decisively
shown in the development of the administrative machine
necessitated by the new principles of State control introduced
by legislation. In fact, English administration was not planned;
it grew. A century ago there was hardly anything which a
Frenchman or a German would recognize as administration.[2]
In 1830 National Expenditure amounted to £50,000,000, of
which the debt absorbed £29,000,000, defence £15,000,000,

---

[1] Cf. C. K. Allen, *Bureaucracy Triumphant*, pp. 145-46.
[2] Cf. G. M. Young, op. cit., vol. ii, pp. 445-47.

leaving but £6,000,000 for collection for the Crown and the whole civil administration. This extraordinarily modest figure is not much enlarged till after the Crimean War. But by 1860 the cost of defence had reached £26,000,000, and a balance of £15,000,000 remained for civil purposes. The later growth of State activity is illustrated by the rapid expansion of the amount required for administrative purposes. Here we give certain figures from the Exchequer returns in various years which show the extent of the change.

Year	Total Expenditure	Expenditure on Civil Services
	£	£
1880–81	80,939,000	23,594,000
1890–91	87,733,000	27,141,000
1902–03	205,236,000	47,767,000
1913–14	197,493,000	83,656,000
1925–26	826,000,000	312,959,000
1929–30	748,712,000	368,095,000
1934–35	688,879,000	345,640,000

The growth in the cost of administration indicated by these figures reflects accurately the rapid extension of State control. In addition they suggest the nature of the new burdens which Parliament has assumed. Moreover, with certain not very significant exceptions, the new administrative services have been created by legislation. The general consequence has been a tendency towards centralization in order to secure uniformity. Every extension of administration has fortified the State.

The inability of the legislature to deal with the increase in its duties is illustrated by two tendencies of recent growth. On the one hand we have an output of delegated legislation whose volume is at least as great as that of ordinary legislation.[1] The practice of legislating by "skeleton acts" is due to the insufficiency of the time of the House of Commons. This is even more decisively illustrated by the second of the two tendencies to which we have referred—namely, the reform

[1] Cf. *Report of Committee on Ministers' Powers*, 1932. Cmd. 4060.

of Parliamentary Procedure. The intention of the successive reforms has been evident. It is their purpose to concentrate control of the parliamentary time-table in the hands of the Cabinet. The House of Commons, it was hoped, would become (in Redlich's words) "an organ of the State with the capacity and duty of providing for the speedy and well-timed dispatch of certain State business."[1] That hope has been only partially realized. Limitations on debate by means of the closure and the guillotine, the standing committees, the control of the executive over time, have not provided a satisfactory solution of the over-work of the House of Commons. Is it possible then that devolution of functions may prove a practical means of relieving the central legislature of excessive business?

THE OUTCOME OF THE INDUSTRIAL REVOLUTION

In the abstract field of political speculation area is a matter of comparative insignificance. But in the affairs of practical government it is of first importance. For long it was held that a large State was incompatible with democratic government. Rousseau, and the thinkers who followed him, maintained that despotism was an almost inevitable consequence of far-flung territories. The history of the United States of America has shown this belief to be ill-founded. There is in it, however, a certain residue of truth, for in large States the security of democratic government is less. The self-government of the Dominions and of Ireland has removed from central control the greater part of the former British Empire. On the other hand, internally we notice the absorption, since 1701, of Scotland under direct government from London. Between 1800 and 1921 Ireland was governed in the same manner. It is evident, however, that actual area did not play a decisive rôle in creating the excessive burdens of the Central Government.

Of far greater significance is the Industrial Revolution. Without the political issues raised by the coming of the Machine,

[1] Redlich, *Procedure of the House of Commons*, vol. iii, p. 22.

a demand for Devolution based on administrative grounds could never have arisen. The Industrial Revolution creates a gulf by which the governmental problems of the eighteenth century are irrevocably separated from ours. After all, *laissez-faire* as a political and economic dogma derived its motive force from the needs of the new manufacturing classes, as later the extension of production tending to monopoly weakened the arguments for its acceptance. Again, the inadequacy of *laissez-faire* as a solution of the new problems thus raised was revealed by the progress of material prosperity due to this Revolution, and to the uneven distribution of wealth which resulted from it. The Factory Acts, the Education Acts, the Poor Laws, Trades Union legislation, even the Reform Bills are all the direct consequences of the Industrial Revolution. It is not a mere increase in area with which the Government was called to deal but an increase both in population and productive capacity such as had hitherto been unknown. Is it surprising that political practice failed to keep pace with such rapid economic development? For Society does not change its institutions as the need arises. There is a period of incubation before the remedy is applied. A prolonged interval on a vital issue is the great danger to Democracy.[1] Like the Prince in the poem, the remedy may come

> Too late for love, too late for joy,
> Too late, too late.

TRADITION OF CENTRALIZATION IN ENGLAND

It is well to remember that there has been in England a tradition of centralization older than any actual political theory of centralization. This significant fact was rightly emphasized by Professor Maitland. "The State that Englishmen knew," he wrote, "was a singularly unicellular State, and at a critical time they were not too well equipped with tried and traditional thoughts which would meet the case of

[1] Cf. Trotsky, *History of the Russian Revolution*.

Ireland or of some communities, commonwealths, or corporations in America which seemed to have wills—and scarcely fictitious wills—of their own and which became States and United States. The modern and multicellular British State—often and perhaps harmlessly called an Empire—may prosper without a theory but does not suggest . . . a theory that is simple enough, and insular enough, and yet withal imperially Roman enough, to deny an essentially state-like character to those 'self-governing colonies,' communities, commonwealths, which are knit and welded into a larger sovereign whole."[1] Though a considerable time has elapsed since Professor Maitland wrote, the truth of his statement will lie plainly revealed when we examine the influence of the Irish Question. Meanwhile, it must be remembered that Bentham, in attempting to solve anew the problem of the relation between central and local government, decided that the central Parliament and its organ, the Ministry, must always preserve a supervisory control over local administration. Here as Redlich emphasizes "he formulates . . . the principle that there is no province or function of public administration in which a central government in its administrative as well as in its legislative capacity is not entitled to interfere.[2] Bentham's theoretic conception bore fruit in practice, for the principle of central authority was first embodied in Poor Law organization and later was extended over the whole field of internal administration.[3]

THE CASE FOR CONSTITUTIONAL REFORM

The classical definition of "Democracy" as the "government of all" amounts from one aspect to a "negation" of all government. This was seen clearly by Bentham who remarked that it was that "sort of government and no other which one can conceive to obtain, where there is no government at all."[4]

[1] From his introduction to Gierke, *Political Theories of the Middle Ages.* [2] Redlich, *Local Government in England*, vol. i, p. 95.
[3] Cf. ibid., vol. i, p. 133.
[4] *Fragment on Government*, Bowring, vol. i, p. 276.

This interpretation achieved a certain air of reality from the creed of the Utilitarians. "The principle of the natural identity of interests where applied to the problem of politics," writes M. Halèvy,[1] "seems logically to lead to the anarchistic thesis." With the philosophic implications of this tendency we are not concerned. Its practical consequences, however, provide the clue to the later administrative demand for Devolution. With that courageous rationalism which is characteristic of the Utilitarian school the anachronisms of the preceding era were removed from the nineteenth-century political structure. In that respect England is much in their debt. But a failure to construct where they had destroyed revealed the incompleteness of the *tabula rasa* which they had laboured to achieve. In the results of their action is to be found the chrysalis of the problem of Devolution. For when constructive political organization became inevitable it was carried through by the Central Government. In an age which found its political inspiration in the State philosophy of T. H. Green and later in Fabian Socialism, the magnitude of the problem tested to the uttermost political conventions and institutions planned to meet the needs of another epoch. Under this test, the flexibility of English institutions has not proved adequate. Centralization of government, concentration of function, have thrown excessive duties upon the legislature. Remedies in detail have been attempted but the major problem remains. How is the efficiency of government, impaired by increasing complexity of its functions, to be restored? The issue lies deep. For a conglomeration of affairs at the centre involves an inflexibility of administration—due largely to ignorance—in the localities. This is coupled with a time-lag between the appearance of a need and the legislative response to it. An analysis of government in Northern Ireland should enable us to judge whether Devolution—the natural remedy for centralization—does offer a reasonable and practical solution.

[1] Op. cit., p. 130.

CHAPTER III

THE INFLUENCE OF THE IRISH QUESTION

WHEN we turn from that field of abstract speculation in which we have discovered the chrysalis of Devolution to the first legislative proposals which came before the Houses of Parliament we are faced with a remarkable contrast. For whatever may be the influence of political theory upon political practice —and the Philosophic Radicals showed that it is by no means inconsiderable—it is certain that only the insistent claims of the Irish Question brought forward the first tentative suggestions. "To analyse the Irish trouble into racial, religious and agrarian is impossible, because in Irish history these three are one, and when England had conceded Catholic Emancipation against her own Protestants, and agrarian reforms against the Irish landlords and both in vain, the logic of history left her no alternative but to concede all the rest, never quite understanding what it was the Irish wanted nor why they wanted it."[1] Because of this failure in political comprehension our history of Devolution opens with the first of the Home Rule Bills in 1886.

THE FIRST HOME RULE BILL

The Act for the Union of Great Britain and Ireland joined the two, hitherto separate, kingdoms into one as from January 1, 1801; and provided for the representation of this United Kingdom in a single Parliament.[2] The history of Ireland in the nineteenth century is the history of an ever-increasing dissatisfaction with this new political organization. Experience of close political union accentuated the demand for complete political separation. But in the middle years of the nineteenth century a triumph for the political ideals of Fenianism was

[1] G. M. Young, *Early Victorian England*, vol. ii, p. 451.
[2] 39 & 40 Geo. III. c. 67.

still far distant. Hence attention was directed toward an attempt to find a compromise between the aspirations of Irish nationalism and the Imperialist conception of the essential unity of the British Isles. The result was the policy first known as the "New Departure" and later as Home Rule.

Here we are concerned neither with the antecedents nor the direct consequences of the Home Rule Bills except in so far as they indicate, on the one hand, the prevalent attitude towards devolved powers and, on the other, the political issues which led ultimately to the Government of Ireland Act of 1920. Throughout it must, however, be remembered that the Home Rule Bills were introduced to solve a problem in politics; that is, a problem which permits only of a political solution. The point is worth making if only because of the prevalent pseudo-Marxist tendency to reduce every question to an economic basis.

The Bill which Gladstone introduced in the Spring of 1886[1] provided that:

(i) An Irish Parliament, consisting of two Chambers, should be established at Dublin with authority over the Irish Executive; control over most local taxation and ultimately over the police.

(ii) No Irish members or Irish Representative Peers should sit at Westminster.

(iii) The Imperial Parliament should deal with questions affecting the Crown, Army, Navy, Colonies, Foreign Policy, Customs and Excise.

(iv) That Ireland should contribute one-fifteenth to Imperial charges.

(v) The Protestant religion should be safeguarded in Ireland.

The Home Rule Bill was followed by an Irish Land Purchase Bill[2] which Mr. Gladstone regarded as integral part of his scheme for the pacification of Ireland. The Bill contemplated the issue of fifty millions of 3 per cent stock for the purpose of buying up the estates of landlords willing to sell their lands at a

---

[1] Bill 181, introduced April 8th.   [2] Introduced April 16th.

cost of from twenty to twenty-five years purchase on the net value of the judicial rent. Rents would be collected by a British Receiver-General and the interest on the loan was to be a first charge on Irish Revenue. This Land Bill is important because its unpopularity reacted unfavourably upon the prospects of the Home Rule Bill. The landlords, whom it was meant to help, would have nothing to do with it, the Radicals disliked buying them out at such a price, the Irish members denounced the appointment of the Receiver-General. The Radicals, who had gained many votes in rural constituencies with the slogan of "three acres and a cow," felt that English Agriculture was being sacrificed, and drew vivid pictures of a train of railway trucks two miles long, loaded with millions of bright sovereigns, all travelling from the pocket of the British son of toil to the pocket of the idle Irish landlord.[1] Even so staunch a supporter of Mr. Gladstone's Irish policy as Mr. Morley felt that "many of the warmest friends of Irish self-government found special consideration for the owners of Irish land bitterly unpalatable."[2] The Nationalists urged that, though Irish Land Reform was long overdue, the scheme for Home Rule should not be overweighted with a controversial measure of this kind.[3] The second Home Rule Bill in 1893 was not accompanied by a Land Act and by the time the third was introduced the Irish Land Question had received a reasonably satisfactory solution in Wyndham's Act of 1903. This collateral issue is mentioned because the Irish Land Question had a very direct influence upon the nature—and the fate—of the Home Rule Bills.

Regarded in the light of later proposals for Devolution, it will be seen that the Home Rule Bill conferred very considerable powers upon the local authority. The defeat of the Government upon this proposal—it was defeated on the Second Reading by 343 votes to 313—reflected a condemnation not of its intrinsic value but rather of the general implications of this

[1] See Morley, *Life of Gladstone*, vol. iii, p. 325.
[2] Ibid., vol. iii, p. 310.   [3] Ibid., p. 325.

solution of a particular question. Lord Randolph Churchill denounced the Bill as "a farrago of superlative nonsense designed to gratify the ambition of an old man in a hurry,"[1] but the true cause of its rejection is implicit in Bright's retort to Mr. Gladstone. "The Prime Minister," he said, "was marching through rapine to the dismemberment of the United Kingdom."

THE SIGNIFICANCE OF THE DEBATE ON HOME RULE

The introduction of the first Home Rule Bill is one of those rare events which serve as a landmark in the history of two nations. This is so, not because of the proposals it contained, nor yet because it brought into rivalry the three great political personalities of the age, but rather because it forced upon public opinion the need for change in political outlook. In the field of active politics it led to a new orientation of parties; in Anglo-Irish relations it settled finally the form of the penultimate solution. Mr. Gladstone's analysis of the Irish Question was both able and substantially accurate, as his long introductory speech in the House of Commons showed.[2] But he was forced to conclusions unacceptable to English opinion. Joseph Chamberlain, "the man who killed Home Rule," in his revolt against the Prime Minister, voiced the predominant attitude of English people towards the Irish Question down to this day. The voting on the Second Reading shows that only 170 English members voted for the Bill, 285 against. Here we are concerned with the Bill, not as a solution of the Irish Question, but as an indicator of public opinion towards Devolution. In fact, as we shall see, the controversy over the Bill extracts indirectly the attitudes of persons and parties towards measures of Devolution. For this reason we shall find the importance of the Bill lies (i) in what it might have achieved, (ii) in what it replaced.

[1] W. S. Churchill, *Life of Lord R. Churchill*, vol. i, p. 118.
[2] *Hansard*, vol. ccciv, April 8th.

WHAT THE HOME RULE BILL WAS INTENDED TO ACHIEVE

For the most authoritative opinion upon the probable effect of the Home Rule Bill we must turn to Mr. Gladstone's speech. He declared:[1] "We have come to the time when we must answer this question—whether we will make one bold attempt to free Parliament for its great and necessary work and to establish harmony by Irish laws for Ireland; or whether we will, on the other hand, continue to struggle on as we have done before, living from hand to mouth, leaving England and Scotland to a famine of needful and useful legislation and Ireland to the continuance of a social disease, that you do not know how to deal with, and of angry discord with Great Britain which you make no attempt to cure."

The Prime Minister had two objects in mind; namely, the pacification of Ireland and the liberation of the House of Commons from the pressure of Irish business. Both these would be achieved once the all-important principle of terminating Irish representation at Westminster by the erection of an independent Parliament at Dublin was allowed. This was the principle which alienated both Chamberlain and Hartington; it was also the principle which bound Parnell. "This Bill," said the latter,[2] "will, I think, be cheerfully accepted by the Irish People and their representatives as a solution of the long-standing dispute between the two countries and . . . will lead to the prosperity and peace of Ireland and the satisfaction of England." But the blessing of Parnell—unexpectedly warm as it proved—served only to accentuate the misgivings of the majority at Westminster. The Bill approached more nearly to a grant of Independence than to an act of Devolution. Criticism is directed against the proposals on the ground that the Parliament at Dublin will prove not a sub-ordinate but a co-ordinate authority.[3] And acting as a collateral power,

[1] *Hansard*, vol. ccciv, col. 1550.   [2] Ibid., col. 1134.
[3] See also speeches of members of Northern Ireland constituencies, ibid., col. 1089–1102.

the probability of conflict or of rivalry between the two Parliaments is a prospect which cannot be disregarded.[1]

Upon the dependent issue, that of relieving the parliamentary time-table, the Prime Minister was assured of support. The obstructionist tactics of the Irish members were naturally unpopular. And moreover, it was felt that if the Irish problem were settled there would be sufficient time for all other business. In fact, as subsequent history has shown, the obstructionist tactics were merely symptomatic of more deeply-laid defects in Parliamentary Procedure. The Irish members by causing the adoption of a series of limitations on debate—from Mr. Speaker Brand's to Mr. Balfour's Reforms—served to hasten the day when the Executive exercises a complete control over the Parliamentary Time Table. But though obstruction might be suppressed the influence wielded by an Irish, or indeed any, Party holding a balance of power could not be diminished. "What will become of the freedom of the great majority . . ." asked Mr. Goschen,[2] "if we acknowledge that our Constitution has come to this point, that whenever 86 determined men in this House say they will have a particular measure, that measure must be granted?" But that raised a problem which has not yet been solved.

WHAT THE HOME RULE BILL REPLACED

But if the Home Rule Bill is important because of what it proposed, it is yet more significant from the point of view of our enquiry, by what it replaced. If, in 1886, Conservatives, Right-wing Whigs and Radicals were united in opposition to Home Rule they were most certainly not in agreement with regard to an alternative policy for Ireland. Where the Conservatives placed their faith in a moderate programme of internal reform, the Radicals suggested constitutional reconstruction. In the former party the most progressive attitude to Irish

---

[1] Cf. J. L. Garvin, *Life of Joseph Chamberlain*, vol. ii, p. 112.
[2] *Hansard*, vol. ccciv, col. 1461.

Affairs was displayed by Lord Randolph Churchill. "In office or opposition, in good fortune or defeat he detested the use of special legislation in Ireland."[1] And although he remained an unwavering opponent of Repeal he did observe the need for social reform. "It has always appeared to me," he said, "that the Tory Party were well qualified to deal with many questions of Irish interest in a manner agreeable to the Irish people and not in the least dangerous to the general welfare of the British Empire. I particularly allude to the question of education and to the question of the land."[2] But this represented the limit of Tory concession; and indeed but few members of the Party were opposed to Coercion or were impressed, like Lord Randolph, by the need for social reform. On the other hand the Radicals proposed a federal scheme of government to be known as Home-Rule-All-Round. This proposal intended, by means of National Councils, to devolve powers upon local legislatures, not merely in Ireland, but also in England, Scotland and Wales. Such powers as the local legislatures exercised would be of a purely domestic character and the integrity of the United Kingdom would be preserved by continued representation at Westminster. At one time the proposal had the qualified support of Mr. Gladstone. He wrote to Lord Hartington with regard to the National Council Plan that he was "deeply convinced that the measure in itself will (especially if accompanied by other measures elsewhere, e.g. in Scotland) be good for the country and the Empire. I do not say unmixedly good, but with advantages enormously outweighing any drawbacks."[3] This qualified approval later made way for Mr. Gladstone's belief that only a radical remedy could solve the Irish Question. It was upon this issue that the Liberal Party split. Mr. Joseph Chamberlain, a strong supporter of the National Council Scheme, believed that no solution

---

[1] W. S. Churchill, *Lord Randolph Churchill*, vol. i, p. 396.
[2] Quoted in above, vol. ii, p. 5.
[3] Letter of Mr. Gladstone to Lord Hartington quoted in Morley's *Gladstone*, vol. iii, p. 198.

of the Irish Question was worthy of consideration unless it preserved intact the integrity of the British Isles. His attitude merits examination. In a notable speech before the General Election he declared:[1]

"We also have to recognize and to satisfy national sentiment, which is in itself a praiseworthy and patriotic and inspiring feeling, and which both in Scotland and Ireland had led to a demand for a local control in purely domestic affairs. And these objects can only be secured, I believe, by some great measure of Devolution by which the Imperial Parliament shall maintain its supremacy and shall nevertheless relegate to subordinate authorities the control and administration of their local business. I look forward with confidence to the opportunity which will be afforded in the new Parliament for the consideration of this most momentous question, and I believe that in the successful accomplishment of its solution lies the only hope of the pacification of Ireland and of the maintenance of the strength and integrity of the Empire—which are in danger, which are gravely compromised, so long as an integral of Her Majesty's dominions can only be governed by exceptional legislation and so long as it, in consequence, continues to be discontented and estranged. . . ."

Such being Chamberlain's attitude it is easy to observe how the split with Gladstone occurred. There is a sharp cleavage on a matter of principle between the two men. Gladstone felt that the Irish Question was a distinctive individual problem. Chamberlain endeavoured to dispose of it as a problem in local self-government which was common to all the component parts of the British Isles. Subsequent political events made it necessary for Chamberlain to enlarge upon his proposals. In a letter to Labouchere[2] he shows the lines along which he hoped to advance.

. . . "There is only one way of giving bona fide Home Rule, which is the adoption of the American Constitution:

[1] This speech is quoted in J. L. Garvin, *Life of Joseph Chamberlain*, vol. ii, p. 9.   [2] Quoted in J. L. Garvin, op. cit., p. 145.

(i) Separate Legislatures for England, Scotland, Wales and possibly Ulster. The three other Irish Provinces might combine.

(ii) Imperial Legislature at Westminster for Foreign and Colonial Affairs, Army, Navy, Post Office and Customs.

(iii) A Supreme Court to arbitrate on limits of authority.

There is a scheme for you. It is the only one which is compatible with any sort of Imperial unity, and once established it might work without friction. But . . . I am not going to swallow separation with my eyes shut."

It was in accordance with the principles thus stated that the "unauthorized programme" had demanded Home-Rule-All-Round, on equal terms for the different nationalities of the United Kingdom, leaving the Imperial Parliament unimpaired in composition and authority as the supreme legislature of the common realm. This meant a scheme of Devolution within the strict meaning of the word. The Home Rule Bill went beyond it. The issue is distinctly stated in practical form by Chamberlain's memorandum to Gladstone in March 1886. In order to define more clearly the points of difference he asked the Prime Minister four questions:[1]

(i) Whether Irish representation was to cease at Westminster?

(ii) Whether the power of taxation, including customs and excise, was to be given to the Irish Parliament?

(iii) Whether the appointment of the judges and the magistracy was to rest in the Irish authority?

(iv) Whether the Irish Parliament was to have authority in every matter not specifically excluded by the Act constituting it or whether it was only to have authority in matters specifically delegated to it by Statute?

Here we have, as Mr. Garvin[2] so justly remarks, "the acid tests of the distinction between Home Rule consistent with federal Union and Home Rule severing or weakening the

[1] J. L. Garvin, op. cit., vol. ii, from Chamberlain's Memorandum.
[2] Op. cit., vol. ii, p. 192.

D

visible links. It was a great and plain issue." To all the questions Gladstone replied in the affirmative and so in the negative to Chamberlain's ideas. The latter at once resigned from the Cabinet, and by this action killed the Home Rule Bill.

The attitude of one party towards Devolution remains to be defined. That party was the Nationalist Party. Parnell, it will be remembered, gave a general approval to the Prime Minister's proposals. What was his attitude to Devolution? In earlier negotiations—in July 1885—Mr. Chamberlain had written to Capt. O'Shea, then Parnell's intermediary, to this effect:[1]

"I have often expressed the conviction that the Irish people are entitled to the largest measure of self-government consistent with the continued integrity of the Empire . . . and with this object in view I ventured myself to sketch a scheme of County Boards and National Councils which I thought might be accepted as a settlement of the Question . . . A complete and effectual system of local government may be, and I hope would be, found sufficient to satisfy Irish National sentiment."

Parnell's reply, communicated through Capt. O'Shea, was chilling.[2] " . . . should satisfactory evidence be forthcoming that legislative independence is likely to be proposed within a reasonable time Mr. Parnell said 'that he thinks it doubtful whether it would be worth while to encumber the Irish Question at present with a larger extension of local government to Ireland than to England.' "

The letter and its reply show exactly what one would expect; namely, that while Chamberlain, endeavouring to preserve the integrity of the British Isles, proposes a devolution of function to local authorities; Parnell emphasizes the distinctive character of the Irish Question.

[1] Letter to Capt. O'Shea, July 11, 1885. Quoted in J. L. Garvin, op. cit., vol. ii, p. 21.

[2] Letter to J. Chamberlain from Capt. O'Shea. Quoted in J. L. Garvin, op. cit., vol. ii, p. 24.

THE CONSEQUENCES

The outcome of the political struggle upon the first Home Rule Bill displayed a characteristic distrust on the part of the British electorate for far-reaching constructive proposals. There were, as we have seen, three different ways of dealing with the Irish Question in 1886. The first was by adopting Mr. Gladstone's Home Rule Bill, the second by legislating upon Mr. Joseph Chamberlain's scheme of general devolution, the third by retaining the *status quo*. Of these alternatives, both the first and the second had much to commend them. They put forward a possible solution of a pressing problem. Mr. Gladstone's proposal had the advantage of securing the support of an Irish majority, Mr. Chamberlain's of preserving the uniformity and integrity of the United Kingdom while at the same time doing something perhaps to mitigate the unpopularity of the Union in Ireland. In addition both alternatives had the incidental advantage of relieving the parliamentary time-table. But ironically enough both constructive proposals were mutually destructive. Both Gladstone and Parnell realized clearly that Chamberlain had killed Home Rule. But Chamberlain himself did not understand till long after that the Home Rule Bill of '86 with equal finality had killed his proposals of Devolution. As Sir William Harcourt declared in the debate, "You may kill this Bill but its record will remain. The history of England and Ireland can never be as if this offer had never been made. You may kill it now but it will ever haunt your festivals of coercion."[1] Despite a melodramatic climax Sir William was unquestionably correct. After 1886, Home Rule alone would satisfy Irish sentiment. Though further proposals of Devolution were to be made, as in Mr. Birrell's Councils Bill, they died of inanition. For the weakness of Chamberlain's conception lay in its demand for uniformity. His inflexible opposition to "separate parliaments," his emphatic assertion of the supremacy of the Imperial Parliament, whatever scheme

[1] *Hansard*, vol. ccciv, col. 1458.

of Devolution might be adopted, meant in the last analysis, so far as Ireland was concerned, that good government was a complete alternative to National government. In that respect as in others he underestimated the strength of Nationalist sentiment. If it could once be shown that Irish Nationality was an ephemeral force then Chamberlain's frequent analogies with States of the American Union would have been pointed. In the circumstances they helped to mislead public opinion in England.

Despite the drastic set-back which each practical scheme of Devolution received, the conception yet displayed a remarkable vitality. Between 1886 and 1920 innumerable proposals along the lines of the first Home Rule Bill or the Radicals' counter-suggestions were brought forward—but none received practical effect. On the whole, British public opinion reacted against Gladstone's conception of fundamental reform and favoured more moderate schemes of Devolution. And in addition, the question of Devolution to local authorities was brought forward after the councils of counties and county boroughs were established in 1889. The Local Government Act[1] of the previous year contemplated that functions of the central Departments might be transferred by Provisional Order. Such a transfer would not involve any redistribution of legislative authority but would merely lead to a transfer of administrative power to the local authorities. As such it was likely to bring about neither a considerable relief of the parliamentary time-table nor an increased efficiency in administration.[2]

THE SECOND HOME RULE BILL

With the second Home Rule Bill, introduced into the House of Commons by Mr. Gladstone on February 13, 1893, we are brought again face to face with the most difficult problem in any scheme of Devolution, namely the problem of representation. The issue, for which the Conference of 1920, relieved as they

---

[1] 1888.   [2] Cf. W. I. Jennings, *Parliamentary Reform*, pp. 40–41.

were of any consideration of the Irish Question, could find
no easy remedy, proved of insuperable difficulty to the Liberals
in '93. The feature of the second Home Bill was the manner
in which it attempted to deal with the crux of Irish Representation. The Irish Parliament in Dublin was retained but so also
was Irish Representation at Westminster. In the latter place
the Irish members were not to have a full right of voting.
By the celebrated "in and out" clause they were not permitted
to vote on any matter affecting Great Britain alone. The proposal
was peculiarly vulnerable as it would give the Irish members
influence but no responsibility in legislation on British affairs.
They could overthrow a Government but could not vote on
a particular part of its programme. In deference to the wishes
of the majority, the Prime Minister amended the Bill by removing all restrictions on Irish voting but reduced the number
of Irish members from 103 to 80. This again was a peculiarly
unsatisfactory compromise.[1] It emphasizes the fact that between
the Liberal-Unionists and Gladstone there was a wide divergence in principle. Consequently, the latter's attempt in
'93 to reduce the difference to one of detail by combining
a "separate parliament" with the continued integrity of the
United Kingdom was doomed to failure. An eclectic selection
of features from a policy of Home Rule and one of Federal
Devolution eliminated all that was valuable in either. The
Bill was defeated in the Lords.

LATER PROPOSALS FOR DEVOLUTION

So far we have observed that the question of Devolution is
inextricably bound up with the question of Ireland. For it was
logical to claim that if any scheme of federalism were introduced it should first take effect in that part of the British Isles
most dissatisfied with the existing form of government. Thus
it is not surprising, when on the retirement of Gladstone the

[1] For the attitude of J. Chamberlain, see J. L. Garvin, op. cit.,
vol. ii, pp. 558–570.

Irish Question ceases to be the central issue in English politics, that at the same time support for Home-Rule-All-Round is less prominent than heretofore. A decade prolific in constructive plans for the settlement of Ireland had passed leaving no practical achievement behind, and so that country was left to find what solace she could in Mr. Balfour's policy of "killing Home Rule by kindness." Two proposals to amend and improve the Act of Union were suggested which merit some attention. The first of these was the "Devolution" scheme put forward in 1904 by the Irish Reform Association under the presidency of Lord Dunraven. The somewhat unexpected success that had attended the Land Conference in the previous year had given rise to a belief that the political problem might also be solved by united action. Its scope was limited. The principal features were—the transfer of Private Bill Legislation to Dublin on the Scottish plan; to hand over the internal expenditure of Ireland, a sum amounting to about £6,000,000 annually, to a financial council of 25 consisting partly of nominated and partly of elected members,[1] and to give to an Irish Assembly the initiative in Public Irish Bills. The Council was to have full control of the money spent in Ireland but its decisions might be reversed in the House of Commons by a majority of not less than one fourth of the total votes given. The merit of these proposals is slight. The first—the transfer of Private Bill legislation—is unobjectionable and might relieve parliamentary time in a small way; but the other two create a divided responsibility. The whole scheme was of a somewhat superficial character. An outcry against it by the extreme Unionists led to its repudiation both by Mr. Balfour and the Irish Secretary, Mr. Wyndham. Ultimately the latter resigned,[2] thus bringing a career of rare promise to a premature close. The later proposals are better known under the title of Mr. Birrell's

---

[1] The Lord-Lieutenant was to be President and the Chief Secretary Vice-President, 12 members were to be elected and 11 nominated.

[2] Because the Under-Secretary, Sir A. MacDonnell, had given some encouragement to the plan.

Irish Council Bill. It was introduced into the House in 1907.[1]
The intention of these proposals was the establishment of an
Administrative Council in Ireland. The Council was to
consist of 82 elected members, 24 nominated members,
and 1 ex-officio member. The Council thus formed was to
control the departments administering local services in Ireland.
Financial responsibility was to be divided. An Irish Fund
was to be created, depending upon annual payments from the
Consolidated Fund of the United Kingdom. The fund was
to defray local expenditure based on estimates made by the
departments, and submitted to the Council by an Irish
Treasury. Needless to say a partly nominated Council, a
financial administration dependent on grants from the Consolidated Fund, did not appeal to Irish sentiment. The proposal
was rejected by a Nationalist Party Convention in Dublin
and then abandoned. It is also to be remarked that the
Committee on National Finance—better known as the Primrose
Committee—concluded upon purely administrative grounds
that the financial dependence of a local upon a central exchequer
was inadvisable. They reported "that the experience of the
last few years amply confirms the theory that a financial partnership with Great Britain does lead in Ireland to a scale of
expenditure beyond the requirements and beyond the resources
of the country itself." Further, subject to certain reservations
in matters of detail, the Committee recommended that "the
power of levying and imposing all taxation in Ireland should
rest with the Irish Government."[2] We shall examine later the
extent to which this recommendation was adopted in Northern
Ireland. Here it is sufficient to observe that the financial
case was strongly reinforced by the development of Nationalist
claims. The issue was perhaps most clearly stated by Sir
Horace Plunkett[3] when he wrote that "the tendency of recent
political thought among constitutional Nationalists had been

---

[1] (Bill 182), May 7, 1907.
[2] *Report of Proceedings of Committee on National Finance*, p. 6.
[3] *Report of the Proceedings of the Irish Convention*, p. 5.

towards a form of government resembling as closely as possible that of the Dominions, and since the geographical position of Ireland imposes obvious restrictions in respect of naval and military affairs, the claim for Dominion Home Rule was concentrated upon a demand for unrestricted fiscal power." But such a devolution of financial control found but little favour at Westminster, where indeed the whole tendency of opinion was towards further financial centralization.

DEVOLUTION NO LONGER PROVIDES BASIS FOR IRISH SETTLEMENT

Throughout the period 1886–1912, Devolution kept its hold on public opinion as a means of conceding Home Rule by instalments. But with the passage of time, it became increasingly evident that, whatever value it might have as applied to England, Scotland, and Wales, it would not settle the problem of Ireland. For this there were in 1912 three outstanding reasons. The first was the growth of Irish Nationalist sentiment. Sinn Fein was founded in 1905 and there followed a revision of the basis of Irish Reform. Arthur Griffith[1] implanted the doctrines of economic nationalism, in which he was an acknowledged debtor to Friedrich List, and so laid the foundation of a movement which was destined to achieve a greater measure of Irish independence than that contemplated in the Home Rule Bills. "We regard Ireland as a Nation," declared the Nationalists in 1918.[2] Their ground of objection to any scheme of Devolution is implicit in these few words. The second reason runs parallel to the first. The delay between the introduction of the first Home Rule in 1886 and the passage of the Act in 1914, militated very seriously against any possibility of its successful application. As Mr. Dillon,[3] a moderate Nationalist, declared in March 1914: "Proposals for Devolution were made in 1886 and after deep consideration rejected. Now the day for it has gone." In

[1] Cf. his pamphlet, *The Resurrection of Hungary*.
[2] *Report of Proceedings of Irish Convention*, p. 5.
[3] *Parl. Debates*, vol. lix, col. 2292, March 1914.

England too it was more and more realized that Sir Henry Campbell-Bannerman had diagnosed the issue accurately in remarking that "to secure good administration is one thing, but good government can never be a substitute for government by the people themselves."[1] The final and most decisive obstacle in the face of a grant of Devolution to Ireland lay in Ulster. The people of the North-Eastern counties of Ireland, differing as they did from the majority of their fellow-countrymen in history and religion, protested against the possibility of government from Dublin. The problem was one of great, but not insuperable, difficulty. Its significance was, however, exaggerated and distorted to serve the interests of political parties. This antagonism would, in any event, have rendered impracticable any scheme of Devolution for the whole island. A speech of Mr. Balfour, a former Unionist Prime Minister, on the third Home Rule Bill in May 1914, passed a judgment which was representative of a very considerable body of English opinion on the all-Ireland scheme of Devolution. Referring to the phrase "Settlement of Ireland" used by a previous speaker, Mr. Balfour said, "I thought this a singularly infelicitous phrase which he used with regard to a Bill which everybody now . . . I believe, on both sides of the House, is of the opinion will settle Ireland only after the horrors of civil war have been experienced, after blood has been shed and property destroyed, and ulterior consequences far greater than any destruction of life or any destruction of property that has been undergone."[2] The natural difficulties of the situation were used in a reckless and melodramatic parliamentary and extra-parliamentary campaign in order to postpone the application of the Home Rule Act. So it was that in September 1914, simultaneously with the Government of Ireland Act, a Suspensory Act was passed, which directed that no steps be taken to put the former Act into operation till the end of the War.[3]

[1] Speech at Stirling, November 1905.
[2] *Parl. Debates*, vol. lxii, col. 966.   [3] 4 & 5 Geo. V, c. 88.

The Home Rule Act[1] of 1914 followed the well-worn path of previous proposals with a few modifications of its own. It set up an Irish Parliament consisting of a Senate of 40 nominated members and a House of Commons of 164 members. External affairs were naturally excluded from its scope, but the reservation of internal services, as the collection of taxes, postal services, police, land purchase, and national insurance, even though in some cases for a limited period, did bring the authority of the local parliament to a low level. This was accentuated by the reservation of the right of absolute veto by the British Government and by the right of the Imperial Parliament to legislate on matters within the competence of the Irish Parliament. The right of fiscal legislation was permanently reserved, though it was proposed to establish a joint Exchequer Board. Representation at Westminster was to be continued but the number of the Irish members was reduced to forty. Executive power was vested in the Lord Lieutenant as the representative of the Crown. In respect of the powers devolved he was to be aided and advised by a Ministry responsible to the Irish Legislature; in respect of the powers reserved, by the British Cabinet.

The purpose of this remarkable constitutional experiment was the preservation of the unity of the British Isles whilst granting a very modest proportion of Irish claims. It is difficult to estimate how it would have operated in practice. Probably considerations of a purely legislative and administrative character would have ultimately necessitated the transfer of certain reserved services, particularly in financial affairs, to the local authority. But while—owing to the restricted application of the Act of 1920—there exists no criterion by which we may answer this hypothetical question, yet there remains the need to emphasize the two capital defects of the Act of 1914. As an Act of Devolution it was unsatisfactory in the essential dualism of its constitutional provisions, in its division of responsibility; as a solution of a particular problem it rested

[1] Government of Ireland Act, 1914, 4 & 5 Geo. V.

upon a mistaken conception of the forces in Irish political life. The Liberal Party calculated that Ireland would be satisfied by a grant of Devolution which, with certain modifications, would later be extended to the other parts of the British Isles. As the Prime Minister pointed out in debate . . . " . . . the importance of the extension of the principle of Devolution in appropriate forms to other parts of the United Kingdom is fully recognized" but "the claim of Ireland is prior in point of urgency and must be dealt with first."[1] This attitude brings to our attention the fact that the difference between the settlement proposed by the supporters of Home Rule and that of the Unionists was one only of degree. The principle underlying both was that of the essential unity of the British Isles. Between them and Sinn Fein with its belief in a national and inalienable sovereignty there was a difference in kind. This conflict in principle explains how it was that the Act of Union was not amended in practice between 1885 and 1920. It also helps us to understand how it was that the English people, rather than accept a fundamental settlement, preferred to live on in the hope that the Irish Question, like the river of the "Garden of Proserpine," would wind "somewhere safe to sea."

[1] *Parl. Debates*, vol. lix, col. 908, March 1914.

CHAPTER IV

THE CONFERENCE ON DEVOLUTION

DEVOLUTION to regional authorities, when untrammelled by national claims, has obvious attractions. Though proposals for Federal Devolution were put forward in the last century to serve ephemeral ends, yet the conception possessed sufficient vitality to survive even when it was no longer possible that it could in any way provide a solution of the Irish Question. What then were the reasons for this sustained vitality? And how was it displayed in practical form?

When it had become evident that the Irish Question was to receive a distinctive solution, then Devolution retained its influence as a means of relieving the time of Parliament. As a consequence the interests of the localities received a very secondary consideration. The actual benefits which might be expected from any general scheme of Devolution are summed up by Professor Ramsay Muir, a prominent advocate of constitutional reform, along these lines. He concludes:

"First, that a large scheme of Devolution is quite practical, but is only worth undertaking if it is applied, not merely to one or two regions, but to the whole country; secondly, that in a closely knit country such as ours it would be essential to preserve in an effective way a real control by the Imperial Parliament over the work of the subordinate legislatures, and that this can be readily done, provided that the Second Chamber problem is satisfactorily solved; thirdly, that such a scheme would give an immense relief to the House of Commons, and enable it to do more thoroughly the work which it now perforce neglects; and finally, that such a scheme would usefully qualify the tendency to excessive centralization which is one of the most unhealthy features of recent development; while it might also provide the means for dealing—not necessarily on uniform lines but with a wholesome variety of method—with the chaos into which our system of local government seems progressively to be falling."[1]

The probable consequences of Devolution reflect clearly the purposes behind it. They do not, however, indicate the complexity of the issue. For a practical scheme of Devolution requires a most careful definition of the relations to be established between the central and the local authority. What functions are to be devolved? What are to be the financial relations? And most important, what considerations are to determine the area under the jurisdiction of the local authority? These are questions which must be answered before Parliament can legislate. It was in order to find a solution of them that after a rather casual debate in the House of Commons in June 1919, a Conference representing both Houses was appointed. The Conference, under the Chairmanship of Mr. Speaker Lowther, presented their Report in April 1920. This document is a landmark in the history of Devolution.

The purpose of the Conference was defined by a Resolution of the House of Commons, in these words:

"That with a view to enabling the Imperial Parliament to devote more attention to the general interests of the United Kingdom and, in collaboration with the other Governments of the Empire, to matters of common Imperial concern, this House is of the opinion that the time has come for the creation of subordinate Legislatures within the United Kingdom, and to this end the Government, without prejudice to any proposals it may have to make with regard to Ireland, should forthwith appoint a Parliamentary body to consider and report:

"(1) upon a measure of Federal Devolution applicable to England, Scotland, and Ireland, defined in its general outlines by existing differences in law and administration between the three countries;

"(2) upon the extent to which these differences are applicable to Welsh conditions and requirements; and

[1] *How England is Governed*, chapter viii.

"(3) upon the financial requirements of the measure."
The Terms of Reference introduced certain limitations into
the scope of the inquiry. The Conference were to consider
and report upon a scheme of Legislative and Administrative
Devolution within the United Kingdom having regard to:

    (i) The need of reserving to the Imperial Parliament the
        exclusive consideration of:—

        (*a*) Foreign and Imperial Affairs: and
        (*b*) Subjects affecting the United Kingdom as a whole.

   (ii) The allocation of financial powers as between the
        Imperial Parliament and the subordinate legislatures,
        special consideration being given to the need of pro-
        viding for the effective administration of the allocated
        powers.
  (iii) The special needs and characteristics of the component
        portions of the United Kingdom in which the
        subordinate legislatures are set up.[1]

The Conference understood, from these Terms of Reference,
that it was not required to pronounce for or against the principle
of Devolution, but only to consider what, if Devolution be
accepted, is the most practicable way of putting it into operation.
It is also to be observed that between the date of the Commons'
Resolution—4th June 1919—and the first meeting of the
Conference on 23rd October of the same year, the Government
proposals with regard to Ireland had taken shape, and for this
reason the Conference felt justified in restricting the scope
of its inquiry to Great Britain alone.
The Report is very instructive. The Conference reached
substantial agreement upon four of the five main questions
at issue, but the subject upon which it was divided is of the
greatest importance. So it is that our most valuable evidence

[1] See the *Report of the Conference on Devolution*, 1920, pp. 2–3.
[Cmd. 692.]

is derived from the character of the disagreement rather than from the extent of the agreement. The Conference was substantially agreed upon:

(i) The Areas which the local legislatures should administer.
(ii) The Powers which should be devolved upon a local legislature.
(iii) The scheme for Financial arrangements as between the United Kingdom and the local Exchequers.
(iv) The scheme for dividing the Judiciary for United Kingdom and local requirements.

The Conference was divided upon:

(v) The character and composition of the local legislatures.

Each of these issues deserves a brief examination.

AREA

At the outset the question presented itself whether the areas should be the three "National" divisions of England, Scotland, and Wales, or smaller divisions delimited for the purpose by the scheme. The former plan was objectionable because of the decided preponderance of England in area, wealth and population; the latter because it necessitated the creation by statute of artificial governmental units. Moreover the Resolution of the House of Commons had expressly declared that the demand for Devolution had arisen "in order to enable the Imperial Parliament to devote more attention to the general interests of the United Kingdom and to matters of Imperial concern." Hence it was the alleged necessity of relieving Parliament and not any desire to gratify the sentiment of nationality that had called the Conference into being. On the other hand the members felt that the "subdivision of England presented such formidable administrative difficulties that, while it might possibly be grafted on to a system of Devolution already in operation, it ought not to form a feature of such a system in its initial stage."[1] Accordingly the Conference reported in favour of the three "National" areas—England, Scotland, and Wales (including Monmouthshire). It is difficult to criticize their conclusion. While it is unfortunate for supporters of Devolution that England overtops the other two combined in size, wealth and population, yet there remains no practical alternative. It has been proposed that by the subdivision of England a more symmetrical system of government might be achieved.[2] This, of course, is perfectly true. It would be possible to delimit autonomous areas with some approach to equality in population and wealth, and with some homogeneity of interest and characteristic in each. Professor Ramsay Muir has outlined on general principles a scheme of Devolution to regional authorities for Scotland, Wales, and seven areas in England.[3] By this means a federation of three unequal members would be avoided and symmetry achieved. This subdivision implies, however, that England is not in fact a single political and economic unit. This is an assumption which is unjustifiable. The progress of economic and social legislation in recent years indicates that decentralization to areas arbitrarily defined is unlikely to serve any useful purpose. After all, federalism in itself is not an aid to government. It survives, as for example in Switzerland or the United States, as a means of preserving the identity of distinct political units. It is the outcome of history. Admittedly the Government of India Act provides a contemporary instance of a reverse process inasmuch as it involves a decentralization of Indian administration. But in this case very unusual conditions prevailed and normally it is a reversal of the ordinary trend of political development to create a federal State. Moreover, the subdivision of England on federal lines would mean the creation of new political units within a single economic unit.

[1] See the *Report of the Conference on Devolution,* 1920, p. 3.
[2] Ibid., Memorandum by Mr. Ronald McNeill.
[3] Op. cit., chapter viii.

POWERS

The conclusion of the Conference in favour of "National" areas is confirmed by the attempt to define powers which might usefully be devolved. This task is one of the greatest difficulty, but after lengthy consideration the Conference reached a large measure of agreement both as to the subjects which ought to be retained by the Central Government and those which might properly be delegated to subordinate authorities. The allocation of powers was fixed upon a threefold foundation. Powers were devolved to the local authority, powers were to be exercised partly by the United Kingdom and partly by the local legislature, and finally, certain powers were reserved. A brief list of the general characteristics of the powers to be devolved is instructive.[1]

(*a*) Powers devolved on Local Legislatures.

1. Regulation of Internal Commercial Undertakings, Professions and Societies (e.g. Licensing, Markets and fairs, etc.).
2. Order and Good Government (e.g. Prisons, Poor Law, Police (other than Metropolitan).
3. Ecclesiastical Matters.
4. Agriculture and Land (e.g. Commons, Drainage, Settled Land Acts, etc.).
5. Judiciary and Minor Legal Matters (e.g. Coroners, County Courts, Criminal Law, Minor Offences, etc.).
6. Education, Primary, Secondary and University (except Oxford and Cambridge).
7. Local Government and Municipal Undertakings (e.g. County Council and Municipal Bills, Municipal Government, etc.).
8. Public Health (e.g. Hospitals, Housing, National Health Insurance, and Lunacy).

[1] Op. cit., Appendix III, where Lists are set out in detail.

E

(*b*) Powers to be exercised partly by Central and partly by Local Parliament.

1. Corrupt Practices.
2. Explosives.
3. Harbours.
4. Land—Acquisition for Public Purposes.
5. Transport—Road and Highways.

(*c*) The Conference did compile a list of subjects to be reserved exclusively to the Parliament of the United Kingdom. It is unnecessary to define them in detail as the Conference, in addition, ruled that *all matters not expressly enumerated are reserved to the United Kingdom Parliament.*

This allocation of powers by the Conference is not open to severe criticism. Recent developments might demand certain modifications, as for example in the control of Agriculture, but on the whole the list commands a general assent. At the same time it must be remembered that its value can be tested only by practical experiment. Abstract speculation cannot foretell the exact balance that would be struck between central and local authority. Moreover, it would be virtually certain that legislation co-ordinating the duties of the respective authorities would occupy an amount of Parliamentary time equivalent to that which is now spent in general legislation for a very considerable period after the establishment of local legislatures. In this event the parliamentary time-table would not be relieved until a satisfactory co-operation between the two authorities had been achieved.

The control of Finance is the vital power in a Parliamentary Democracy. For this reason the decisive feature in any experiment of this nature is the extent of the financial responsibility enjoyed by the local authorities. The Conference dismissed the facile plan of a lump-sum Grant-in-Aid representing the whole of the existing and contemplated expenditure of each National Parliament. Such a plan, it was rightly assumed, would ensure neither finality for the Imperial Exchequer not independence and scope for the growth of the National Parliaments. At the same time the Conference was not prepared to impair in the smallest way the authority of the Imperial Parliament. The central Exchequer must control resources essential for Imperial purposes. Thus the Conference dismissed "the equally facile but infinitely more fatal plan" of leaving each nationality with the revenue assumed to arise within its borders.[1] The principle which determined the accepted solution of the problem was that each Nationality should be able to count on an income which, while sufficing for its existing needs, is yet elastic enough to provide that reasonable expansion of responsible expenditure, which National policy may demand and be prepared to pay for, from the taxation of its own Nationals. For this reason the Conference concluded that those sources of revenue which clearly arise from and within the National territory and at the same time do not form an integral part of the Imperial fiscal system, might conveniently be transferred. It was recommended that the following sources of revenue should be handed over to the local authorities to meet the expenditure on the transferred services:

1. Liquor Licences.
2. Establishment Licences.
3. Traders' Licences.
4. Entertainments Duty.
5. Inhabited House Duty.
6. Land Values Duty.

The deficit was to be made up by the transfer of so many pence in the pound Income Tax (excluding Super Tax) as might be needed to balance the account. At the end of five years the whole situation with regard to allocated funds and allocated taxes was to be reviewed.

These suggestions with regard to the allocation of financial

[1] Op. cit., Appendix IV. Report of Lord Chalmers, Committee on Finance.

powers are extremély tentative. The sub-committee appointed
to enquire into the question had recommended that Death
Duties should be transferred. This suggestion was not adopted
by the Conference as a whole, no doubt both because of the
fluctuating yield of the duties, and because of obvious difficulties
in assessment. This meant, however, that the deficit between
local revenue and local expenditure would be very large.
In the financial year 1919–20, the Conference estimated that
total expenditure and revenue in the National areas would be
as follows:

	England	Scotland	Wales
	£	£	£
Expenditure	52,664,500	9,100,000	3,988,000
Revenue	13,350,000	1,585,000	914,000
Deficit	39,314,500	7,515,000	3,074,000

Thus there is a very large deficit indeed to be met by grants-in-
aid from the Exchequer. This would certainly be increased
by the addition of extra charges entailed by a grant of Devolution; as election expenses in the National areas, additional
National Ministers, new parliamentary expenditure, and
probably new buildings. It is difficult to give a close estimate
of the extra expenditure involved by the creation of subordinate
Governments. But experience in Northern Ireland shows that
it would be by no means inconsiderable. The general conclusion
to be drawn from the financial proposals of the Conference
is that they err emphatically on the side of caution. Local
responsibility would be almost non-existent. At the same
time no proper check would be placed on extravagant administration, for a deficit would be met by the central Exchequer.
The task of allocation is, of course, by no means simple and
even in Northern Ireland—where political considerations
encourage a very close co-operation—it has given rise to many
problems. But carefully restricted financial powers foredoom
any experiment of this kind to failure.

THE JUDICIARY

The Judicial recommendations of the Conference suggest how the systems prevailing in Scotland and Wales might be adapted to a scheme of Devolution.[1] These particular considerations need not detain us. On the wider issue of principle the Conference suggested that the definition, punishment, and regulation of procedure in the trial of major crimes—*mala in se*—should be reserved to the United Kingdom Parliament, while such changes as might be found desirable in other matters should be left to the authority of the local legislatures.

THE COMPOSITION OF THE LOCAL LEGISLATURES

The Conference, having determined the nature of the powers that might be delegated to subordinate legislatures in the three "National" areas, were unable to reach substantial agreement upon the constitution of these legislatures. Two proposals were put forward. The first, associated with the name of Mr. Murray Macdonald, attempted a radical solution. In it the establishment of local legislative bodies with separate elections was advocated. The opponents of this solution were so impressed by its disadvantages that they felt driven to opposing the principle of Devolution itself. In order to bridge this divergence of view the Chairman of the Conference, Mr. Speaker Lowther, submitted an alternative proposal of more modest character. The issues raised reveal the difficulty of imposing a scheme of Devolution upon a priori grounds and therefore deserve some little attention.

Mr. Speaker Lowther's proposals were not put forward as a final solution, but rather as a means whereby a practical trial of the working of Devolution might be carried out by responsible persons with political experience. The principal features of his scheme are as follows:[2]

[1] Op. cit., Appendix v. Report of Lord Stuart of Wortley's Committee on the Judiciary.   [2] Op. cit., Appendix i.

1. There shall be established local subordinate legislatures for the three "National" areas.
2. These legislatures shall be styled "Grand Councils."
3. A "Grand Council" shall consist of two Chambers.
4. The first Chamber, called the "Council of Commons," shall consist, for each of the three Areas, of all the members returned to the House of Commons to sit for constituencies in that area.
5. The Second Chamber, called "The Council of Peers," shall consist, for such areas, of a number of members of the House of Lords equal to half the number of Members of the House of Commons for that area, and chosen for the duration of each Parliament by a Committee of Selection of the House of Lords.

Since the "Grand Councils" are constituted, not by special election, but of persons who are members of the United Kingdom Parliament it follows that during a session of Parliament the sittings of the Grand Council must be suspended. It was suggested, as a general rule, that the spring and summer months should be reserved for the ordinary session of Parliament and the autumn for the ordinary sessions of the Grand Councils. Finally it remains to be observed that the Grand Councils were to fill a definitely subordinate rôle. Parliament might legislate on devolved subjects, might pass legislation over-riding a Grand Council Act, and the Cabinet might advise the exercise of the Royal Veto on matters of policy.

The intention of Mr. Speaker Lowther's proposals is clear enough. The "Grand Councils" made the least possible change in constitutional structure compatible with any scheme of Devolution. They used the experience of members of both Houses of Parliament. They involved an extension of the Standing Committee system, but not a new departure in principle. The supremacy of Parliament would be unchallenged. Moreover, the scheme promised a certain measure of relief to members. English members would no longer be concerned with Welsh and Scottish affairs and in the same way the others also would be relieved. Finally, the scheme was definitely of a transitional character. After a limited period of trial it laid upon each of the Grand Councils the duty of deciding, in the light of practical experience, the permanent constitution of the legislative bodies for their respective areas. Thus it would be possible for each of the areas either to adopt a constitution involving separate elections, or to revert to the position prior to Devolution, or to continue as constituted. This element of flexibility is indeed the chief attraction of the "Grand Council" proposal.

The proposals associated with the name of Mr. Murray Macdonald were of a more radical character. Their adoption would involve a drastic change in English constitutional practice. The general trend of these proposals is shown in the following provisions:[1]

1. There shall be established legislatures subordinate to, but separate from, the Parliament of United Kingdom—in England, Scotland, and Wales.
2. Each subordinate legislature shall have a directly elected chamber.
3. Each chamber shall consist of the same number of members as represent these three areas in Parliament.
4. The members of each chamber shall be elected for the same constituencies and by the same electors, within the several countries, as now return members to Westminster.
5. The legislatures may be either uni-cameral or bi-cameral according as the Government shall decide.
6. In either event peers shall not be disqualified for election to the popularly elected Chambers.
7. The subordinate legislatures shall determine the question of payment of members.
8. The subordinate legislatures shall sit for five years unless sooner dissolved.

[1] Op. cit., Appendix II.

9. Each subordinate legislature shall have an executive Committee responsible to it.

10. The members of the Executive Committees shall be appointed by H.M. the King in accordance with existing constitutional practice.

Such is the main outline of Mr. Macdonald's scheme for the creation of subordinate but independent local legislatures. In it the same precautions are taken to preserve "absolutely unimpaired" the inherent and supreme powers of the Parliament of the United Kingdom. Its intention is to secure effective relief of the existing parliamentary congestion and at the same time to give the local legislature—and indirectly the local electors—an effective control over their executive. The scheme, it will be noted, has a certain similarity to the form of government now in force in Northern Ireland. In both instances there is a local legislature, a local executive responsible to it and double representation. In the latter case, however, a different principle obtains in Northern Ireland to that proposed by Mr. Murray Macdonald. But without desiring to press the analogy too far it is yet evident that government in Northern Ireland provides the material essential to a realistic judgement upon the issues involved.

Meanwhile it remains for us to indicate the rather evident objections to both the proposals laid before the Conference. Mr. Speaker Lowther's scheme is open to severe criticism in that the Grand Councils would be unlikely in a real sense to relieve the pressure of parliamentary business. As the Conference had been appointed with this as its principal objective, the criticism goes deep. After all, while it may be admitted that the scheme would divest a large amount of business from the House of Commons itself, yet this relief would be effected only by imposing the same business on its members acting in a different capacity. In the normal course autumn sessions are regarded with disfavour, but under the Grand Council scheme they would become permanent. It is hardly probable that the quality of legislation in the areas affected would be improved by the increase in the duties of members of Parliament. There is, moreover, a further vital objection to Mr. Speaker Lowther's scheme, and it may be stated in one word—confusion. In the three stages in the life of a Parliament—at election time, during the session, and at the dissolution—this undesirable result would be liable to occur. Technically the "Grand Councils" and Parliament have clearly defined and independent spheres of action. In fact, it is reasonable to assume that the duplication of membership would erase from the popular mind any such clear-cut distinction. At election time there would be a dual appeal to the electors, one local and the other central. Candidates would have to define their attitude to two Executives. Again local issues would inevitably cut across Imperial issues. The electors would have but one vote, though acting in two capacities, and consequently would have the unenviable task of weighing the importance of local as opposed to central policy. This is a test too severe for any democratic electorate. During the session the same difficulties are liable to recur. Members would have a double responsibility to the electors and to the Executive Governments. Finally this dual status would raise problems with regard to the dissolving power. The councils could be dissolved independently by the Sovereign. Consequently, the Executive would be hampered in the exercise of its power. Whatever the internal difficulties of a Grand Council might be, it would be dependent entirely upon the dissolution of the House of Commons for an appeal to the sovereign people. These remarks indicate the character of the defects liable to be encountered in the actual operation of Mr. Speaker Lowther's scheme. They seem of a nature so formidable as to preclude any possible adoption of the Grand Council system.

Meanwhile, when we turn to Mr. Macdonald's proposals we are faced by difficulties of a no less intimidating kind. The English Parliamentary System is the growth of centuries of political evolution and the break with its tradition of centralization involved by the adoption of these proposals would be abrupt. The novelty of the conception is of course no argument against it, but it does mean that the case for subordinate legislatures must be well proved. In fact, this is what Mr. Macdonald was unable to do.[1] On analysis certain serious obstacles to an acceptance of the scheme present themselves. The first arises in respect of the local legislature in England. How is England to be persuaded to ask for or to accept and work such a scheme of Devolution? And even if it were established, would it not tend either to attract no public attention at all or else to rival the Imperial Parliament itself in importance? These questions cannot be answered with finality, but the whole balance of probability is against the ready acceptance and smooth working of such institutions by the "predominant partner." A second objection to these proposals is to be noted in respect of their cost. The practical operation of the experiment would demand an almost prohibitive financial expenditure, once more especially in the case of England. Houses of Parliament would be required in the three "National" areas, a not inconsiderable staff of officials to work the organization, and salaries for the Ministers and members. In England, where the membership of the lower House of the legislature would be approximately 500, these charges would be no light burden. In addition, as elections to these bodies and the Imperial Parliament would not be contemporaneous in the ordinary way the cost of elections in each of the areas would be doubled. A final objection may be raised with regard to the effect of such an experiment upon the Parliamentary System. In the first place, since the number of members of legislative bodies within the United Kingdom would be doubled, it would appear inevitable that their quality would decline. Since public opinion has no great respect for the intellectual calibre of members today, a further lowering of the standard is a prospect which friends of parliamentary government could not envisage with confidence. In the second place there is a danger that,

---

[1] Op. cit., Memorandum by Mr. Murray Macdonald, pp. 31–35.

in England at any rate, the increase in the electoral duties of citizens might well create an apathetic attitude towards democratic government. It is for these reasons we feel that Mr. Macdonald's proposals do not carry the conviction which so bold an experiment demands.

CONCLUSION

The Conference added a great deal to our knowledge of the problems which a system of Devolution would involve in the British Isles. It did not, however, present a solution of them likely to command any wide measure of support. The Report as a whole is unconvincing. For this reason the discussion in the House was indefinitely postponed. The problem was certainly one of great complexity. But the Conference failed in two vital respects to present an acceptable conclusion. With regard to the allocation of financial powers it erred greatly on the side of caution by recommending that the Local Government should in the normal course meet, at the most, a quarter of its expenditure out of revenue. This strikes at the root of any measure for self-government. Since the Committee on National Finance had previously recommended the transfer of direct taxation the Conference here displayed a retrogressive outlook. Again, in respect of the composition of the local legislatures neither of the proposals sponsored by members of the Conference seems practical. Here the predominance of England presented the most serious problem. And by failing to make allowances for the difference in wealth and population between the "National" areas, both the proposals opened themselves to unanswerable criticisms. Scotland would never be satisfied with a "Grand Council"; England would never work a local legislature. Hence it would appear that a less symmetrical but more realist solution is the only means by which Devolution might be given practical effect. Might not a more profitable avenue of approach be opened by suggesting that, while the Grand Council scheme be applied to England, local legislatures be established in Scotland and Wales?

PART II

THE ULSTER QUESTION

". . . all whose names are underwritten, men of Ulster, loyal
subjects of H.M. King George V. . . . do hereby pledge
ourselves in solemn covenant to stand by one another in
defending for ourselves and our children our cherished position
of equal citizenship in the United Kingdom and in using all
means which may be found necessary to defeat the present
conspiracy to set up a Home Rule Parliament in Ireland."

The Covenant.

"We declare the right of Ireland to the ownership of Ireland,
and to the unfettered control of Irish destinies, to be sovereign
and indefeasible. . . . We hereby proclaim the Irish Republic
as a sovereign Independent State and we pledge our lives and
the lives of our comrades-in-arms to the cause of its freedom,
of its welfare, and of its exaltation among the nations."

*The Proclamation of the Provisional
Government of the Irish Republic to
the People of Ireland.* Easter 1916.

"Wait and see."

H. H. ASQUITH.

CHAPTER V

THE GENESIS OF THE ULSTER QUESTION

IN the British Isles today there is one example of Devolution in practice, namely, the Government of Northern Ireland. Its existence is due, not to the inspiration of a constitutional doctrine, but to the events of a remarkable history. To understand the form and mechanism of the Constitution of Northern Ireland, it is essential to bear in mind the characteristics of her people and the political aims to which they have aspired. For these reasons a survey of recent events in Northern Ireland must be reckoned a necessary preliminary to any judgment upon the merits of its Constitution. For it is in the historic forces which have moulded Ulster, which have determined her religion, her economy, her social structure, which have decided her relationship both with Great Britain and the Irish Free State, that we ought to be able to discover the premises which made possible both the creation and the continuance of her Government. The existence of a subordinate Government at Belfast is the great enigma in Irish political life today. To explain it one must recall certain of the dominant tendencies in Anglo-Irish relations more especially during the last half-century. Such an objective historical summary has the additional advantage of enabling us to decide to what extent the phenomena displayed by the subordinate Government in Belfast are characteristic results of such constitutional machinery or are due to the peculiarities of historical development.

THE FOUNDATION OF ULSTER

The differences in race and creed, which have combined to effect the political division of the Irish nation, are not likely to be minimized during the existence of the present phase of the Irish Question. The danger, indeed, lies in exaggeration rather than in understatement. For the creation of independent Governments at Dublin and Belfast is now commonly held to have been the inevitable consequence of an historical process rather than the immediate solution of a pressing problem. The former view depends in the last analysis upon a supposed predominance of racial and religious ties over the influence of environment. It represents at best only a half-truth. For a cursory examination of the history of the province of Ulster reveals two forces striving for supremacy—the one having for its object association with the rest of Ireland; the other aiming at exclusion. The former attained its apogee of success in Grattan's Parliament, the latter in the building of Stormont.

The plantation of Ulster with settlers of Scottish and English birth was more successful than those in any other part of Ireland. The methods adopted were brutal. Lord Deputy Chichester left a record of the means whereby the foundations of modern Ulster were laid. "I burned," he reported, "all along the Lough (Neagh) within four miles of Dungannon, and killed 100 people, sparing none, of what quality, age or sex soever, besides many burned to death. We killed man, woman and child, horse, beast and whatsoever we could find." The later infusion of Scottish settlers, mostly Presbyterian in creed, added a third element to an already difficult situation. So it was that in the civil wars which succeeded the fall of Strafford, the Protestants in Ireland were divided into two hostile camps, Episcopalian and Puritan. That division has proved of enduring significance in Ulster. During the Interregnum the Ulster settlers united with the Scots in their quarrel with the Long Parliament, thereby calling down the wrath of John Milton, who denounced them as "a generation of Highland thieves and red shanks who, being neighbourly admitted . . . by the courtesy of England, to hold possessions in our province, a country better than their own, have with worse faith than those heathen, proved ungrateful and treacherous guests to their best friends and entertainers."[1] During the same period

[1] John Milton, *Observations.*

they came into conflict with the Anglican Church. In a Petition of 1641 from "some Protestant Inhabitants of the counties of Antrim, Downe, Derry, Tyrone, etc.," to the Long Parliament, toleration of Catholics was described the sovereign crime of "the children of Ishmael and Esau."[1] This unflattering description of the Bishops of the Established Church indicates the peculiarities of the Presbyterian position in Ireland. They were out of sympathy with the Independents in England, they resented the Episcopalian jurisdiction of the Established Church, they were bitterly opposed to toleration of Catholics in a predominantly Catholic country. There remained one ally to which they were bound by ties of blood as well as of religion—the party of the Covenant in Scotland. But it was evident that on political questions the interests of Scottish and Ulster Covenanters would sooner or later diverge.

THE PERIOD OF ASSOCIATION

A century and a half after the Interregnum association between settlers and Irish led to common action against the incompetence and injustices of British rule in Ireland. The Northern Dissenters realized that a divided nation could provide no defence against Castle rule. As Grattan declared, "the Irish Protestant could never be free till the Irish Catholic ceased to be a slave." The Volunteers secured a nominal parliamentary independence but failed in the two all-important issues— emancipation and reform—which alone could make representative government in Ireland a reality. The influence of the French Revolution among the Dissenters of the North was very great and in the Belfast of 1791 democracy was the popular creed. The Chief Secretary denounced Belfast "as the source of all the mischief" and pointed to the menace of "these levellers of the North." At the same time the Presbyterian Synod of Ulster made it their "earnest prayer that the time may never more return when religious distinctions shall be

[1] Quoted in J. W. Good, *Ulster and Ireland*, p. 8.

F

used as a pretext for disturbing society, or arming man against his neighbours; that intolerance of every kind may be trodden under foot; and every equally good subject shall be equally cherished and protected by the State."[1] The anti-climax which followed this movement for a United Ireland need not concern us here. It is sufficient to recall that there was a period, not long distant, when the aspirations of Ulster coincided with those of the rest of Ireland.

Throughout the nineteenth century the prospect of a united Ireland became increasingly remote. The Act of Union proved the culminating catastrophe to Irish patriotic hopes, for with its passage there passed also something of that generous enthusiasm which had for one flickering moment illuminated the Irish political scene. Wolfe Tone had convinced Catholics and Dissenters alike that they had "but one common interest and one common enemy; that the depression and slavery of Ireland was produced and perpetuated by the divisions existing between them, and that, consequently, to assert the independence of their country and their own individual liberties it was necessary to forget all former feuds, to consolidate the entire strength of the whole nation, and to form for the future but one people." After 1801, the will to unity disappeared. Mistrust was sown, religious bitterness revived, while at the same time the progress of the Industrial Revolution created a cleavage in economic interest. Three provinces in Ireland remained predominantly agricultural whilst the fourth, Ulster, found a new prosperity in rapid industrial expansion. Thus between Ulster (or rather the four north-eastern counties of that province) and the rest of Ireland there exists a difference in religion, in race, in economy. Individually, these contrasting elements would be of no great significance; collectively they do provide a possible basis for division. Whether a policy of separation would triumph over a policy of association was one of the great problems of Irish history in the nineteenth century. It was an issue which

[1] Ibid., pp. 52–3.

demanded, in no stinted measure, creative statemanship and popular good-will. The circumstances of Irish government made the one impossible and the other difficult. It is improbable that the internal history of Ireland would have led to Partition; it is certain that the intervention of English parties made it inevitable.

ULSTER AND HOME RULE

The Home Rule controversy revealed a certain rigidity of out-look, a certain barrenness in political thought which made it patent that the failure of England to provide a solution of the Irish Question was not a failure for which this or that statesman could be held responsible, but it was a failure in the political conception of a nation. Professor Maitland[1] maintained that the want of a theory about Ireland which would have mediated between absolute dependence and absolute independence was the origin of many evils, and though subsequent history may not have proved the accuracy of his diagnosis in its entirety, yet it has emphasized at every turn the existence of a regrettable *lacuna* in English political thought. A people which prides itself on a genius for political compromise displayed a legal pedantry which precluded compromise on the most significant problem in politics of the last century. Reservation of final political authority to Great Britain; denial of responsible self-government to Ireland; these were reckoned the essential bases of any political reform. A problem which demanded for its solution a great effort of creative imagination was approached with caution and an enduring pessimism.

From this indictment of British statesmanship Mr. Gladstone stands excepted, for the Home Rule Bill, whatever its defects, showed two essential qualities—imagination and courage. To this day one cannot read unmoved his peroration on the Second Reading in the House:[2]

"As to the harvest of the future, I doubt if you have so

---

[1] Op. cit., p. xx.　　　　[2] *Hansard*, vol. ccciv.

much confidence, and I believe there is in the breast of many a man who means to vote against us to-night a profound misgiving, approaching to a deep conviction, that the end will be as we foresee and not as you—that the ebbing tide is with you, and the flowing tide with us. Ireland stands at your bar, expectant, hopeful, almost suppliant. Her words are the words of truth and soberness. She asks a blessed oblivion of the past, and in that oblivion our interest is even greater than hers. . . . Go into the length and breadth of the world, ransack the literatures of all countries, find if you can a single voice, a single book . . . in which the conduct of England towards Ireland is anywhere treated except with profound and bitter condemnation."

It is possible that by one bold act of statesmanship Mr. Gladstone might have changed the destiny of two nations. It is certain, even without the intervention of the Ulster Question, that the English people preferred a conservative to a courageous policy.

The year 1885 might be held to mark the genesis of the Government of Northern Ireland as we know it today. For in that year the prospect of Home Rule led to serious riots in Belfast. At once it was evident to Unionists in England that the opposition of Orangemen to Home Rule would prove an invaluable weapon in party warfare. Lord Randolph Churchill, with characteristic acuteness, wrote early in the following year: "I decided some time ago that if the G.O.M. went for Home Rule, the Orange card would be the one to play. Please God, it may turn out the ace of trumps, and not a two!"[1] In addition the election of 1885 revealed the comparative strength of parties in Ireland. Of 89 contested seats the Nationalists won 85, mostly by overwhelming majorities. The Province of Ulster returned 18 Nationalists as against 17 of the opposite persuasion. These returns warn us emphatically against the assumption that Ulster was unanimous in

[1] Letter to Lord Fitzgibbon, February 16, 1886, quoted in W. S. Churchill, op. cit.

its opposition to Home Rule. At no time during the past half-century was there a certain majority against Home Rule within that province. Three of its nine counties—Donegal, Cavan and Monaghan—had large Nationalist majorities. In two of the remaining six—Fermanagh and Tyrone—opinion on the balance slightly favoured the Nationalists. In the remaining four the Orangemen had a decisive majority. Thus though it is convenient to speak of this issue in Irish politics as the "Ulster Question," it is inaccurate. For the province, as a whole, was not opposed to Home Rule. In four counties the bulk of the population was Unionist, whilst in two others very considerable sympathy was felt for their cause. Needless to say, the geographical subtleties of the situation were not readily understood in Great Britain. This in itself, being a question of detail and not of principle, was of no great consequence, but it did occasion in Great Britain an over-estimation of the numerical strength of the Unionists in Ulster. Thus it was a matter of some comment that the exclusion of Ulster from the operation of the third Home Rule Bill meant the exclusion at most of the six north-eastern counties of that province. Had it been generally known in addition that the Unionist leaders in 1914, as well as in 1920, demanded from the Cabinet the exclusion of six counties and *no more* it would have caused very considerable surprise in England and no little resentment amongst Unionists in other parts of Ireland. The Unionist rulers maintained that in a larger area their political supremacy would be challenged; within the six counties their position would be impregnable.

Throughout the modern phase of the Irish Question territorial issues have played a very secondary rôle to religious division in Ulster. Lord Morley has recorded his impression of the sectarian bitterness in the Belfast of half a century ago. " . . . Strange to say," he wrote,[1] "this great and flourishing community where energy, intelligence and enterprise have achieved results so striking, has proved to harbour a spirit

---

[1] *Recollections*, vol. i, p. 222.

of bigotry and violence for which a parallel can hardly be found in any town in Western Europe." To this day hostility and bitterness between the Churches exercises a dominant influence upon Ulster politics.[1] One may despise this survival of medieval intolerance, one may condemn or scorn the attitude of mind which makes it possible, but one cannot ignore its existence. This is the legacy of the fierce fanaticism of the religious wars, fostered and nourished through the centuries by a chain of calamitous circumstance, till today it has become embedded as a well-nigh ineradicable habit in the Ulster mind. After the introduction of the Home Rule Bill religious antagonisms were hardened by the division of political parties. Before 1801, Ulster Protestants rallied to the Nationalist cause; since 1885 the terms Unionist and Protestant, Nationalist and Catholic have become synonymous. Religious and political divisions coincide; and by this unreal and artificial alignment of forces the history of Ulster has been moulded.

THE INTERVENTION OF THE ENGLISH PARTIES

It was very fitting that Mr. Gladstone's speech in the House introducing the first Home Rule Bill was followed immediately by speeches from two members for Co. Antrim.[2] At the very beginning of the Home Rule controversy they protested in the name of the northern counties against the conception of an all-Ireland Parliament. Thus both friend and foe were made aware that in Ulster was to be found a vulnerable joint in the armour of Home Rule. To the Conservatives, opposed in principle as they were in any event, it provided an invaluable political weapon, but what was of far greater significance. it sowed misgiving in the minds of many Liberals and Radicals. In a letter to the Prime Minister, Mr. John Bright expressed what many Englishmen felt to be the most profound objection to Home Rule.

[1] The riots in July 1935 provide a recent illustration.
[2] Vide *Hansard*, vol. ccciv, cols. 1089–1102.

"I cannot consent," he wrote,[1] "to a measure which is so offensive . . . to the whole sentiment of the province of Ulster so far as its loyal and Protestant people are concerned. I cannot agree to exclude them from the protection of the Imperial Parliament." It is evident now that had the first Home Rule Bill contained provisions designed expressly to safeguard the interests of the Ulster Unionists the case for its adoption would have been immeasurably strengthened. At that time the Ulster Unionists had not yet acquired that feverish antagonism to Irish proposals emanating from a Liberal Government which they were later to display, and consequently a "special treatment" basis might have received consideration. But whatever may have been the chances of establishing a Home Rule Parliament for all-Ireland in the spring of 1886, they had passed by the close of the year. For in the meantime certain of the Conservative leaders had suggested that constitutional opposition was not the only means by which Home Rule might be defeated.

In England Conservatism owes its strength to the consistently moderate tone of its programme. The narrow distinction between conservatism and reaction is understood. As a consequence it is rare that the pronouncements of the extreme Right influence the policy of the party as a whole. There is, however, one exception. The attitude of the Conservative Party towards the Ulster Question was determined by the opinions of the extreme Unionists. Therein lies the significance of Lord Randolph Churchill's superficial but militant letter. It was not the statements; it was the tone that expressed the attitude of the new Unionism. Lord Randolph wrote:[2]

"If political parties and political leaders . . . should be so utterly lost to every feeling and dictate of honour and courage as to hand over coldly, and for the sake of purchasing a short

[1] Letter of May 18, 1886, quoted in Morley, *Life of Gladstone*, vol. iii, p. 327.
[2] Letter to a Liberal-Unionist member, 1886. Vide W. S. Churchill, op. cit., vol. ii, p. 65.

and illusory Parliamentary tranquillity, the lives and liberties of the loyalists of Ireland to their hereditary and most bitter foes make no doubt on this point. Ulster will not be a consenting party; Ulster at the proper moment will resort to the supreme arbitrament of force; Ulster will fight; Ulster will be right; Ulster will emerge from the struggle victorious, because all that Ulster represents to us Britons will command the sympathy and support of an enormous section of our British community and also . . . will attract the admiration and approval of all free and civilized nations."

The jingling phrase "Ulster will fight, Ulster will be right" evoked an immediate response. The north-eastern counties rallied to this flamboyant appeal, thus throwing into relief the undeniable weakness in the Liberal proposals. A statesman of Mr. Gladstone's insight, had he given the issue consideration, could not have persisted in the belief that the best way to solve an inconvenient political problem is to ignore it. Yet that was the method adopted in 1886. The Prime Minister promulgated his principle, he failed to take count of the detail. The omission is understandable—as it was Home Rule was coupled with complicated land proposals—but it was, none the less, disastrous. Had some form of federalism been proposed; had the Ulster Unionists been safeguarded by the express terms of the Bills; a reasonable basis for amendment and discussion would have been provided. In the event the extreme Unionists and the Orangemen felt that the failure to take any account justified an appeal to unconstitutional agitation. The belief thus planted was not to be eradicated easily. Lord Randolph Churchill had not sown the dragon's teeth; but he had tilled the soil that was to bring forth armed men.

Nothing is more remarkable in the penultimate phase of the Ulster Question than the inelasticity of Liberal proposals. Partly, no doubt, the claims of social reconstruction and constitutional reform in England occupied the attention of a Cabinet fertile in political expedient, but to a far greater extent was this rigidity due to the memory of a historic controversy and to the shadow of a great name. The events of 1886 had determined the lines of Unionist opposition; Mr. Gladstone had invested Home Rule with all the sanctity of a traditional Liberal cause. So it was that when Parliament assembled on February 14, 1912, there awaited the Government the most formidable of all its legislative tasks. The third Home Rule Bill was the final attempt to settle the Irish Question by the establishment of a subordinate Parliament in Dublin. In the intervening years the demand of the Irish majority had not weakened, whilst the Unionist party, "unrepentant in its opposition to Home Rule in any form, had, if anything, rather hardened in its attitude."[1] Moreover, the passage of the Parliament Act gave a new edge to the controversy. No longer now could the Unionist Party rely on the House of Lords to block the way, in the event of their opposition being overborne in the Commons. Hence the probability was that within two years the Home Rule Bill would become law.

The more melodramatic episodes in the Unionist resistance to Home Rule in the few years before the War have received more than a due share of attention. In themselves they are of no great significance, but they did succeed on the one hand in reviving sectarian bitterness in all its former intensity and on the other in discrediting once for all the honour and prestige of British government amongst the vast majority of the Irish people. The Unionist Party throughout the controversy played their one invaluable card—the card Lord Randolph has designated "the ace of trumps." For this reason no one who desires to understand the motive force behind the Government in Belfast can afford to ignore the events of 1912–14.

THE POLICY OF THE LIBERAL GOVERNMENT

The Home Rule Bill, which the Liberal Government introduced, was not an extreme one; on the contrary, the main question about it, as an administrative measure, was whether after the

[1] Cf. J. A. Spender, *History of Our Own Times.*

numerous concessions to Unionist sentiment made in the original proposal and afterwards in Committee it would have been a workable measure. But the Prime Minister was well aware that the objection of the Unionist Party to Home Rule was not an objection to the extent of the powers to be surrendered, but an objection to the principle of an independent Parliament in Dublin. In addition he knew that Unionist opposition would concentrate on the Ulster Question in the belief that without Ulster a Home Rule Parliament could not function. So it was that during February 1912 the Cabinet anxiously debated whether Ulster or those counties in which the Prostestants were in a clear majority should be given an option to contract out, in the Bill as introduced, or whether this should be reserved as a concession at a later stage.[1] Eventually the Ministers decided that the Bill should be applied to all-Ireland.[2] At the same time the Cabinet felt bound to warn the Nationalist party that "the Government felt themselves free to make changes, if it became clear that special treatment must be provided for the Ulster counties, and that in this case the Government will be ready to recognize the necessity either by amendment or by not pressing it (the Bill) on under the provision of the Parliament Act."[3] The calculations which induced the Prime Minister to sponsor this unstatesmanlike course of action deserve attention because of the light they throw on the contemporary phase of the Ulster Question. The events of 1886 had shown that there was a *prima facie* case for a certain form of local autonomy in Belfast under the central aegis of an all-Ireland Parliament in Dublin. From the earliest discussions on the Home Rule Bill in 1909, Mr. Churchill declares that he and Mr. Lloyd George had always advocated the exclusion of Ulster on a basis of county option or some similar process. But "we had been met by the

---

[1] Cf. Spender and Asquith, *Life of Lord Oxford and Asquith*, vol. ii, p. 111.   [2] Ibid., vol. ii, p. 15 sq.

[3] Cabinet Letter to the King, February 6, 1912. Quoted in Spender and Asquith, op. cit.

baffling argument that such a concession might well be made as a final means of securing a settlement, but would be fruitless till then."[1] Mr. Asquith rejected the case for special treatment in the original draft of the Bill firstly because of a strong personal preference that the Government policy should be a policy for the whole of Ireland, and secondly because of certain more ephemeral but none the less weighty political circumstances. The former reason was creditable but not realist, as the Cabinet letter to the King expressly admitted. The political reasons, moreover, have not been entirely substantiated. Mr. Asquith gave special weight to three elements in the Ulster situation, namely:

1. That there were Nationalist and Catholic majorities in considerable parts of Ulster and that in the province as a whole representation was equally divided.
2. That Exclusion would be deeply resented by the Nationalists.
3. That it would be unlikely to propitiate the Ulster extremists (as Carson).

These considerations led the Prime Minister to frame a Home Rule Bill without special treatment for the Ulster minority. The wisdom of this course has been a matter of controversy. In retrospect it does appear with regard to (1) that the admixture of parties in the north provided a strong case for guarantees to the minority both there and in the rest of Ireland; and that thereby the difficulty contemplated in (2) would disappear, while the followers of Sir Edward Carson in the event proved irreconcilable.

But if Mr. Asquith miscalculated in the weighing of political forces, he did not, as his opponents, underestimate the complexity of the issue. The Prime Minister acknowledged that "minorities have their rights; and they have not only their rights but susceptibilities which ought to be considered and provided for"; but he also claimed that a minority had no

[1] *The World Crisis*, p. 104. Revised edition.

right "to thwart and defeat the constitutional demands of a great majority of their fellow-countrymen."[1] At every election for 26 years fourth-fifths of Irish people had voted for representatives pledged to Home Rule. Was it reasonable to suppose that the Irish people would view with equanimity the destruction of hopes constitutionally expressed? Was it just that a parliamentary majority at Westminster should submit passively to "the naked veto of an irreconcilable minority"?

THE ATTITUDE OF THE UNIONIST PARTY

It is inaccurate to suggest, as is frequently done, that the Unionist Party had no positive proposals for a final settlement of the Irish Question. The predicament of the Party lay not in its lack of policy, but in the fact that its policy, having been put into practice under exceptionally favourable conditions, had failed. It is as unnecessary, as it would be unjust, to minimize the benefits conferred on Ireland by Mr. Balfour's reforms from 1887 onwards, in order to maintain that his policy of "killing Home Rule by kindness" did not provide any possible basis for the final settlement of Ireland. Good government is not a substitute for national government, and it was the latter which attracted all the aspirations of the Irish people. So it was in the critical pre-War years that the Unionist Party, confirmed in its opposition to Home Rule, was faced with the political failure of its ameliorative measures. A continuance of the Union on its old basis was no solution. Mr. Asquith had asked at the beginning of the Balfour régime (1887) "what conceivable advantage can there be either to Ireland or Great Britain from the continuance of this gross caricature of the British Constitution? There is much virtue in government of the people, by the people, for the people. There is also much to be said for a powerful and well-equipped autocracy; but between the two there is no logical or states-manlike halting-place. For the hybrid system which the Govern-

[1] Speech in Dublin, July 14, 1912.

ment is about to set up . . . a system which cannot either be resolutely repressive or frankly popular . . . is reserved the inexorable sentence which history shows must fall on every form of political imposture."[1] This admittedly hostile analysis gives a clear idea of the character of the Unionist failure. In addition it explains how it was that the Party had to concentrate the whole of their opposition on the Ulster Question. From coercion to social reform, every policy consistent with the maintenance of the Union had been tried and every such policy had failed. Therefore the Unionist Party could not counter Home Rule with a more attractive alternative; but it could and did insist that the evils of the Union were insignificant in comparison with the disasters which Home Rule would entail.

"If Ulster succeeds," said Sir Edward Carson in a long-remembered speech,[2] "Home Rule is dead." He believed that a Dublin Parliament could not function were Belfast and the surrounding districts outside its jurisdiction. This view, widely accepted as it was among the followers of both parties, provided the predominant motive for resistance in Belfast. Distrust of government exercised by a Catholic majority in Dublin was the original—and genuine—cause of Ulster opposition. But by 1911 the Orange leaders hoped to use this antipathy not in order to secure special safeguards for the minority or even exclusion of the Protestant counties from the jurisdiction of the Dublin Parliament, but for the purpose of wrecking Home Rule. It was this objective, frankly unconstitutional in character, that created an atmosphere of intensified bitterness in the Irish Debates. When Sir Edward Carson declared that "Ulster asks to remain in the Imperial Parliament and she means to do so,"[3] the majority of Englishmen felt an active sympathy with this claim. But when it was apparent that the Opposition intended to use the Ulster Question in order to

---

[1] Spender and Asquith, op. cit., vol. i, p. 65.
[2] October 10, 1911, in Dublin. Quoted Colvin, op. cit., p. 104.
[3] Quoted Colvin, op. cit., p. 104.

defeat Home Rule for Ireland then the issue was no longer one of political controversy but of constitutional principle. It was this attitude which led the Prime Minister to write that between the supporters and opponents of Home Rule there lay "a deep and hitherto unbridgeable chasm of *principle*."[1] The claim of Ulster to be excluded from the Home Rule Parliament merited consideration; her ambition to wreck Home Rule for Ireland could allow of no compromise. As Mr. Churchill said, "the utmost they can claim is for themselves. Ulster cannot stand in the way of Ireland."[2]

THE CONFLICT

So much of the political life of Northern Ireland today is dominated by the memories of pre-War years that one must attempt to recapture something of the outlook of those days. The biographies of the Orange leaders, the political memoirs of that time, give us a picture of a controversy whose features were decided, whose character was simple.[3] To us the problem may seem complex; to contemporaries all was plainly black or white. Here, they felt, was no issue that could be solved by diplomatic subtlety or by the wisdom of political experience; here was no occasion for a careful balancing of argument or for an attempt to weigh imponderables. Instead there was displayed an outward confidence in a cause so assertive as to preclude all possibility of settlement. In Belfast the Nationalists were cast in the rôle of arch-villains in the drama. Incredible tales of their duplicity were circulated and it was felt that there was no trickery to which they would not stoop in order to gain their ends. The Orangemen, on the other hand, went, as their Covenant declared, "in the sure confidence that God will defend the right." The atmosphere of the North permeated the whole Unionist Party, and produced a militant

[1] *Memorandum*, September 1913. Quoted in Spender and Asquith, op. cit.   [2] *Parl. Debates*, vol. xxxvii, col. 1720.
[3] Cf. Colvin's *Life of Carson*. Birkenhead, op. cit. R. McNeill, *Ulster's Stand for Union*.

ardour strangely out of step with the leisurely march of English politics. The response of the Orangemen to the introduction of the Home Rule Bill had been the formation of a Provisional Government in Belfast in the autumn of 1912. The Rev. J. B. Armour, a Presbyterian minister as well known in Ulster for an unflinching sincerity in the expression of Liberal—and unpopular—opinions as for the pungency of his oratory, declared in the following year that "Carsonism is not really popular outside the ranks of Orange Lodges . . . and his Provisional Government is the most outlandish proposal ever made by a sane man. But the terror is so great that sane men prefer to sit silent and say nothing. The right of free speech does not exist in Ulster at present." These words explain, in part, how the Liberal-Unionist minority acquiesced in the leadership of the Orange extremists. But in any event the first Home Rule Bill had signed the death warrant of Liberalism in Ulster. In 1886, the decisive year in the history of Anglo-Irish relations, Mr. Armour had said in the General Assembly of the Presbyterian Church—"We are in the presence of great and sweeping changes in the government of our country, and I could not fancy that, whatever powers swayed the destinies of Ireland, the members of the Presbyterian Church could be worse treated than they have been by the ring esconced in the purlieus of Dublin Castle." But the flood-tide of Unionist sentiment swept Presbyterian and Liberal-Unionist alike into the ranks of Carson's followers. And so by 1912 the material that would normally exercise a moderating influence no longer survived as a distinct political unit. When the Bill came near to its third rejection in the Lords, Ulster armed in earnest. Regiments were openly enrolled and drilled, arms were landed surreptitiously in large numbers, all the accessories for a campaign were collected. Ulster, in a cause she considered just and loyal, took every step, as Lord Midleton has written,[1] which she had for centuries condemned in her southern neighbours. In both cases the law of the sovereign power was challenged

[1] *Ireland*, p. 108.

though this did not, in the Ulster view, affect the argument. For Ulster was in the right; the South in the wrong.

The Conservative Party at first giving a tacit assent to the Orange preparations in Belfast, later openly encouraged the whole movement, Mr. Bonar Law's speech at Blenheim on July 27, 1912, is the most striking instance of the violence which the Ulster question had brought into English politics. The Leader of the Opposition there described the Government of the day as "a Revolutionary Committee which seized by fraud upon despotic power." He continued:

"In our opposition to them we shall not be guided by the considerations, we shall not be restrained by the bonds, which would influence us in an ordinary political struggle. We shall use whatever means seem to us most likely to be effective. . . ."

This Blenheim speech, characterized by the Prime Minister as "a declaration of war against constitutional government,"[1] is a fitting indication of the influence of Ulster Unionism on English politics. Its tone is paralleled by that of the Covenant which was signed by most of the responsible leaders of Church and State in Belfast in September 1912.[2] It read:

"Being convinced in our consciences that Home Rule would be disastrous to the material well-being of Ulster as well as the whole of Ireland, subversive of our civil and religious freedom, destructive of our citizenship, and perilous to the unity of the Empire, all whose names are underwritten, men of Ulster, loyal subjects of His Gracious Majesty King George V, humbly relying on the God in whom our fathers in days of stress and trial confidently trusted, do hereby pledge ourselves in Solemn Covenant throughout this, our time of threatened calamity, to stand by one another in defending for ourselves and our children our cherished position of equal citizenship in the United Kingdom and in using all means which may be found necessary to defeat the present conspiracy to set up a Home

[1] Spender and Asquith, op. cit., p. 107.
[2] Certain of the clergy of the Church of Ireland and a large minority of Presbyterian ministers declined to sign.

Rule Parliament in Ireland. And in the event of such a Parliament being forced upon us we further solemnly . . . pledge ourselves to refuse to recognize its authority. In sure confidence that God will defend the right. . . ."

The political opposition to Home Rule was reinforced by a religious sanction. The Primate of the Church of Ireland writes in his autobiography that "a truly religious conviction animated the opposition," and records that solemn religious services were held before the signing of the Covenant. Almost everywhere in Protestant Ulster a Bill sponsored by the Government of the day, supported by a majority of British, as well as of Irish, members, was described as a "great conspiracy."[1] It is so described even in the reminiscences of an Archbishop. This attitude rendered the task of the Liberal Government one of supreme difficulty. By the autumn of 1913, the Prime Minister was well aware of the magnitude of the crisis.[2] He admitted that if the Bill was passed there would be a serious danger of organized disorder in the four counties. But it was not a case of a "homogeneous people resisting a change to which they are unitedly opposed" since the proportion of Unionists to Nationalists in that area is about 7 to 3. On the other hand the defeat of Home Rule seemed to hold out prospects much more grave. In that event it would not be too much to say that Ireland "would become ungovernable." After all four-fifths of her electorate together with a substantial British majority would be content with nothing less than a subordinate legislature with a local executive responsible to it. Could not this constitutional demand be satisfied without civil war in the North?

EXCLUSION

It was evident throughout the controversy that there was one means by which the full consequences of this political dilemma

---

[1] Cf. *The Adventures of a Bishop*, by Dr. D'Arcy, chapter xiii.

[2] Cf. his Memorandum of September 1913. Quoted in Spender and Asquith, op. cit., vol. ii, pp. 31–33.

might be avoided—namely by excluding Ulster from the full operation of the Home Rule Bill. This involved in some form a political partition of the island—a prospect odious to all the parties involved. The Liberal Government disliked it because of a strong preference that their policy should be one for the whole of Ireland; the Unionists disliked it because it was their aim to wreck Home Rule altogether; the Nationalists regarded it as a disaster which would counteract all the benefits of self-government. None the less, in spite of an aversion that was well-nigh universal, the failure of Mr. Asquith's Government either to conciliate or to repress the Ulster Volunteers left no profitable opening for discussion except along the lines of some such proposal.[1] In addition, by the autumn of 1913 the attitude of both Unionists and Liberals was somewhat modified. The former had not failed to notice that the Southern Irish Loyalists declined to accept the leadership of Sir Edward Carson. Their claims were more moderate, their tone more conciliatory than that of the Ulstermen and, moreover, they felt a certain sympathy with the Nationalist cause. The breach was significant in that it compelled the Ulster leaders to speak for Ulster and not for Irish loyalists as a whole. At the same time the Liberal Government were well aware of the dangerous impasse towards which events in Ireland were moving. Lord Loreburn's letter to *The Times* in the autumn of 1913 revived the public interest in various possibilities of settlement by means of Devolution and federation.[2] Could the Government do nothing but watch the play of irreconcilable forces in a spirit of indolent resignation?

The first practical suggestion for Exclusion is believed to have come from the Nationalist Party. This rather surprising fact deserves some explanation. Apparently the Nationalist leaders —especially Mr. Devlin—reckoned that Ulster could be per-

---

[1] Cf. J. A. Spender's criticism in *The Public Life*, vol. i, p. 111. He argues that the whole question of Ulster resistance "should have been tested at the moment of challenge."

[2] Cf. *The Times*, September 11, 1913.

suaded to accept the principle of Home Rule for all-Ireland
provided that the northern-eastern counties enjoyed a more
or less substantial measure of self-government within this
new constitutional entity. In other words, they recommended
some form of "Home Rule within Home Rule." Their suggestion, through confusion with the Prime Minister's proposals
for "veiled exclusion," was later described in the misleading
word "exclusion." But after all the aim of Nationalists was
to secure by some means or other the *inclusion* of the Ulster
counties in the Irish Parliament and not their exclusion.

"Exclusion" was rendered a practical policy only because of
the fears of civil war entertained by all three parties. Lord
Hugh Cecil analysed the situation accurately when he said:
"the exclusion of Ulster would not satisfy the Unionist Party
but . . . it would avoid Civil War, because if you cut out
Ulster there is nothing for Ulster to fight against, and it takes
two parties to make a Civil War."[1] It was in the autumn of
1913 that the Prime Minister received the first serious intimation
that the Unionist Party might waive its objection to Home Rule
for the rest of Ireland if Ulster were treated separately.[2] The
new basis of discussion did not prove very promising. The
Prime Minister's proposals with regard to legislation for statutory Ulster were conceived with the double purpose of giving
to the Ulster majority the substance of their claims whilst
inflicting as little violence as possible on Nationalist sentiment.
They amounted roughly to "veiled exclusion." "I thought
personally," he wrote, "that there ought to be at any rate a
better chance of settlement along these lines than any other."[3]
But Carson destroyed these hopes in declaring that he could
only proceed on a basis of "naked exclusion."[4] The same
fate overtook the Prime Minister's plan of Federation with
a supreme Imperial Parliament, for Sir Edward Carson "flatly
refused anything short of exclusion." An escape from the dead-

---

[1] *Parl. Debates*, vol. lxii, cols. 1004–5.
[2] Cf. Spender and Asquith, op. cit., vol. ii, p. 34.
[3] Ibid., p. 37.   [4] Colvin, op. cit., vol. ii, p. 269.

lock was sought in various "permutations and combinations" of the Exclusion policy. These plans may be classed under two heads. On the one hand it was proposed that Ulster should be included in the Home Rule Government with an option to secede after a certain number of years; on the other that Ulster should be excluded at the beginning and later a final decision be taken by the people of that province. Mr. Redmond desired "Home Rule within Home Rule."[1] Discussion of the various alternatives narrowed the issue. The Nationalists were "reluctantly persuaded as the price of a peaceful settlement" to agree to giving to the Ulster counties the right by plebiscite of excluding themselves for a term of years.[2] Accordingly on March 9, 1914, when the Home Rule Bill was proposed for a Second Reading on the third and last occasion under the Parliament Act, the Prime Minister announced his intention of proposing an amendment giving the Ulster counties the right to vote themselves out for a period of six years.

The progress of private negotiations for settlement on the basis of Exclusion affected neither the public utterances of statesmen nor the bitterness of party feeling. In 1913 Lord Lansdowne, a Unionist leader, declared the proposed contracting out for Ulster to be "absurd and impracticable." As late as May 1914 Mr. Bonar Law, Leader of the Unionist Party, declared in the House:[3]

"The position of the Unionist Party on that question (i.e. Exclusion) has never been in doubt and has never changed. We have always said . . . that we are utterly opposed to Home Rule, with or without Exclusion, and that we will not in any shape or form and to no degree accept any kind of responsibility for any kind of Home Rule."

This uncompromising attitude was reinforced by the new difficulties to which the delimitation of the area of statutory

---

[1] Cf. Gwynn, *Redmond*, chapter iii.
[2] Spender and Asquith, op. cit., vol. ii, p. 38.
[3] *Parl. Debates*, vol. lxii, col. 966.

Ulster gave rise. The Ulster leaders demanded six counties, that is, the four north-eastern counties together with Fermanagh and Tyrone. The Nationalists insisted on Fermanagh and one half of Tyrone. No agreement was found possible as between these rival claims. In order to stem, if possible, the rising tide of party feeling a Conference composed of the leaders of all parties assembled at Buckingham Palace on July 21st, but the conversations that took place achieved no practical result. The discussions turned entirely, so Mr. Asquith tells us,[1] on the geographical demarcation of the area to be excluded temporarily or permanently from the operation of the Home Rule Bill. There was a debatable territory, particularly in the two counties of Fermanagh and Tyrone, where "the racial and religious intermixture presented exceptionally intricate difficulties." Upon the question of boundary and of time-limit British statesmanship had to declare itself helpless.

THE OUTCOME

In the summer of 1914 the margin in dispute in these fierce antagonisms appeared to English statesmen "inconceivably petty." Mr. Churchill has recorded with unconcealed disgust that "upon the disposition of these clusters of humble parishes" in Fermanagh and Tyrone "turned at that moment the political future of Great Britain."[2] Then, as on many other occasions, matters of comparative insignificance decided great events. The future of British government in Ireland was the issue at stake; and the interminable dispute over minor territorial adjustments was symbolical of the political bankruptcy of a system of government. It was essential to secure a settlement by consent in order to restore the crumbling prestige of British statesmanship in Ireland. And it was with this aim in view that in July 1914, "turning this way and that in search of an exit from the deadlock, the Cabinet toiled around the muddy

[1] Lord Oxford and Asquith, *Fifty Years of Parliament*, vol. ii, pp. 157 ff.   [2] *The World Crisis*, p. 109.

by-ways of Fermanagh and Tyrone."[1] When war broke out on August 4th, this—the penultimate attempt to reach agreement on the Irish Question—had already failed.

The National Convention, which assembled in Dublin in 1917, was faced with the thankless task of making the final attempt. Here we are concerned, not with the course of its discussions but with the attitude of the Ulster representatives. From the earliest days of the Convention it was seen that the success of the Ulster Unionists in thwarting the policy of the Liberal Government had reinforced the claim for complete exclusion. The securing of an agreement to establish a single Legislature for a united Ireland was, as the Prime Minister wrote, an essential element of a settlement.[2] It was hoped at first that a scheme of Irish self-government might be framed to which the Ulster Unionists would give their adherence. But such hopes proved illusory.[3] The only scheme of Irish government which the Ulster representatives presented to the Convention was confined to the exclusion of their entire province.[4] Hence the Ulster members in the Convention remained there only in the hope that some form of Home Rule would be proposed which might modify the determination of those they represented to have neither part nor lot in an Irish Parliament. The Nationalists strove to win them by concessions; but they found themselves unable to accept any of the schemes discussed. The "inexorable opposition" of Ulster to any form of Home Rule, however diluted, eventually caused her representatives to vote against the scheme embodied in the Report of the Convention. In it the interests of Ulster were protected by the most elaborate safeguards; by additional representation secured through nomination, by artificial majorities, by special consideration for legislative or administrative acts affecting that province.[5] The rejection of these

---

[1] *The World Crisis*, p. 109.
[2] Letter to Sir Horace Plunkett, February 25, 1918.
[3] Cf. *Report of Proceedings of the Irish Convention*, Cmd. 9019, pp. 4–5.
[4] Ibid., Appendix XIV.
[5] Ibid., Cf. The Statement of Conclusions, pp. 29 ff.

proposals marked the final cleavage between the Northern and Southern Unionists. On an issue of principle they voted in opposite camps. Lord Midleton, leader of the Southern Unionists, criticized the action of Ulster in these words: "She went into the Convention in 1917 with stated willingness to consider reasonable terms of settlement; she did not contribute a single concrete proposal in eight months; she ended it by voting against the most advantageous and best-guarded scheme which has yet been devised to keep Ireland united."[1] "This is an opportunity for a settlement by consent," wrote Mr. Lloyd George with more truth than perhaps he guessed, "that may never recur, and which, if it is allowed to pass, must inevitably entail consequences for which no man can wish to make himself responsible."[2]

At first sight the Home Rule controversies may appear to have a somewhat tenuous relation to a study of the form of government now in force in Belfast. To us the struggles of pre-War politics seem curiously remote. So much has been achieved in Irish government that seemed totally impracticable to all the protagonists in that fierce party-warfare that we tend to minimize the significance and to doubt the reality of the issues involved. It is as though in 1935 and 1914 men speak in different political languages. In Belfast alone the outlook is unchanged. The atmosphere is that of the Covenant; the spirit is that of Sir Edward Carson and the Volunteers; the menace is still the Nationalists both within and across the border. Without an understanding of the Home Rule conflict the politics of Northern Ireland would be unintelligible, the very existence of a Government at Belfast would be incomprehensible.

[1] Op. cit., p. 109.
[2] From a letter quoted in *Proceedings of the Irish Convention*, p. 22.

CHAPTER VI

THE CONSTITUTION OF NORTHERN IRELAND

It will be remembered that the Home Rule controversy was shelved in September 1914 by the simultaneous passage of the Government of Ireland Act, 1914,[1] and a Suspensory Act,[2] which directed that no steps should be taken to put the former Act into operation until the end of the European War. The outbreak of the Anglo-Irish war in 1919 and the serious menace to the continuation of British rule in Ireland which it contained, necessitated a radical revision of Government policy. In addition, the Act of 1914 could not be kept in perpetual abeyance, since the fixing of the legal termination of the War automatically set a limit to the period during which its suspension might continue. Consequently the Coalition Government were faced with the alternatives, either of putting the Act of 1914 into operation, or of introducing new legislative proposals for Ireland. The Government decided in favour of the latter; and the Government of Ireland Act, 1920, which it sponsored has provided the framework of the Constitution of Northern Ireland. Before outlining its provisions so far as they affected Ulster it is well to notice how the area of jurisdiction of the Northern Government was fixed.

AREA

From Mr. Gladstone's Bill of 1886 to the Government of Ireland Act of 1914, none of the various proposals for establishing Home Rule in Ireland contained provisions for excluding Ulster—or any part of it—from the jurisdiction of the Irish Parliament. When such exclusion had become a practical issue in politics then it was obviously of importance to envisage some means whereby the area to be excluded might be defined

---

[1] 4 & 5 Geo. V. c. 90.   [2] Ibid., c. 88.

precisely. Lord Crewe's amending Bill of 1914,[1] which provided for the exclusion of Ulster for a limited period, proposed that this should be done by county option. Under this scheme the Lord Lieutenant was empowered upon petition from not less than one-tenth of the parliamentary electors of any county in the Province of Ulster to cause a poll of the parliamentary electors in that county to be held. The issue was to be placed before the electorate in a direct question: "Are you in favour," or alternatively, "Are you against the exclusion of your county from the operation of the Government of Ireland Act, 1914, for a period of six years?" In the abstract such a plebiscite, if carried out under proper conditions, would provide an equitable basis for arriving at a decision. In the particular case for which it was devised it would have meant a spectacular gamble. The four north-eastern counties would almost certainly have voted for exclusion by comfortable majorities. But there was no such certainty about Fermanagh or Tyrone. In both instances a few votes would probably turn the scale. Such a prospect did not appeal to the politicians on either side. Consequently it is not surprising that county option disappears from the later proposals. In certain "Headings of a Settlement as to the Government of Ireland,"[2] which were circulated amongst members of both Houses of Parliament in 1916, there appeared the first definite suggestion for the separate treatment of the six-county area in Ulster. The proposals, highly significant as they were in indicating the future course of events, proved abortive. Two years later the Ulster members of the Convention proposed the exclusion of the whole Province of Ulster.[3] It is safe to remark that had this proposal been accepted the Government in Belfast would have ceased to exist many years ago. The Act of 1920 did not prove so blind to Orange interests. In the debate in the House Sir James Craig said:

"We had to take the decision a few days ago as to whether we shall call upon the Government to include the nine counties

[1] Bill intituled an Act to amend the Govt. of Ireland Act, 1914. Introduced June 23, 1914. [2] Cmd. 8310. [3] Cmd. 9019, p. 23.

in the Bill or be satisfied with the six . . . The majority of
Unionists in the nine counties is very small. . . . We admit
quite frankly that we cannot hold the nine counties. Therefore
we decided that, in the interests of the greater part of Ulster,
it is better we should give up the three counties."[1]

The area of jurisdiction of the Northern Government
comprises the six counties of Antrim, Armagh, Down,
Fermanagh, Londonderry, and Tyrone, and the cities of Belfast
and Londonderry. Thus the dispute of 1914 over the disposition
of "the clusters of little parishes" in Fermanagh and Tyrone
was decided by statute entirely in favour of the Unionists.

THE STRUCTURE OF THE NORTHERN GOVERNMENT

The Act of 1920 is a landmark in the history of Ireland for
the one reason that it brought into existence the local Parliament
which now functions in Belfast. The outline of the constitutional
structure to be established follows closely the model of the
British Dominions. The Legislature consists of the Crown
and two Houses of Parliament.[2] It is the duty of the Governor
as Representative of the Crown to summon, prorogue and
dissolve the Parliament in the name of the King.[3] In addition
he enjoys the right of giving or withholding the Royal Assent
to Bills passed by the two Houses of Parliament. This power
is to be exercised subject to two statutory limitations; the
Governor-General must comply with any instructions given
by the King in respect of any Bill, and must, if so directed,
reserve any Bill for the signification of His Majesty's pleasure.[4]
There must be a session of Parliament once at least in every
year.[5] The Senate, or Upper House, is composed of two
ex-officio Senators together with twenty-four Senators elected
by the House of Commons according to the principles of
proportional representation. The term of office of the elected
members is eight years. One half of the members of the Senate

---

[1] *H. of C. Debates*, 1920, vol. 127, col. 991.   [2] Act of 1920, s. 1.
[3] Ibid., s. 11.   [4] Ibid., s. 12.   [5] Ibid., s. 11.

retires every four years.[1] The House of Commons is the more influential Chamber. It consists of fifty-two members elected, originally according to the principles of Proportional Representation, but now under the simple majority system. Every citizen who has reached the age of 21 years is eligible as a member. Universal suffrage is in practice. The total number of members is fixed by the Act of 1920 and may not be altered by the Parliament of Northern Ireland.[2]

The Parliament of the United Kingdom reserved to itself very considerable authority in Northern Ireland. In order that such authority might not be exercised regardless of opinion in that province, the Act made provision for the continued representation of the Northern Ireland constituencies at Westminster.[3] The number of members was, however, reduced from 30 to 13. The members for the Imperial Parliament were elected by the same electors, voting in the same constituencies as those of the Northern Parliament, the one difference being that the elections for the latter were conducted under the principles of P.R. Since 1929, when P.R. was abolished, the constituencies are no longer co-terminous.

The actual form of the Executive has been somewhat amended since 1920. The Act of that year contemplated the appointment of one representative of the Crown—the Lord Lieutenant— as the chief Executive Officer over all-Ireland. It was intended that he should act as the Representative of the Crown both in North and South.[4] The course of events in the South, however, precluded the possibility of this constitutional proposal being translated into practice. Actually one Lord Lieutenant, Lord FitzAlan, was appointed in April 1921. His tenure of office was legally terminated when the Constitution of the Irish Free State came into force in December 1922.[5] The new office of Governor of Northern Ireland was then created.[6]

[1] Act of 1920, s. 5.   [2] Ibid., s. 14.   [3] Ibid., s. 19.
[4] Ibid., s. 8.   [5] Cf. 13 Geo. V. c. 2.
[6] Cf. Quekett. *Constitution of Northern Ireland*, for description of legal course of events.

The Governor is endowed, as respects Northern Ireland, with the rights and duties of the Lord Lieutenant. All executive and administrative powers in respect of matters within the jurisdiction of the Northern Parliament are vested in the Crown and are exercised by the Governor, as the Representative of the Crown, through the various departments of State. In general the Governor acts upon the advice of the Northern Cabinet. The Ministers are responsible to Parliament and must be members either of the Senate or the House of Commons. A Minister may sit and speak in both Houses but he may move and vote only in that House of which he is a member. There are seven Departments of State. A Minister is appointed head of each department and is responsible for its work in the Legislature.

LEGISLATIVE POWERS

The Parliament of Northern Ireland is not a legislature enjoying sovereign power. Its Constitution is framed by an Act of the Imperial Parliament. It is within the competence of the latter either to amend or to withdraw the grant of self-government given to the north-eastern counties of Ulster. It is not within the power of the Northern Parliament to alter the essentials of its constitutional structure. It is not endowed with the constituent power. In accordance with the Act of 1920, the Parliament has power to make laws for the peace, order and good government of Northern Ireland in matters relating exclusively to Northern Ireland. The phrase "peace, order and good government" is used in its restrictive sense. In addition, certain matters are definitely excluded from the competence of the local legislature.[1] Such matters, under the terms of the Act, fall into three classes:

1. Matters of Imperial concern which are called *excepted* matters. They include the Crown; the making of peace and war, the control of the Army, Navy and Air Force, foreign affairs and certain questions of somewhat lesser importance

[1] Govt. of Ireland Act, 1920, s. 4, s. 19.

2. Certain matters which are *reserved* to the Imperial Parliament. Under this category fall questions arising out of reserved taxation; the general subject-matter of the Land Purchase Acts pending the completion of land purchase and other issues of ephemeral importance. Among the latter are to be noticed certain matters whose transfer to the Northern Parliament was delayed in view of the possibility of the creation of an all-Ireland Parliament under the terms of the Act.

3. Matters within the legislative powers of the Council of Ireland. These powers were later transferred to the Northern Parliament in view of the fact that the Council was never properly constituted.

These provisions of the Act of 1920 constitute a direct limitation of the powers of the Parliament of Northern Ireland. There are other provisions which by implication impose similar restrictions. The latter were introduced mainly in order to safeguard the rights of minorities. They are intended to provide a guarantee for religious liberty by prohibiting all legislation which interferes with religious equality or which discriminates between members of different creeds.

THE ACT OF 1920 AND IRISH UNITY

The Government of Ireland Act of 1920 is popularly referred to as the "Partition Act." Though this may be an accurate description of the consequences which the Act entailed, it gives, none the less, a misleading conception of its actual provisions. For the Act contained elaborate, though unstatesmanlike, proposals whose professed objective was the ultimate unity of Ireland. The impression that these clauses were introduced in the hope—entirely futile though it proved—of placating opinion in Southern Ireland is one that subsequent events do nothing to dispel. The official summary of the Act describes the intention of the Government in these words:[1]

[1] Govt. of Ireland Act, 1920, Summary of Main Provisions.

"Although at the beginning there are to be two Parliaments and two Governments in Ireland, the Act contemplates and affords every facility for Union between North and South, and empowers the two Parliaments by mutual agreement and joint action to terminate partition and to set up one Parliament and one Government for the whole of Ireland."

With a view to facilitating the eventual unity of Ireland, a bond of union was created for the intervening period by the Council of Ireland. This Council was to consist of twenty representatives elected by each Parliament and a President nominated by the Lord Lieutenant. It was its function to initiate proposals for united action on the part of the two Parliaments. Further, in the hope of securing uniform administration three matters (Railways, Fisheries, and Contagious Diseases of Animals) were placed within the exclusive jurisdiction of the Council. The plan might have met with deserved success had it been applied a decade earlier. In the event it met none of the needs, nor the difficulties, of the contemporary situation in Ireland. Thus it is not surprising to find that the Council, though in law it enjoyed a prolonged, if chequered, career until 1926, in fact never functioned at all.

THE TRANSFER OF SERVICES

The Act of 1920 involved very considerable changes in administrative practice in Ireland. Originally it was intended that the transfer of services to the respective Irish Governments should take palce contemporaneously, but when it became evident that Parliament of Southern Ireland as envisaged in the Act would in fact never be constituted, it was decided to proceed with such alterations as were necessary for the establishment of the Northern Government. In order to enable the constitutional changes to be made gradually the Act gave authority to His Majesty in Council to bring its provisions into force by declaring a series of "appointed days."[1] Under

---

[1] 1920, s. 73.

these provisions a considerable interval was permitted to elapse before the final consummation of the Act. May 3, 1921, was fixed as the appointed day for the establishment of the Northern Parliament, and on the 4th a proclamation was issued by the Lord Lieutenant making provision for the elections to be held for the Northern Legislature. The new Parliament assembled on June 27, 1921, and on the same day the Lord Lieutenant established the departments and appointed the Ministers as heads of their respective departments. The elected members of the House of Commons then proceeded to the election of the 24 members of the Senate. The Parliament was formally opened by the King on June 22nd. The transfer of the administration was delayed for several months in order to facilitate certain negotiations in which the British Government was then engaged. The Prime Minister hoped that Northern Ireland might be induced, whilst retaining her own Constitution, to become a component part of an Irish Federal Dominion. The course of Anglo-Irish negotiations and the form of the Anglo-Irish Treaty show that this objective was used as a diplomatic lever of no little value in the discussions preceding the emergence of the Irish Free State. For this reason, therefore, the transfer of the various administrative powers to the Northern Government was not completed till March 1, 1922.

THE POLICY OF THE FIRST GOVERNMENT OF NORTHERN IRELAND

The returns for the first election to the Northern Ireland House of Commons, which was held in 1921, resulted in a large majority for the Unionists. Of the fifty-two members returned forty were members of that party, six were Nationalists and six representatives of Sinn Fein. Sir James Craig, as leader of the Unionists, was called upon to form a Ministry. His Cabinet was constituted as follows:

Prime Minister .. .. Sir James Craig
Minister of Finance .. .. Mr. H. M. Pollock

Minister of Home Affairs	..	Sir R. D. Bates
Minister of Labour ..	..	Mr. J. M. Andrews
Minister of Education	..	The Marquis of Londonderry
Minister of Agriculture..	⎫	Mr. E. M. Archdale
Minister of Commerce ..	⎭	

The strength of the Cabinet thus formed depended upon the predominance given with one accord by the electors of the six counties to a single political issue. That issue was the existence of a Government in Northern Ireland. The Unionists received the grant of self-government with outward reluctance. Their leaders neglected no single opportunity of reminding the British people that in accepting the Act of 1920, Ulster had made the "surpreme sacrifice." The official attitude was explained by Sir James Craig in a letter to Mr. Lloyd George. He wrote:[1]

"In order that you may correctly understand the attitude we propose to adopt . . . it is necessary that I should call to your mind the sacrifices we have so recently made in agreeing to self-government and in consenting to the establishment of a Parliament for Northern Ireland. Much against our wish but in the interests of peace we accepted this as a *final settlement* of the long outstanding difficulty with which Great Britain has been confronted." Mr. Armour's comment was less unctuous. "I am not saying that they did not do right in starting their Government," he remarked in the General Assembly, "they were compelled to do it because they had yelled about 'No Home Rule' for a generation and then they were compelled to take a form of Home Rule that the Devil himself could never have imagined."[2]

Once self-government had been established Sir James Craig and his colleagues devoted their energies to maintaining intact the Constitution outlined in the Act of 1920. The inclusion of the six counties in an all-Ireland federation was regarded

[1] Quoted, *N.I., H. of C. Debates*, vol. i, col. 48.
[2] Quoted W. S. Armour, *Armour of Ballymoney*, p. 332.

by the Cabinet with the most profound aversion. No Governmentment has ever had a more settled policy than that of Ulster, claimed Sir James Craig, and he added—"That policy is to retain a Parliament of our own and not to come under a Dublin Parliament."[1] In the course of the next few years the Unionist Party laid less emphasis upon the "supreme sacrifice" but more upon the "final settlement" that had been achieved. One political party at any rate was content.

With the character and aims of the Nationalist Opposition we shall deal later. Here it is sufficient to point out that their aversion to self-government in the six counties was extreme. Not only were they politically severed from the vast majority of their creed and party, but also they were cast for the rôle of a permanent minority in Northern Ireland. In no conceivable circumstances could the Opposition become the Government. The bitterness of the Nationalists was intensified by the knowledge that the area of jurisdiction of the Northern Government had been dictated by the Ulster Unionist Council in order that their party might govern as large a population as was consistent with continued Unionist supremacy. The aim of the Nationalists was to end Partition. So it was that the existence of self-government in Belfast became, and has since remained, the supreme issue in Northern politics. In the first House of Commons the members of the Nationalist and Sinn Fein parties, adopting a policy of non-recognition, declined to take their seats. Thus the House consisted of a single party with no definite Opposition. As an immediate consequence the 24 elective members of the Senate were chosen from among the Unionist Party. So all the members attending both Houses were supporters of the Act of 1920 and followers of a Government pledged to put it into execution.

The events which led to local self-government in Belfast rendered it inevitable that this cleavage of opinion on the supreme constitutional question should provide the one vital issue in Ulster politics. Since there is no agreement on essentials

[1] Quoted *N.I., H. of C. Debates*, vol. ii, col. 553.

between the rival parties the survival of the Northern Parliament depends upon the continued success of one party at the polls. Parliamentary Democracy cannot function properly under such frozen political conditions.

PUBLIC OPINION AND THE ACT OF 1920

It is needless to remark that it was the political proposals, and not the constitutional experiment contained in the Act of 1920, that attracted the attention of public opinion. The reaction which the former provoked deserves some attention. In Ireland, the reception was uniformly hostile. "The Act of 1920," Captain Redmond remarked some time later, "was condemned in every corner of Ireland, and it had not even the support of a single Member whether he came from the North or the South."[1] This is not surprising since the Act paid no attention whatever to contemporary Irish opinion. The six counties preferred the Act of Union; the Nationalists still supported those proposals for Home Rule which they had so nearly realized in the heyday of their power; whilst Sinn Fein, now the largest and most influential party in Ireland, contemptuous of the parliamentary manœuvres of the last decade, advocated complete separation. For these reasons the Bill was received with distaste in the North, with derision in the South. Even amongst those prepared to judge upon its merits a Bill proposed by the British Government there seemed serious ground for criticism. It was one thing, as Mr. Hammond has written,[2] to leave the Ulster counties outside a Home Rule Bill by the methods discussed at the Buckingham Palace Conference; it was another to set up a Parliament in Ulster and so give strength and permanence to Partition. This arrangement seemed to Irishmen, suspicious by nature and still more suspicious by experience, not, as it seemed to the Prime Minister, a way out of a difficulty, but as a deliberate blow

[1] *H. of C. Debates*, 1922, vol. 151, col. 1408.
[2] Cf. *C. P. Scott, of the "Manchester Guardian,"* p. 273.

at Irish unity. Both critics and supporters agree that the "practical and irrevocable" importance of the Bill lay in its consequence—the creation of self-governing institutions in Belfast. From that moment, wrote Mr. Churchill,[1] the position of Ulster became unassailable. No longer could it be said that the Ulster Protestants barred the way of their Southern fellow-countrymen. "They were masters in their own house, and small though it might be, it was morally and logically founded upon a rock. The Act of 1920 ended for ever this phase of the Irish problem." But it was this very aspect of finality, so attractive to Mr. Churchill, that was so alarming to all who sympathized with the ideal of Irish Unity. In a letter to Mr. Dillon dated May 30, 1920, Mr. C. P. Scott analysed his objections to the Bill. He wrote:

"As you say, the present Bill has no relation to the needs of the situation. Its real objects, so far as I can make out, are, first to get rid of the Home Rule Act, and secondly to entrench the six counties against Nationalist Ireland. Its effect, one fears, will be not to make a solution easier but to make it harder, by creating a fresh and powerful obstacle. Why not take Carson at his word and simply leave the six counties as part of the United Kingdom and establish one Parliament for the rest of Ireland? . . . The six counties would not for ever stay out, it would be found too inconvenient, and when they came in it would be on their own terms—that is, on terms agreed upon with the Irish Parliament, by Irishmen, with Irishmen."[2]

Mr. Scott believed that if the Prime Minister could be persuaded to leave the six counties out of the Bill it would thereby be rendered a good deal less dangerous. The settlement then would be obviously provisional and Ulster extremism would be less firmly entrenched.[3] At this present moment the Ulster Nationalists, despairing of any immediate reunion

---

[1] *The World Crisis*, "The Aftermath," p. 286.
[2] Quoted in J. L. Hammond, op. cit., p. 273.
[3] Cf. his letter of June 29, 1920, to Mr. Dillon.

with the Free State, desire a return to this policy. They would prefer to be governed from London rather than from Belfast. But when Scott wrote the Cabinet had decided upon its policy. Mr. Dillon's foreboding reply was only too accurate. "Banish from your mind," he wrote,[1] "all ideas of modifying the present Home Rule Bill. The Irish situation has reached a stage now in which there is not the slightest hope of any beneficial effect except from heroic measures."

ULSTER AND THE ANGLO-IRISH TREATY

Neither of the historic English parties was without a theory of government based in each case upon a diagnosis of the conditions of English Society. But both parties were more than hesitant in applying their respective theories to the problems of Ireland. More especially since 1914 a certain fatalism had deadened the policy of successive Governments. Those circumstances that fostered the growth of a national sentiment irreconcilable with British rule account for this inertia. But they do not justify the lack of a constructive policy, based upon the frank acceptance of the actual state of public opinion in Ireland. Both Mr. Asquith's Cabinet and its successor accepted the inevitableness and foresaw the confusion; but both allowed that the new Ireland which was to rise out of the ruins of the old must be left to come into existence of itself. They cared only to stave off the calamity of change, and so prolonged the travail and birth-pangs of the new Ireland.

The opportunist policy of the Coalition Government alone enables one to understand the rather curious part which Ulster played in the Treaty negotiations. Both the principal parties at the Conference were agreed as to the ideal solution—severance of Ulster from the United Kingdom and incorporation in a United Ireland Dominion—but neither side separately, nor even both in concert, could move towards this consummation

[1] Quoted in J. L. Hammond, op. cit., p. 276.

without the consent of a third party.[1] Ulster had accepted the
Act of 1920 unwillingly, but on the explicit understanding that
her status once acquired was permanently assured. It was
inconceivable that she should be coerced by an English Government. Mr. Lloyd George, while admitting that "the form in
which the settlement is to take effect will depend upon Ireland
herself," made it quite clear that "it must allow for the full
recognition of the existing powers and privileges of the Parliament and Government of Northern Ireland, which cannot
be abrogated except by their own consent."[2] At the same time
Sinn Fein could accept no settlement as final which did not
secure the essential unity of Ireland. "As regards the question
at issue between the political minority and the great majority
of the Irish people," replied Mr. de Valera, "that must remain
a question for the Irish people themselves to settle. We cannot
admit the right of the British Government to mutilate our
country, either in its own interest or at the call of any section
of our population. We do not contemplate the use of force.
If your Government stands aside, we can effect a complete
reconciliation."[3] But it is plain now both that previous pledges
would in any event have prevented the British Government
from "standing aside," and at the same time that Sinn Fein
would not have been able to reach agreement with the North.
What then were the practical alternatives with regard to the
future of Ulster which faced the negotiators? There appeared
to be three possible courses: (1) Forcible incorporation of
Ulster with the South; (2) Subtraction from Ulster of the
two predominantly Catholic counties or their equivalent;
(3) The retention by Ulster of all her existing area.[4] The first
alternative was ruled out by all parties. The second was attractive to Sinn Fein, not merely because of the territorial gain,
but also because it might well render the economic position

[1] Cf. F. Pakenham, *Peace by Ordeal*, p. 107.
[2] Proposals of the Brit. Govt. for an Irish Settlement, July 20,
1921. Cmd. 1470.
[3] Letter to P.M., August 10, 1921. Cmd. 1470.
[4] Cf. Pakenham, op. cit., pp. 163–4.

of Northern Ireland intolerable and thus indirectly lead to reunion. The Northern Government, on the other hand, maintained that the third alternative alone was consistent with the Prime Minister's pledge for the full recognition of the "powers and privileges" of Northern Ireland. In a letter of November 11th, Sir James Craig wrote:[1]

"We observe with considerable concern that the area within the jurisdiction of the Northern Parliament is referred to as being open to possible revision. This question was carefully and fully considered in all its aspects . . . and the area decided upon is defined in the Act and it forms no less essential a part of the Act than the powers conferred upon the Northern Parliament." One may doubt, as Mr. Lloyd George did, the full validity of this contention, but mere doubts were insufficient should the Northern Government prove recalcitrant. And the correspondence which passed between Mr. Lloyd George and Sir James Craig prior to the Treaty showed that no conciliatory move was to be expected from the North. The Prime Minister's invitation to Ulster to come into Conference was declined on the ground that any such discussion would be fruitless unless the Cabinet withdrew the proposals for an all-Ireland Parliament. "Such a Parliament," wrote Sir James Craig,[2] "is precisely what Ulster has for many years resisted by all the means at her disposal, and her detestation of it is in no degree diminished by the local institutions conferred upon her by the Act of 1920." As an alternative Sir James suggested that the six counties should be vested with constitutional powers similar to those proposed for the South, even though this involved the loss of representatives in the Imperial Parliament. In fact, though not in name, he suggested that the six counties no less than Southern Ireland should be given Dominion status. Mr. Lloyd George refused; pointing out quite rightly that the proposal "would stereotype a frontier

---

[1] Correspondence between H.M. Government and the Prime Minister of Northern Ireland. Cmd. 1561.
[2] Letter of November 11, 1921.

based neither upon natural features nor broad geographical considerations by giving it the character of an international boundary."[1] Further correspondence ensued but no results were achieved save that Ulster was assured that "her rights will be in no way sacrificed or compromised."

The constitutional status and area of Northern Ireland played a large part in the conversations between the English and Irish delegates. Mr. Pakenham has shown in his dramatic reconstruction of the course of the negotiations that "Sinn Fein, seeing that British Liberal and world opinion was likely to be against her in seeking a Republic, and with her in seeking a United Ireland, planned early that it should be on the latter head that the break, if break there must be, should come."[2] In the event the Irish delegates were unable to carry out this plan, but its existence explains how it was that they were induced to accept the boundary clause in the Treaty. The British proposals of November 10th provided, in the event of a Boundary Commission being appointed, that "it should determine in accordance with the wishes of the inhabitants the boundaries between Northern and Southern Ireland." But in the Treaty this provision read that the Commission "shall determine in accordance with the wishes of the inhabitants, *so far as may be compatible with economic and geographical considerations*,"[3] the boundary between North and South. It was these economic and geographical considerations that later were to prove decisive in losing the Irish Free State every scrap of her anticipated territorial gains.

In the Treaty the Sinn Fein postulate of the political unity of Ireland was formally accepted. Under Article 1, the Irish Free State was to embrace the whole of Ireland, and thus the *principle* of Partition embodied in the Act of 1920 was nullified. Needless to say, this assertion of principle was accompanied by no prospect of a practical realization. But it was consistently

---

[1] Letter of November 14, 1921.   [2] *Peace by Ordeal*, p. 109.
[3] Articles of Agreement for a Treaty between Great Britain and Ireland, clause 12.

applied throughout the Treaty. This is most strikingly shown in the provisions regulating the future relationship between the Free State and Northern Ireland.[1] The Treaty, having defined Ireland as the area of jurisdiction of the Free State Government, had to ensure the maintenance of the constitutional status of Northern Ireland by specific measures of exclusion. In the first instance, the exercise of the legislative and executive powers of the Free State in relation to Northern Ireland were excluded until the expiration of one month after the ratification of the Treaty by the British Parliament. Within this month—which was subsequently made to run from December 5, 1922—Northern Ireland was given the alternative either of excluding itself from the Free State by a special address presented to the King by both Houses of its Parliament, or of remaining in the Free State with wide powers of local self-government. It was certain at the time of the signature of the Treaty that Northern Ireland would exclude herself, and in this case it was provided she should do so subject to a subsequent revision of her frontiers by a Boundary Commission.

In the event the solution envisaged by the Treaty was not put into operation in its entirety. The relevant address to the King was passed by both Houses of the Northern Parliament on December 17, 1922, but the appointment of the Boundary Commission did not take place until November 1924. The setting up of the Commission was in itself a task of some difficulty, in that the Northern Government refused to appoint its Commissioner in accordance with the terms of the Treaty. By a supplemental agreement, however, the two signatory Governments arranged that the power of the Government of Northern Ireland to appoint a Commissioner should be transferred to the British Government.[2] The Commission thus created, with Mr. Justice Feetham, of South Africa, as Chairman, conducted elaborate investigations but were unable to arrive at an agreed solution. Since 1914, said Mr. Churchill:

[1] Clauses 11 to 16.
[2] Scheduled to the Treaty, Act No. 51 of 1924.

"Every institution, almost, in the world was strained, great empires have been overturned. The whole map of Europe has been changed. The position of countries has been violently altered. The mode and thought of men, the whole outlook on affairs, the grouping of parties, all have encountered violent and tremendous changes in the deluge of the world, but as the deluge subsides and the waters fall we see the dreary steeples of Fermanagh and Tyrone emerging once again. The integrity of their quarrel is one of the few institutions that have been unaltered in the cataclysm which has swept the world."[1] No report of the Commission was published owing to the resignation of the Free State nominee. An agreed solution was, however, accepted by the three Governments concerned and thereby the provisions of the Treaty were considerably modified.[2] In the issue at stake this agreement confirmed the existing boundary as defined in the Act of 1920. This involved the retention of all disputed areas in the two counties of Fermanagh and Tyrone within the jurisdiction of the Northern Government. In the Free State it was felt that the Treaty had been broken in spirit if not in letter. For the Sinn Fein delegates had signed in the belief that the Boundary Clause secured the "essential unity" of Ireland. They understood from the words of the Prime Minister that the clause was weighted in their favour and that the British Government had taken a definite political decision to give them the two counties provided their contention as to the wishes of the inhabitants proved correct.[3] But Mr. Justice Feetham, in a subsequent letter to *The Times*, made it clear whatever the statistical facts that the transfer of substantial areas from Northern to Southern Ireland was precluded, in his view, by the wording of the clause. So ended a most unfortunate chapter in Anglo-Irish negotiations.

The Treaty in all essentials confirmed the constitutional

---

[1] *The Aftermath*, p. 319.
[2] Scheduled to the Treaty, Act No. 40 of 1925.
[3] Cf. Pakenham, op. cit., p. 346, and Appendix 8.

position established in Northern Ireland by the Act of 1920. But with regard to status it entailed a considerable modification of the earlier settlement. Under the latter Ireland had been divided into two political and administrative units of equal authority, but now the balance is changed in that one of the units has become a virtually independent State whilst the other remains a semi-autonomous province within a larger political entity.

PART III

GOVERNMENT IN NORTHERN IRELAND

"Belfast . . . the city which has been the refuge of the oppressors and the necropolis of Liberalism."

"There are many in Ulster unamenable to reason, as they are so poisoned with whirling speeches that they believe that their prejudices have the sanction of Sinai."

Armour of Ballymoney.

"I long to see Belfast the freest place in Ireland. May there be given to us a vision of our city, as it might be, a city of justice, a city of plenty, a city of peace, where all success should be founded on service, and all honour given to nobleness alone, where the sick and the weak and the poor should be succoured by men and women who had felt, and were filled with the love of Christ."

JOHN MACNEICE,
Bishop of Down.

CHAPTER VII

THE ELECTORAL SYSTEM

TODAY the years 1918–21 assume all the qualities of an epilogue; then it was hoped they would bring to birth a golden age of parliamentary democracy. The emergence of the submerged nationalities of Central and South-Eastern Europe evoked a demand for the principles of Representative Government which brought about the acceptance of even the more fanciful devices of paper democracy. Less than a decade sufficed to show that the post-War Constitutions created the illusion, but not the reality, of parliamentary government. But at the same time this phase in the history of Democracy affected the outlook of the age; even in countries, such as Great Britain, which remained consciously aloof from the enthusiasms of the new Europe. If this influence is most decisively shown in the larger issue of Anglo-Irish relations yet it is also reflected in the narrower constitutional field of Northern Ireland. The Constitutions of post-War Europe showed a remarkable unanimity in prescribing, for the elections to the popular Assembly, direct election on the principles of Proportional Representation or with "representation of minorities."[1] And moreover, to such an extent had P.R. become part of the accepted machinery of the Modern State that it was included in the new Constitutions almost without discussion.[2] This popularity, though it did not shake the loyalty of the United Kingdom to the simple majority system, did lead to the introduction of P.R. in Ireland under the 1920 Act.

In Northern Ireland, the electoral system is a matter of peculiar significance both because of the number of electorates and the need for the proper representation of minorities. There are, in fact, no less than four elected assemblies.

[1] Cf. Yugoslav Constitution, Art. 69.
[2] Cf. Headlam-Morley, *The New Constitutions of Europe*, p. 101.

Three of these are elected by the direct vote of the people and one by members of the House of Commons of Northern Ireland. The representatives of Northern Ireland returned to the Parliament of the United Kingdom are elected, like their colleagues at Westminster, under the simple majority system. The members of the House of Commons in Belfast, though originally elected according to the principles of P.R., are now elected in the traditional English manner. The members of both Parliaments are elected by universal adult suffrage. In Local Government a restricted property franchise is in force. Here again, as in the Northern Ireland parliamentary elections, P.R. was abandoned, after a brief trial, in favour of the simple majority system. The Senate is elected by the members of the Lower House and in this instance alone has P.R. been retained. It is to be remembered throughout that the relative merits of the alternative systems of election were not the only consideration which guided the Imperial Government. For in addition, full representation of the Opposition was felt to constitute an essential feature of the Settlement. Sir. L. Worthington Evans stated in 1920 that: "P.R. was introduced into the Government of Ireland Act as one of the safeguards by which it was intended to protect minorities." After all, the peculiarity of the Ulster Question lay not in the existence of a political minority but in the fact that it was likely to prove a permanent minority. So long as party divisions remain irreconcilable, so long as self-government in Belfast is co-terminous with the continued electoral success of one party, then P.R. does appear to offer the best means of securing such a minority *some* representation. Electoral machinery must be subordinated to political needs.

LOCAL GOVERNMENT

The first experiments designed to test the suitability of P.R. in Ireland were carried out in Local Government elections. It had been felt since before the War that the fierceness of

Irish party strife demanded an absolute accuracy in election returns. For this reason P.R. was prescribed as the electoral system in the Home Rule Act. This legislation of the Liberal Government was endorsed by a large majority in the Irish Convention.[1] It was not, however, till 1919 that the first practical experiment was carried out in the Sligo municipal elections. The success of this trial led to the passage of legislation prescribing P.R. for all local elections in Ireland.[2] The elections for the urban and municipal councils were held early in 1920; the County Council elections in the summer of the same year. The results showed that P.R. was definitely favourable to minority representation both in North and South. They also served to dispel the illusion that the north-eastern counties of Ulster were entirely Unionist. Public interest centred largely upon a dramatic contest which decided the party majority in the Tyrone County Council election. In this county the Nationalists had gained a recent but slight numerical advantage. Under P.R. the party, composed of constitutional Nationalists and Sinn Fein working in co-operation, secured the majority to which their voting strength entitled them. The new electoral system was received with favour by all parties other than the Ulster Unionists.

Local Government bodies in Northern Ireland are elected upon a restricted property franchise similar to that in force throughout the United Kingdom. Till 1922, elections were carried out according to the principles of P.R. Since then the simple majority system has been restored. The purpose and the consequences of this change may be discussed more conveniently in connection with the similar alteration in parliamentary electoral machinery.

HOUSE OF COMMONS—NORTHERN IRELAND

The number of members, the system of election, the delimitation of constituencies in Northern Ireland were determined by

[1] By 45 votes to 20.   [2] Local Government (Ireland) Act, 1919.

the Act of 1920.[1] The House of Commons consists of 52 members. They are elected upon the same franchise as members returned to serve in the Imperial Parliament. The House is elected for a period of five years, unless sooner dissolved. The Act of 1920 provided that contested elections should be held according to the principles of Proportional Representation. The actual system enforced was that of the Single Transferable Vote. There were ten constituencies each returning not fewer than 4 nor more than 8 members.

At the outset, the Parliament of Northern Ireland had not the power to alter the prescribed electoral laws. It had been decided at Westminster that all matters relating to the franchise, to the system of election, to the size of constituencies and the distribution of members amongst them should lie outside the jurisdiction of the Northern Parliament for a period of *three years*, dating from the first meeting of the Parliament in Belfast. In addition the Act of 1920 ruled that, in any new distribution sanctioned by the Northern Parliament after the lapse of this probationary period, the number of the members should not be altered and that due regard should be paid to the populations of the constituencies. The power thus granted was exercised by the Northern Government in 1929[2] for the purpose of abolishing P.R. and restoring the simple majority system as it remains in force today. This change entailed certain consequential alterations, the most important of which was the creation of single-member, in place of the original multiple, constituencies. In the University alone was P.R. retained.

By providing that the franchise for the election of members to the Northern Ireland House of Commons should be identical with that of the United Kingdom, the Act made it practicable that the register of electors compiled for the latter election should also be used for the former. This was possible until a change was made either by the Imperial or the local Parliament. In 1928 the Representation of the People Act was amended

[1] Sec. 14.   [2] 19 Geo. V. c. v.

so as to assimilate the United Kingdom franchise for men and women by conceding the "flapper" vote. In order to preserve the same electoral roll, the Northern Ireland Parliament passed a parallel Act giving an equal franchise.[1]

This brief outline of the history of representation in Northern Ireland provides the background against which the validity of the reasons advanced for the Amending Act of 1929 may be tested in the light of experience; and against which the operation of the respective electoral systems may be analysed. The form of Proportional Representation, recommended in the Act of 1920, is the system known as the Single Transferable vote. Under it constituencies return several members. The elector in voting places the number 1 opposite the name of the candidate he likes best, and is invited to place the number 2 opposite his second choice, the number 3 opposite his third choice, and so on, numbering as many candidates as he pleases. The Returning Officer ascertains the result of the election in the following manner. He counts each ballot paper as one vote to the candidate marked 1 thereon. He also counts the total number of votes. He ascertains the quota. This figure is obtained by dividing the votes cast by the number of seats to be filled plus one, and adding one to the result. Thus if there are 100 votes cast and two seats to be filled the quota will then be $\frac{100}{2+1} + 1 = 34$, a number which can be obtained only by two candidates. The candidates who have received the quota are then declared elected. The surplus votes of those candidates who have received more than the quota are transferred in strict proportions, and credited to the unelected candidates indicated by the figures 2, 3, and so on as the next preferences of the electors whose votes are transferred. Then those candidates who after the transfer of surplus votes have obtained the quota are declared elected. The candidates lowest on the poll are now eliminated one after another by transferring their votes, in accordance with the wishes of their supporters, to the candidates indicated

[1] 18 & 19 Geo. V. c. 24.

I

as next preferences. This process is continued until either the
required number of candidates, having each obtained the quota,
is elected, or the number of candidates not elected is reduced
to the number of seats still vacant. In the latter event, the candidates not eliminated are declared elected.

This system of election by the Single Transferable Vote
requires that the electoral area should be divided up into constituencies each returning several members. In Northern Ireland
the number of members returned for each constituency varied
from 4 to 8. The actual distribution of seats was as follows:

	Number of Members returned
Belfast County Borough—	
East	4
North	4
South	4
West	4
Antrim County	7
Armagh County	4
Fermanagh and Tyrone Counties	8
Londonderry County (including the County Borough of Londonderry)	5
Down County	8
The Queen's University of Belfast.. ..	4
Total	52

The constituencies were defined so as to coincide in the
majority of cases with the county boundaries. This was unfortunate in that it involved the creation of constituencies of
unwieldy size as Fermanagh–Tyrone, and Down. To mark
as many as eight preferences is a task imposing a certain strain
on the average elector—and as a consequence, such large
constituencies play into the hands of the party organizations.
A four to five member constituency appears to provide the
most convenient area for the operation of the Single Transferable vote, and in the Irish Free State, where the system has
given considerable satisfaction, it has been found desirable
to abolish the larger constituencies.[1]

Two elections in Northern Ireland were held under P.R.
They provide a reasonably clear indication of the influence

[1] Vide Electoral (Revision of Constituencies) Bill, 1934.

such a system of voting might have exercised on Ulster politics.
The first was held on May 24, 1921. Sinn Fein and the Constitutional Nationalists were united in opposition to the Unionist
party. Under P.R. it was possible for both the Nationalist
groups to put forward their own candidates without playing into
the hands of their opponents. 89 per cent of the electorate voted.
The Unionists secured 40 seats; the Opposition parties 12. The
former obtained a majority everywhere except in the two constituencies of Armagh and Fermanagh–Tyrone. At the same
time, the minority received representation everywhere outside
Belfast City. If one omits the voting in the Queen's University—
where seats are not in accordance with a quantitative population
basis—it appears that an assignment of seats strictly proportional
to votes would have given the Unionists 32 representatives
instead of 36, and the Nationalist 16 in place of 12. This
inaccuracy, which is considerable in a small area, was caused
almost entirely by the returns of the Belfast constituencies.
The city was split up into four 4-member constituencies
and the Nationalist vote was so divided amongst them that the
party returned only one member although just failing to poll
the quota in the other three constituencies. The second and last
election held under P.R. took place in 1925. On this occasion the
returns were substantially accurate. The figures were as follows:

GENERAL ELECTION, 1925
Figures for contested County and Borough Constituencies

Parties	Votes	Seats Won	Seats in proportion to votes
Unionist	211,662	22	22·0
Nationalist	91,452	9	9·5
Independent Unionist	42,902	5	4·5
Republican	20,615	1	2·1
Labour	18,114	3	1·9
Total	384,745	40	40·0

These figures indicate that the results obtained under the
Single Transferable Vote are substantially accurate. The value

of the votes polled for the larger parties shows a very close approximation to equality, and although the returns for the smaller parties reveal certain discrepancies this is a matter of rather secondary importance. The system, whilst giving an opportunity to small parties, does not favour them. In the 1925 election the Republicans nominated candidates in several constituencies, but only in one did they poll a quota of votes. This consequence of a split vote cannot be avoided other than by the introduction of further refinements in electoral machinery. However suitable these may have proved in a large nation, as the German Republic, they do appear unduly elaborate in so small an area as Northern Ireland. Moreover, it may well be claimed that the destination of a single seat is, in itself, a matter of no vital significance. After all, under P.R. both Republicans and Labour secured reasonably fair representation. Further, in no contested constituency did one party monopolize representation—a fact which might in time have blunted the edge of party feeling, and did, in fact, prevent an exaggeration of the geographical divisions of party strength. Moreover, so long as P.R. remained in force it provided a guarantee that a small turnover in votes should not achieve results out of all proportion to voting strength. The returns of the 1931 General Election in Great Britain bear witness to the remarkable mathematical inaccuracy possible, in certain circumstances, under the Simple Majority system.

GREAT BRITAIN AND NORTHERN IRELAND—GENERAL ELECTION, 1931

Party	Votes polled	Seats[1]	Seats in Proportion to Votes
Government Parties (Conservative, Liberal, National Liberal)	14,531,925	493	368
Labour	6,648,023	46	168
Independent Liberal ..	106,106	4	3
Others	371,252	5	9
Totals	21,657,306	548	548

[1] Not including 67 uncontested seats (61 Government, 6 Labour).

The English system of voting does not stand condemned because it exaggerates majorities. On the contrary, this very lack of proportion is widely held to be one of its peculiar merits, in that the system thereby tends to ensure stable government. But this virtue—if virtue it be—does render the simple majority system quite unsuitable for use in countries where there exist minorities, whether racial or religious, sensitive to their rights.

From the first, the introduction of P.R. was opposed by the Ulster Unionists. They were unwilling that it should be inserted in the Act of 1920 and the party leaders publicly announced their intention of abolishing P.R. before the second General Election held in Northern Ireland. The surprise lies, therefore, not in the fact that the electoral law was amended but in that it remained unamended till 1929. For three years admittedly the Northern Parliament had not the constitutional power to alter the system of election, but then that period had elapsed by 1924. Later, Sir James Craig was challenged by his supporters as to the failure of the Government to abolish P.R. before the second election. He replied that "there are certain very grave considerations which I am not at liberty to announce in the House that made it necessary to carry out the last election under P.R., much as I object to the system."[1] These considerations, it may be assumed, took count of the possibility that the abolition of P.R. might be viewed with disfavour in London—a consequence that could not be regarded with equanimity in Belfast at a time when the Boundary clause still held out possibilities of territorial readjustment. The Unionist denunciations of P.R., however, continued unabated; and at the Orange celebrations in 1927 Lord Craigavon (formerly Sir James Craig) announced the forthcoming abolition of P.R. The Prime Minister pointed to the desirability of eliminating all minorities except that represented by the Nationalist Party.[2] This would mean that Ulster's political life would continue to consist of a straight fight on the traditional Protestant-Catholic Unionist-Nationalist lines; and that in this struggle the Unionists were

[1] Cf. *N.I., H. of C. Debates*, April 21, 1925.
[2] Cf. *Belfast News-Letter*, July 13, 1927.

assured, on a population basis, of certain victory. While the consequences of electoral reform thus held obvious attractions for the Prime Minister, they could not be viewed with favour by the Labour Party, whose political existence the measure was intended to terminate. As early as 1926 the Belfast Trades and Labour Council protested strongly against the declared intention of the Government to abolish P.R.,[1] and in the autumn session of the Commons in 1927 the leader of the Labour Party moved the appointment of a Select Committee to enquire into the authority of the Government to carry out electoral reform on the lines proposed.[2] The debates both on this motion and subsequently on the Government's Electoral Amendment Bill were marked by extreme bitterness. Mr. Kyle, the leader of the Labour Party, admitted that in practice P.R. might not be perfect but held that it was not entirely its merits that were under discussion. There was also the question of minority rights guaranteed in the Act of 1920. "It seems to me," he said, "that the abolition of P.R. is deliberately designed to favour the Unionist Party in that it will make it the more difficult for minorities to secure representation."[3] Mr. Devlin, leader of the Nationalists, adopted a similar attitude. "I think," he said in the House, "that this is a mean, contemptible and callous attempt by the majority which you now have to rob the minority . . . of the safeguard which was incorporated in this measure . . . as an essential feature in the task of national pacification."[4] Outside the House equally vigorous protests were made. It is sufficient to refer to one of them. In January 1928, a Manifesto addressed "To the People of the Six Counties" was published under the signature of fourteen members of the House of Commons. The signatories included nine Nationalist M.P.s, three Labour M.P.s, an Independent Unionist and an Independent.[5] This document protested against the "glaring injustices" suffered by minorities in Ulster

---

[1] Cf. *Belfast News-Letter*, April 7, 1926.
[2] Cf. *N.I., H. of C. Debates*, October 25–26, 1927.
[3] Ibid., vol. viii, col. 2268.   [4] Ibid., vol. viii, col. 2280.
[5] Cf. *Irish News*, January 30, 1928.

and specially condemned the proposed abolition of P.R. "an eminently fair system of representation." "All this hideous campaign of intolerance and wrong," the manifesto proceeds, "now seeks its culminating triumph in the abolition of P.R., which the British Legislature embodied in the Act of 1920, and which was intended for, and by the minority accepted as a safeguard of their meagre rights." It is to be noted that the vigour of the minority protests was occasioned in no small measure by their experience of similar change in electoral practice which had taken place in Local Government elections in 1922.

The reasons given by the Prime Minister for the abolition of P.R. were such as are usually advanced by its opponents. He claimed that the cost was excessive, that the constituencies were too large and as a consequence that members "feel, as conscientious Ulstermen, that they are not able to give to the whole of those wide constituencies that meticulous care and attention that the electors are really entitled to receive." In addition, Lord Craigavon pointed to the menace of a multiplicity of parties such as P.R. is generally supposed to create, he argued that the system was bound "in the end to result in confusion amongst the electors, who will hardly know who they are voting for," and finally, that as "loyal Ulstermen" they would prefer to vote under the same system as that in force in Great Britain.[1] Certain of the Unionist criticisms of P.R. were undeniably just. The introduction of P.R. did, in fact, involve a certain financial outlay, though the cost of subsequent elections can hardly be termed excessive.[2] Further, certain of the constituencies were unquestionably large and unwieldy; but then that might be remedied by reducing their size instead of by abolishing P.R. The loss of the personal touch between members and their constituencies is a real defect in P.R. and does provide a very legitimate ground for criticism. But here again smaller constituencies would have diminished the force of this objection. For the rest the Prime

[1] Cf. *N.I., H. of C. Debates*, vol. viii, cols. 2276–82.
[2] The initial expenditure was necessitated by administrative work connected with the creation of a new electoral system. It was non-recurrent.

Minister appeared to underestimate the intelligence of the Ulster electorate. In 1925 there was a heavy poll and less than 2 per cent of the votes were invalid. Moreover, as experience in the Free State has shown, a growing familiarity with P.R. has reduced the number of spoilt votes to a quite insignificant level. However, the debates in the House of Commons reveal clearly that neither the Government nor the Opposition were deeply concerned with the more particular consequences of different electoral systems. The issue was, in fact, more simple. The Prime Minister desired to abolish P.R. because he believed that it would create a multiplicity of parties; that as a result the stability of the Government would be threatened, and that ultimately the traditional divisions in Ulster politics would disappear. The Opposition defended P.R. because they believed that it constituted a guarantee to minorities. But it is to be observed that while the proposed change was unlikely to affect the actual representation of the Nationalist minority it was expected —and expressly intended—to wipe out all other minority representation. It was the continued existence of the Labour and Republican not of the Nationalist Party that was in jeopardy.

Two elections to the Northern Ireland House of Commons have taken place under the simple majority system. The results show to what extent the aim of its supporters and the fears of its opponents have been realized.

GENERAL ELECTION, 1929
(Single-member constituencies; but 4 University members still elected by P.R. not included)

Party	Votes	Contested Seats	Seats in proportion to Votes	Uncontested Seats
Unionist	146,899	18	13	16
Independent Unionist	41,337	2	4	—
Nationalist	34,069	5	3	6
Labour	24,960	1	2	—
Liberal	21,645	—	2	—
Others	21,187	—	2	—
Total	290,697	26	26	22

GENERAL ELECTION, 1933[1]

Party	Votes	Contested Seats	Seats in proportion to Votes	Uncontested Seats
Unionist	72,133	6	6·5	27
Independent Unionist	35,774	2	3	—
Nationalist	22,269	3	2	6
Republican ..	20,510	2	2	—
Labour	14,436	2	1·5	—
Independent ..	2,211	—	—	—
Total	167,333	15	15	33

These election returns indicate that no radical change was effected by the alteration in the electoral system. At the same time it is evident that the Government was correct in supposing that the single-member constituencies would favour the two larger parties. In the 1929 election the Unionists were very considerably over-represented, and in both elections the Nationalists benefited slightly. These gains have meant corresponding losses to the smaller parties. Labour, for example, has not been able to retain the number of seats it won in 1925, owing to the division of the larger constituencies. But on the whole—in so far as two elections afford sufficient evidence upon which to form a judgment—it may be said that both the hopes of the majority and the fears of the minority have been only in small measure fulfilled. There has been, however, one significant consequence of the change, namely a rapid increase in the number of uncontested seats. In 1923 there were no uncontested seats; in 1925 there were 8; in 1929 there were 22; in 1933 there were 33. In other words, just 70 per cent of the borough and county seats were not contested at the last election.[2] The reason is evident. When party divisions are based upon religious professions the result of an election in most single-member constituencies is a foregone conclusion. It is one of the

[1] These figures are derived from publications of the Proportional Representation Society.
[2] The University seats are not counted in these calculations.

more notable defects of the simple majority system that it has increased the stagnation of political life in Northern Ireland.

The alarm which the minority showed at the proposed abolition of P.R. in parliamentary elections was due very largely to their experience of a similar change in Local Government elections. The Manifesto of the National League of the North, published in 1928, gives us a conception of their attitude. It reads:[1]

"The Government has announced its intention of introducing a measure for the abolition of Proportional Representation in parliamentary elections and of carrying out a scheme of gerrymandering constituencies that will secure the same indefensible and discreditable result as in the case of Local Government elections." This, of course, is the statement of a party case. None the less, so much bitterness was aroused— and still survives—because of the introduction of the ward system in local elections that one must refer to certain of the results of the change. The abolition of P.R. necessitated a redistribution of the seats in the various electoral districts. The boundaries of the new areas were drawn, so it is claimed by the minority, in such a way as to place the Opposition parties in a position of inferiority even in districts where they enjoyed major voting strength. The bitterest indignation was aroused by what appeared to be, upon an examination of the distributions, a carefully calculated gerrymandering of the areas. A scrutiny of the redistribution of areas carried out by the Government reveals that there does exist very considerable justification for the complaints of the minorities. In several districts, as, for example, in the city council of Derry, in the County Council of Tyrone, where under P.R. the Nationalists had controlled the local councils, they were placed in a minority by the new distribution. One illustration is sufficient to bring home the reality of the Nationalist objections.

[1] Signed Joseph Devlin, M.P., C. Healy, M.P., P. O'Neill, M.P., and others. See *Irish News*, November 3, 1928.

OMAGH DISTRICT COUNCIL[1]

	Nationalist	Unionist
Population—35,519	21,854	13,675
L.G. Voters—13,480	8,459	5,381
Number of Elected Representatives under P.R. System	26	13
Under New System	18	21

"There is nothing in the history of gerrymandering so monstrous as this," declared the Chairman of the Tyrone County Council; and even when one has discounted the characteristic exaggeration of political utterances one must admit that the Unionist majority have followed an electoral policy which can serve only to intensify the mistrust and bitterness of the minority.

It remains to be noted that in local elections also the introduction of the simple majority system has led to a very rapid increase in the number of the uncontested seats. The following figures[1] of the Belfast City elections illustrate this tendency.

CITY OF BELFAST
WARDS CONTESTED IN ELECTION OF COUNCILLORS
(Aldermanic seats not included)
Councillors

	1923	1924	1925	1926	1927	1928
Wards Contested ..	10	10	4	10	8	6
Wards Uncontested ..	5	5	11	5	7	9

	1929	1930	1931	1932	1933	1934	1936
Wards Contested ..	3	4	2	3	5	2	5
Wards Uncontested ..	12	11	13	12	10	13	10

[1] Derived from publications of the Proportional Representation Society.

Aldermen

After the first election in 1923, seven wards and eight wards hold
Aldermanic elections alternately at three-year intervals

	1923	1926	1929	1932	1936
Wards Contested ..	7	2	4	—	1
Wards Uncontested ..	8	5	4	7	6

Thus in 1934 only two of the fifteen wards electing
councillors in Belfast were contested. In 1936, on an average
less than 50% of the electors per contested wards recorded a
vote.[1] Elsewhere the same lack of political vitality is evident.
There were no contests in Londonderry, Bangor, Carrick-
fergus, Cookstown, Lurgan, Newtownards, Portrush, Port-
stewart and Whitehead. Needless to say, the responsibility
does not lie entirely with the electoral system. But it may fairly
be maintained that under the peculiar conditions of political
life in Ulster it does emphasize this tendency towards rigidity
in representation. The 1920 local elections held under P.R.
provide an instructive contrast. Then the city was divided
into nine wards returning from six to eight members each.
There were no "clean sweeps." In each ward the minorities
secured representation; the Labour Party, for instance, securing
one or two seats in every case. This diffusion of representation is of considerable value in local government.

THE SENATE

The Senate is composed of two ex-officio members (the Lord
Mayor of Belfast and the Mayor of Londonderry) together
with twenty-four elected members. The term of office of every
elected member is eight years. One-half of the members retire
every fourth year. These Senators are elected by members
of the House of Commons voting according to the principles
of Proportional Representation. Several elections have taken

[1] Vide *Northern Whig*, May 16, 1936, for figures.

place under these provisions. None of them possess much interest either from an electoral or a political aspect. The first was held in 1921. At that time both Nationalist and Sinn Fein members of the House of Commons, pursuing a policy of non-recognition, declined to take their seats. As a consequence, the twenty-four elective members of the Senate were all Unionists, nominated by the Unionist Party. After the second Senatorial election held in 1925 the Senate remained Unionist with the exception of one member. Since then the Opposition has increased its strength in the Senate only to a very small extent. In these circumstances the system of election has received no adequate test and as a consequence no material exists whereby one may form a judgment as to its suitability. The more obvious criticisms against this form of indirect election have no weight, so long as the Second Chamber remains for all practical purposes a one-party House. In the Irish Free State a similar system of election proved unsatisfactory, in that it rendered it probable that the majority in the Upper House would be opposed to the Government of the day. This was so because the partial election of the Senate at stated intervals made it representative of no body of opinion; while at the same time its majority would tend to reflect the party outlook predominant in Dáil Eireann several years previously. But in Ulster no such conflict between the two Houses is possible, for the same Government has held office for close on sixteen years.

THE HOUSE OF COMMONS OF THE UNITED KINGDOM

Northern Ireland is represented by thirteen members at Westminster. The Act of 1920 made provision for reducing the representation of her constituencies in the House of Commons from thirty members, which was the number fixed in 1918,[1] to this new figure. The Northern Ireland members are elected upon the same franchise and under the same electoral law as

[1] Redistribution of Seats (Ireland) Act, 1918.

their colleagues at Westminster. The constituencies fixed
in 1920 are as follows:

Belfast County Borough—	Number o Members
East	1
North	1
South	1
West	1
Antrim County	2
Armagh County	1
Fermanagh and Tyrone Counties ..	2
Londonderry County	1
Down County	2
The Queen's University of Belfast	1
Total	13

These elections do not arouse much interest in Ulster. It
is felt that most matters directly affecting the electorate will
be discussed and decided at Stormont. As a result the polling
is invariably light and the Imperial elections are regarded with
considerable indifference. The returns at the 1931 General
Election are instructive. Of the 13 seats, 11 were won by the
Unionists, 2 by the Nationalists. Of the former, 9 were
uncontested. Thus only in four constituencies did polling
actually take place. Out of an electorate of 784,698 only 135,159
votes were cast; or alternatively about 17 per cent of the
electorate was actually called upon to exercise a vote.[1] In 1935,
polling was heavier, but 7 of the 13 seats were uncontested.

CONCLUSION

The interest in the electoral systems in Northern Ireland has
been concentrated on those adopted in local government and
in the local parliamentary elections. In both instances Proportional Representation was prescribed by legislation of the
Imperial Parliament but was later abandoned in favour of

[1] These figures exaggerate the number of persons voting as each
elector may exercise 2 votes in the 2-member constituency of Fermanagh-Tyrone which was contested.

the Simple Majority system by the Ulster Legislature. From
a purely electoral aspect there is much to be said both for and
against such a change. The alternative merits of the rival
systems have been so fully discussed elsewhere that it is
necessary to recall only one particular consideration here.
The most forceful objection to the adoption of P.R. in the
United Kingdom is the possibility that it might promote
instability of government. Even were this criticism well founded
—which is doubtful—yet it has little force in Northern Ireland.
For the stability of a subordinate Government exercising
limited powers in a small area is obviously not a matter of
comparable significance to the stability of the Imperial
Government. Even confirmed opponents of P.R. allow that
it is the system of election most suitable in all forms of local
government. However, it would be idle to pretend that the
electoral are the only, or even the most important, considerations
involved. The value of P.R. in Northern Ireland depended
almost entirely upon its political implications. It was inserted
in the Act of 1920 as a guarantee for minorities; it gave them
both in local and parliamentary elections a reasonably fair
representation; its operation—even if cumbersome, as its critics
claim—was so obviously equitable in intention as to give a
sense of security. The peculiarities of the situation appeared
to *demand* some such system of election. The minority,
embittered by the partition of the country and resentful of
government by their traditional opponents, were naturally
sensitive to the smallest infringement of their rights. In such
circumstances the Government displayed a frankly aggressive
attitude in abolishing P.R. for local government elections
in 1922 and for parliamentary elections in 1929. Even if there
had been no accompanying injustices of any kind, this action
revealed a complete lack of sympathy with the minority outlook.
At the worst it was a party manœuvre; at the best a psychological mistake. A comparison between the electoral returns
before and after 1929 reveals that the change has affected
neither the accuracy of representation nor the number of the

small parties to the extent that was anticipated. It has, however, drawn attention, and added to, the frozen condition of Ulster's political life. This is most clearly indicated by the very large proportion of uncontested seats in local, parliamentary and Imperial elections. When 70 per cent of the members of the House of Commons of Northern Ireland—admittedly the most important legislative body in the province—are returned, as in 1933, without a contest, then indeed there is just occasion for the democrat to fear for the future of representative government.

CHAPTER VIII

THE LEGISLATURE: ITS STRUCTURE AND POWERS

THE Parliament of Northern Ireland is not a sovereign Legislature. It came into existence in accordance with the provisions of an Act of the Imperial Parliament. And the Legislature which passed the creative Act can also repeal it. Thus the constituent power in its absolute form lies with the Parliament at Westminster and not with the Parliament at Stormont. Furthermore, the Legislature of Northern Ireland does not enjoy legislative, as distinct from constituent, sovereignty, since certain legislative and fiscal powers are reserved specifically to the Parliament of the United Kingdom. In this federation, if one may so term it, of two unequal powers the line of demarcation between the sphere of action of the respective legislatures is drawn in the Constituent Act, as modified by two amendments of somewhat minor importance.[1] In an examination of the legislative authority in Northern Ireland interest therefore must be directed in turn to (*a*) the allocation of powers as between the two Parliaments; (*b*) the actual structure and procedure of the Parliament of Northern Ireland and to (*c*) the work accomplished in the Imperial Parliament. Such a survey should bring out the practical merits and defects of the division of legislative power prescribed in the Constituent Act. It is well to bear in mind throughout this survey that in Northern Ireland public interest is centred almost exclusively upon the operation of the local parliamentary institutions. Thus even at an election for the return of members to the Imperial Parliament candidates define their policy in relation to local issues. There is no discussion, sometimes not even a casual reference, to the wider questions of the day. So in 1929 and 1931 electors in Northern Ireland heard nothing of the arguments for or against the enactment of the India Bill; in 1935 the burning

[1] Miscellaneous Provisions Acts of 1928 and 1932.

question of the objective of British foreign policy was barely
mentioned and certainly no candidate made it a plank in his
election platform. This prevalent indifference to the prominent
issues of National and Imperial policy reacts decisively upon
the balance of legislative authority. For public opinion in the
North has enjoyed the power, indefinable, but none the less
real, of interpreting the Constituent Act; and that public
opinion (especially Unionist opinion) has decreed that interest
shall be directed towards the local parliamentary institutions
and the activities of their members. As a consequence the subordinate Legislature has filled a more important rôle than that
foreseen by British statesmen in 1920.

THE ALLOCATION OF LEGISLATIVE POWER

In general, the Parliament of Northern Ireland has power to
make laws for the peace, order and good government of Northern
Ireland, except in such matters as are explicitly excluded from
its jurisdiction by the Constituent Act.[1] These excluded
matters may be classified conveniently according to the following
definition:

(a) *Excepted Services.* Under this title are included matters
of Imperial concern as : The Crown or the succession to the
Crown; the making of peace and war; the Navy, Army and
Air Force; treaties and relations with foreign States, or with
other parts of H.M. Dominions; dignities or titles of honour;
treason, alienage; trade with any place outside Northern Ireland;
submarine cables; wireless telegraphy; aerial navigation;
lighthouses, buoys and beacons; coinage, legal tender; standards
of weights and measures; trade-marks; patent rights and other
matters of lesser importance.

(b) *Reserved Services.* Under this category are included
services which are reserved to the Imperial Parliament as:
Postal Services; Post Office and Trustee Savings Banks;
designs for stamps; Registration of Deeds; Supreme Court
of Judicature and the Land Purchase (Ireland) Acts.

[1] Act 1920, s. 4, s. 9.

Reserved Taxes. This category includes the more important types of direct and indirect taxation as: Customs duties; Excise duties on articles manufactured or produced; Income tax including Surtax; and any tax on profits or a general tax on capital.

It will be noticed that the matters excluded from the jurisdiction of the Northern Parliament affect the actual government of the Province in varying degrees of intensity. Thus, for example, Northern Ireland as a self-governing area is not normally concerned to any great extent with the disposition of the fighting services or the succession to the Crown, or the coinage; but it is affected very clearly in its daily life by the forms of direct and indirect taxation, by the Judicature, by the postal services. Then again certain differences logically involve important issues of administrative organization. Thus certain of the services administered by the central authority are local to Northern Ireland, others are common to all parts of the United Kingdom. Under the former category are to be found the Supreme Court of the Judicature and the Land Purchase Commission; in the latter all the Excepted Services as well as the Reserved Taxes. Such services as are "local" have an administrative organization in Northern Ireland even though they are under the control of the United Kingdom authorities, whilst the remainder of the services are administered, and the reserved taxes are collected, by departments having their headquarters in London. This difference in type in the administrative machinery for the reserved services suggests undue complication but in fact it has worked with efficiency. The distinction between excepted and reserved services was introduced into the Act in order to segregate powers that were to be administered in perpetuity by Whitehall from those that might be transferred in the event of an all-Ireland Parliament becoming an accomplished fact.

In addition to the specific limitations imposed by the terms of the Constituent Act upon the authority of the Legislature of Northern Ireland, there are also certain restrictions by implication. The latter were intended to safeguard the rights of minorities. They prohibit Parliament from making laws that interfere in any respect with religious equality. In this way not only is sectarian legislation rendered unconstitutional, but also any discrimination in State grants to schools or other institutions of different religious denominations, likewise is illegal. The Parliament is prohibited also from taking property without giving compensation.[1]

A mere statement of the limitations imposed upon the Legislature gives no real criterion whereby the extent of the authority of the local Parliament may be estimated, unless it be accompanied by a summary of the actual operation of the fiscal system. Elsewhere the rather elaborate financial relationship between the two Governments is analysed in some detail.[2] Here it is sufficient to indicate the relative responsibility of the central and local governments in the imposition of revenue taxation. The forms of taxation that are *reserved* include customs and certain excise duties, income tax (including surtax), and any general tax on profits. The larger proportion of taxation in Northern Ireland rests therefore with the Government of the United Kingdom; and the proceeds of these taxes are paid, in the first instance, into the United Kingdom Exchequer. There a separate account is kept of the total amount of these revenues attributable to Northern Ireland. From this is deducted the cost of the reserved services—as the Supreme Court, the Post Office and the Land Purchase Commission—in addition to the Imperial Contribution and other charges payable by Northern Ireland to the United Kingdom. The balance that remains to the credit of Northern Ireland subsequent to these deductions is termed the "Residuary Share of Reserved Taxes." It is issued from the Consolidated Fund of the United Kingdom and paid into the Exchequer of Northern Ireland. By this process Northern Ireland covers her administrative expenditure by means of revenue raised within her area, since the expenditure on the *reserved* services is paid as a first charge upon

[1] Act of 1920, s. 5.   [2] Chapter x.

the proceeds of the *reserved* revenue; while the cost of the *transferred* services is covered in part by the proceeds of *transferred* revenue and in part by the "Residuary share of the Reserved Taxes." These items do not, however, comprise the full liability of the Northern Ireland taxpayer, in that the six counties compose no more than a small self-governing unit within a large State. As a consequence Northern Ireland, as part of the United Kingdom, is bound logically to pay a proportion of the expenditure necessary for the upkeep of the Imperial Services as a whole. These services, which are defined in the Government of Ireland Act, include the Fighting Services, Foreign and Colonial Relations, War Pensions and the National Debt. The liability in respect of these Services is met by an annual payment known as the "Imperial Contribution." The amount of this contribution is not static. It is calculated each year by the Joint Exchequer Board in accordance with a prescribed formula. The general principle governing this annual payment is that the amount should equal the excess of total revenue over actual and necessary expenditure in Northern Ireland so long as similar rates of taxation are levied, and so long as the same or equivalent social services are undertaken in Northern Ireland and the United Kingdom. The Imperial Contribution is not paid out by the Exchequer at Stormont, but is deducted from the amount of the reserved taxes received into the Exchequer of the United Kingdom.

As a result of these financial arrangements only a small field is left within the absolute control of the local Parliament. Its normal means of raising revenue are confined to the following taxes:

(*a*) Death Duties.
(*b*) Stamp Duties.
(*c*) Motor Vehicle Duties.
(*d*) Entertainments Duty.
(*e*) Excise Licence Duties—other than those "reserved."
(*f*) Mineral Rights Duty.

The yield from this "Transferred Taxation" is increased

to some extent by various fixed charges paid into the Northern Exchequer. But the amount of "Transferred Revenue" forms only a small proportion of the total revenue raised in Northern Ireland. In 1933–34 the latter amounted to £11,002,583. Of this £2,383,144 was derived from Transferred Revenue; whilst £8,610,554 came under the category of "Reserved Revenue." Thus, in that particular financial year, only 21 per cent of the total Revenue was "Transferred" while 75½ per cent was Reserved.[1] Throughout the period of operation of the Northern Ireland Government the percentage yields from these two types of taxation have remained almost unchanged, and so the figures quoted provide a valid criterion of the limitation of financial authority imposed upon the local Parliament. But it is well to observe that a similar balance of financial authority is not to be found on the Expenditure side. For although in 1933–34 the Northern Ireland Parliament raised by its own authority only 21 per cent of the total Revenue levied within its area, yet the Northern Ireland Executive had control over the Expenditure of 84 per cent of the total Revenue in the same financial year. Thus in a very real sense the Government of Northern Ireland enjoys a wider power on the financial than on the legislative side.

This brief résumé of some aspects of the financial system brings into relief certain remarkable features in the distribution of legislative power. The general effect of the main financial provisions is to withdraw powers, normally exercised by a legislative assembly, from the jurisdiction of the Parliament of Northern Ireland. Financial authority is divided in accordance with the dictates of financial convenience and not with regard to the time-honoured traditions of English parliamentary practice. Thus, while the "Reserved Revenues" are raised by authority of the Parliament of the United Kingdom and while they are paid into the Exchequer of the United Kingdom, the residuary share of such revenue—comprising as it does the larger part of the total revenue from the six counties—

[1] The small remaining percentage is placed to a Reserve Fund.

is paid into the Exchequer of Northern Ireland and its expenditure is authorized by the Parliament of Northern Ireland. So it is that the Legislature which authorizes State expenditure does not impose the major portion of the taxation required to meet it. Likewise the administration of the reserved services constitutes a further divergence from the accepted forms of financial responsibility. These services, it will be remembered, though local to Northern Ireland, are administered from Whitehall. The expenditure on them is authorized by the Parliament of the United Kingdom. Neither the Parliament nor the Government of Northern Ireland exercises any control over them. None the less, the expenditure necessary to their administration is covered by the Northern Ireland taxpayer in that it is deducted from the total sum of the reserved taxes. Thus the general principles of British public finance are observed in so far as all public revenues are paid into the Exchequer and no money can be withdrawn from the Exchequer except on the authority of Parliament expressed either in permanent legislative form, as in the case of Consolidated Fund charges, or by annual appropriation Acts; but they are neglected in so far as the Parliament which authorizes such expenditure either does not impose or does not enjoy a sovereign control over the taxation designed to meet it. As a consequence this hybrid system of financial control reacts upon the power of the Parliament at Stormont since an absence of final responsibility involves a diminution of authority. And so, ultimately, a wide discretionary power is vested in the non-democratic body—the Joint Exchequer Board—which determines each year the liabilities of the respective Governments.

Since 1920 it has been found that some of the restrictions and reservations inserted in the Constituent Act interfered with the proper administration of the transferred services, and accordingly the Parliament of the United Kingdom passed two amending Acts with the intention of overcoming such difficulties. The Acts were passed in 1928 and 1932 respectively.[1]

[1] Northern Ireland (Miscellaneous Provisions) Acts, 1928 and 1932.

They aimed, not at any redistribution of legislative power, but at the interpretation of certain provisions in the light of administrative experience. Thus the amendment passed in 1928 contained a clause designed to facilitate the export of agricultural produce. It had been found that in order to maintain the level of agricultural exports in post-War years it was necessary to introduce some measure of grading. The Constituent Act permitted legislation for this purpose for internal marketing but prevented the extension of such grading to the export trade.[1] Accordingly, in 1928, it was enacted that:

"The restrictions contained . . . in the principal Act on the power of the Parliament of Northern Ireland to make laws, shall not be construed as preventing that Parliament making laws for the purpose of ensuring that live stock and agricultural produce shall not be sent to Great Britain, the Irish Free State, the Isle of Man except under such regulations as to standards of quality, inspection or compulsory insurance as may be made by or under the authority of that Parliament."[2]

This interpretation proved of no little assistance in the rationalization of the agricultural export market. Other provisions amending the original Act were inserted in the Act of 1928 as well as in that of 1932.[3] They possess no general interest and lead one to infer that the division of power carried out in 1920 has proved reasonably satisfactory in the day-to-day work of government.

THE CONSTITUENT POWER

The Parliament of Northern Ireland does not exercise the Constituent Power. Its right to make laws for "the peace, order, and good government" of Northern Ireland is subject to the overriding authority of the provisions of the Constituent Act.[4] It may not repeal or amend any such provision unless

---

[1] Cf. s. 4, Act of 1920.
[2] Govt. of N. Ireland (Miscellaneous Provisions) Act, 1928.
[3] Ibid., 1932.   [4] s. 4.

specifically permitted to do so by the Act itself. In addition, a full reservation of the Constituent power is made in favour of the Parliament of the United Kingdom.[1] It reads:

"Notwithstanding the establishment of the Parliament of Northern Ireland . . . or of anything contained in this Act, the supreme authority of the Parliament of the United Kingdom shall remain unaffected and undiminished over all persons, matters and things in Northern Ireland and every part thereof."

These statements suggest a rather more drastic limitation of authority than is in fact the case, inasmuch as the Constituent Act is haphazard rather than inclusive in character. For example, the Parliament of Northern Ireland enjoy, by a right explicitly conferred,[2] the power to amend their electoral system, and this power has been exercised. In the majority of post-War Constitutions the electoral system is inserted as an integral part of the Constitution. Thus in Poland, in Czechoslovakia, in the Irish Free State and in Yugoslavia, direct election on the principles of Proportional Representation or with "representation of minorities"[3] is prescribed in the respective Constitutions and may not be altered except by the process of constitutional amendment. In this respect, therefore, the Constituent Power in Northern Ireland is interpreted within narrower limits than on the Continent. Special provisions are in force for determining the constitutionality of legislation passed by the Parliament of Northern Ireland. In the normal course the validity of legislation may be tested in the Courts. In such an event an appeal lies (with certain exceptions) from the Court of Appeal—the Appellate Court of Northern Ireland—to the House of Lords. Such an appeal lies only by leave of the Court.[4] At the same time there exists a more general method of testing the validity of legislation. Should the Governor or a Minister consider it expedient in the public interest that steps be taken to determine the validity of any

[1] s. 75.   [2] s. 15.
[3] Cf. Yugoslav Constitution, Art. 69.
[4] The Act of 1920, s. 49.

particular Act of the Parliament of Northern Ireland, they may refer the issue to His Majesty in Council and then, if it is so decided, the question may be referred to the Judicial Committee of the Privy Council. In the hearing the Judicial Committee are empowered to allow any persons who are interested in the question to appear and to be heard. The same course may be followed by the Joint Exchequer Board should any two members of it be desirous of obtaining a decision of any question of the interpretation of the Act of 1920, or any other question of law that may arise in connection with their duties. In a similar way any person may petition His Majesty in Council to refer any question of law arising out of any decision of the Joint Exchequer Board to the Judicial Committee.[1] The decision of the House of Lords or of the Judicial Committee as to the validity of any law is final and conclusive.[2] In practice, the reference of an issue arising out of the constitutionality of legislation to the Judicial Committee has proved satisfactory but costly. So far the only instance was provided in 1936 in the hearing by the Judicial Committee of a special case brought forward at the instance of the City of Belfast, who challenged the competence of the Government of Northern Ireland to require local authorities to levy a rate for education. The Judicial Committee gave judgment in favour of the Government.

THE STRUCTURE OF THE LEGISLATURE

(a) *The Representative of the Crown*

The Parliament consists of the King and the two Houses. The King is represented by the Governor of Northern Ireland. The latter fills a rôle similar in all important respects to that played by the Governors-General of the British Dominions. He summons, prorogues and dissolves the Parliament in the name of the King. As representative of the Crown he gives

---

[1] Act 1920, s. 51–52.   [2] Ibid., s. 53.

or withholds the royal assent to Bills sent up by both Houses. In the exercise of this duty the Governor is bound to comply with any instructions given by the King in respect of any Bill; and further, he must, if so directed, reserve any Bill for the signification of the King's assent.[1] Since December 1922 the Duke of Abercorn has been Governor of Northern Ireland. The term of office is normally six years but the Duke has been reappointed twice on the expiry of his term of office.[2] The powers of veto, and of reservation, vested in the Representative of the Crown, have not as yet been used. Originally it was intended that such powers might be exercised on matters of policy, but it is doubtful whether such an interpretation would now prove acceptable in Northern Ireland.

(b) *The Senate*

The Senate is composed of 26 members. Of these 24 are elected by Members of the House of Commons, voting according to the principles of Proportional Representation. The remaining two, the Lord Mayor of Belfast and the Mayor of Londonderry, hold office ex-officio. The term of office of every elected Senator is eight years and it continues independently of the life of Parliament. One half of the members retire every fourth year.

The powers of the Senate in important respects are similar to those of the House of Lords. Bills, other than Money Bills, may be introduced in the Upper House. With a similar exception it enjoys also a full power of amendment on all Bills sent up by the House of Commons. Bills imposing taxation or appropriating revenue must, however, originate in the Lower House, and further the Senate may not amend such Bills or amend any Bill in such a way as to increase proposed charges or burdens on the people. As a safeguard for Senatorial rights it has been provided that any Bill which appropriates revenue must deal only with that appropriation.[3] In this way the insertion of extraneous matter under cover of a financial Bill is prevented.

[1] Act 1920, s. 12.　　[2] In 1928 and 1934.　　[3] Act of 1920, s. 16.

In one matter of considerable constitutional importance, the status of the Senate differs from that of the House of Lords. Since 1911 a time-limit has been imposed upon the legislative veto of the latter. In the case of the Senate no such restriction exists. In its place a means has been devised whereby differences between the two Houses may otherwise be settled. If a public Bill sent up by the Commons is rejected by the Senate in two successive sessions then a joint sitting of the two Houses is held. At this sitting members deliberate and vote together upon the Bill as last proposed by the Commons and upon such amendments as were made by one House and not agreed to by the other. Any amendments supported by a majority of the members present are taken as carried. In the same way the fate of the Bill itself is decided by the vote of the majority of the total number of members present. If it is accepted then it is taken to have been duly passed by both Houses. In the event of the Senate rejecting a Money Bill, the joint sitting of both Houses may be convened during the same session.[1] Owing to the continued supremacy of the Unionist Party in both Houses of the Parliament of Northern Ireland no occasion has yet arisen for the summoning of a joint meeting of all members of the Legislature.

No special qualification in respect of age, residence, distinction or office is legally required of candidates for the Senate. Consequently a full power of nomination rests with the electoral assembly, that is, the House of Commons. This freedom of choice stands in sharp distinction to the elaborate system of functional representation prescribed for the formation of the Senate of Southern Ireland in the Act of 1920. The difference in composition is accounted for in part by the restricted area under the jurisdiction of the Northern Government, and in part by the confidence of the British Government in a prolonged Unionist supremacy in the House of Commons of Northern Ireland. In practice the system of election has given neither great satisfaction nor great dissatisfaction. The elections do

[1] Act of 1920, s. 17.

not occasion much outside interest in that the party majority is even more secure in the Upper than in the Lower House. Since two or three votes from the Commons are sufficient to elect a Senator, an undesirable element of intrigue is introduced, perhaps inevitably, at election time.

The powers and privileges of members of the Senate are similar to those enjoyed by the House of Commons of the United Kingdom.[1] When it assembles the Senate elects one of its members to be Speaker and he retains the office so long as he remains a Senator, unless removed by a Resolution passed by a majority of the total number of the members of the House. Since the volume of business transacted by the Senate is slight it has been found convenient that the Speaker should act as Chairman when the House is in Committee.[2] The Speaker receives a salary of £1,000 per annum. Normally no salary attaches to the office of Senator, but two guineas per diem is allowed for travelling and incidental expenses—subject to a maximum of eighty guineas in any one year. These expenses are paid only to members who take the Oath of Allegiance and their seat, and who are not in receipt of an official salary. This allowance was provided by a Resolution adopted by the House of Commons in 1924. Four years later the House of Commons resolved that an additional £100 per annum should be paid to any member of the Senate declaring an insufficiency of means. This latter allowance was subjected to a temporary reduction of 15 per cent, but this was restored in 1936. Thus it is possible for a Senator to receive up to £180 per annum. The Senate has proved the less influential House. Apart from the limitations imposed upon its financial power, it has suffered from a lack of vitality. This is due in part to the absence of an effective opposition. For the first few years of its existence, there was, in fact, no opposition at all.[3] Later the minority secured some representation, but it remains rather insignificant. The present strength of the respective parties is:

[1] Act of 1920, s. 18.   [2] Standing Orders.
[3] As the Mayor of Londonderry did not take his seat.

Unionist	..	..	.. ..	14
Independent Unionist		..	..	7
Nationalist ..	..	..	..	5

In turn this absence of opposition leads men of vigour and personality to seek election to the Lower House. Thus, for example, in 1934 Mr. T. J. Campbell, K.C., the leader of the Nationalist Party, resigned his seat in the Senate in order to contest a Belfast constituency and so secure election to the House of Commons. On occasion important pronouncements of policy have been made in the Senate, but such events are exceptional. The sessions of the Senate are short. In the whole of 1933 the House sat only on 26 days; in 1935, only on 29 days. And on the majority of its rare sessions the House sits for a very brief period indeed. Ministers may speak in either House but may vote only in the House of which they are members. A valid criterion of the lesser importance of the Senate is provided by the fact that only one Cabinet Minister, Lord Charlemont, the Minister of Education, is a member of that House. In any event, the Senate is condemned to play a minor rôle as a political assembly since the fate of Ministries is decided by vote of the House of Commons. It is, therefore, in its capacity of a "revising" chamber that one must look for the more valuable contribution of the Senate to the political life of Northern Ireland. In many respects it is admirably equipped for this task. Its membership is small; it enjoys, as a consequence, opportunities for calm deliberation such as are unknown in larger chambers; it is not swayed, as the more democratic House, by the fluctuating violence of party passion; its term of membership is so long as to enable Senators to obtain a full knowledge of legislative practice as well as to preserve continuity of policy. Unfortunately the Senate does not accrete to itself the type of member that would counteract effectively the prevalent senatorial tendency toward somnolent inertia. The actual achievement of the Senate may best be gauged by reference to the number of Bills initiated in that House and by reference to the number of amendments inserted in Bills sent up by the Commons.

Year	Number of Bills introduced in the Senate	Number of Bills introduced in the House of Commons
1926	4	17
1928	5	28
1930	4	24
1931	7	27
1935	1	30

These figures show conclusively that only a small proportion of Bills—and even then almost invariably Bills of somewhat minor importance—are introduced in the Senate. Its most important function, therefore, lies in amendment. The statistics over a period of years are as follows:

Year	Number of Amendments inserted by Senate	Number agreed to by the House of Commons
1932–33	32	32
1933–34	30	30

The large majority of the amendments inserted are amendments of minute detail, devised to improve the phrasing of Bills or the quality of legislation. There exists too close an agreement in political opinion as between the members of the party predominant in both Houses for the Senate to exercise its powers in matters of principle.

THE HOUSE OF COMMONS

The House of Commons consists of 52 members elected by universal suffrage. The House may, unless sooner dissolved, continue in existence for a period of five years. For three years after the first meeting of the Parliament the Legislature of Northern Ireland had no power to amend the law relating to elections, constituencies and the distribution of members amongst them.[1] Since 1924 the Parliament has enjoyed and

[1] Act 1920, s. 14.

exercised the right of amending the electoral system; but it is expressly ruled that such legislation shall not alter the total number of members and shall pay due consideration to population in any redistribution of seats amongst the constituencies. A member of the House of Commons is not paid in that capacity, but in 1923 the House resolved that "provision should be made of £200 a year in respect of expenses to every Member who has subscribed to the necessary oath and has taken his seat." A member who is in receipt of a salary either as an officer of the House or as a member of the Government does not receive such an allowance.[1] During the slump, this payment was subjected to a 15 per cent cut. This was restored in 1936.

The Speaker presides over the House of Commons and exercises duties in all respects similar to those performed by the Speaker of the House of Commons of the United Kingdom. The Speaker is given a certain discretionary authority in the application of the closure.[2] The debate on the Redistribution of Seats Bill, which proposed to abolish Proportional Representation for parliamentary elections in 1929, was the first occasion on which it was found necessary to resort to the guillotine closure. Also he exercises the power of selecting amendments for debate known as the "Kangaroo."[3] The Speaker's salary of £2,000 per annum is charged upon the Consolidated Fund. A Chairman of Ways and Means is also appointed with duties modelled on those of his counterpart at Westminster. The salary of the latter is £1,500 per annum and is voted annually. The greater part of the business of the Legislature is done downstairs either in the ordinary session of the House or in Committee of the whole. It is true that *ad hoc* Committees are appointed from time to time, but they deal only with matters of lesser importance. And the size of the House eliminates the possibility of referring Bills to Standing Committees in the normal course of business, since there are not sufficient members to man them. No Select

---

[1] Cf. Resolution of H. of C., March 29, 1923.
[2] Standing Order 24.   [3] Ibid. 26.

Committee may consist of more than five members except by special permission of the House.[1] The most important of such Committees is the Select Committee on Public Accounts, which is appointed annually by the House to review the expenditure of the administrative departments. A House of 52 members composes a very suitable unit for debating purposes. As a consequence a large proportion of parliamentary business is transacted in the informal atmosphere of the Committee of the whole.

As in every modern legislative chamber the Executive exercises a very complete control over the allocation of parliamentary time. In Northern Ireland this has not, however, as elsewhere led to an undue restriction of the opportunities afforded to private members. In a House of 52 representatives faced with a legislative programme of clearly-defined dimensions there exist plentiful facilities for private members both to take part in debate on Government measures and to introduce Bills of their own. In practice the debates are generally informal in character without long set speeches from the front benches and almost all members speak with some frequency. On the other hand little advantage is taken of the facilities that exist for the introduction of Private Members' Bills. This is due partly to difficulties in drafting but even more to the well-known limitations of such legislation. The actual figures over a period of years are as follows:

Year	Number of Bills Introduced by Government	Number of Bills introduced by Private Members
1932–33 Nov. 23rd to Nov. 7th	25	1
1933–34 Dec. 18th to Nov. 14th	23	3[2]

[1] Standing Order 50.
[2] These figures are extracted from the *Journals of the House of Commons* (*N.I.*), vols. xv and xxi.

The traditional English practice in the introduction of financial legislation is observed at Stormont. Bills imposing taxation or appropriating revenue must be introduced by a Minister of the Crown, and further such Bills may originate only in the House of Commons.[1] As at Westminster, it has been found necessary to impose a limit on the period to be devoted to a discussion of the estimates. At Stormont not more than ten days may be allotted for the consideration of the annual estimates, though it is possible, by a motion made after notice, to obtain an additional time not exceeding three days.[2] At Westminster the House is confined to twenty sitting days, also with a possible extension of three days.

In Private Bill legislation there are certain modifications of the procedure in force at Westminster. Every Private Bill is originated in the House of Commons, and a further important modification of the practice at Westminster is provided by the fact that each Bill undergoes only one Committee stage after having previously been introduced and read a second time in both Houses. Proceedings in Committee are conducted before a Joint Committee of both Houses. In the case of an unopposed Bill the Committee consists of two Senators, one member of the House of Commons, and the Chairman of Ways and Means, who presides; in the case of an opposed Bill the Committee consists of three Senators, three members of the House of Commons, and a Chairman elected by the Committee itself.[3] A somewhat similar procedure is followed in the case of Divorce Bills.

The House of Commons is the focal point of the legislative system in Northern Ireland. Not only does it enjoy special privileges in the all-important field of finance but also it controls the Executive. Its status is exhibited in many fields. In the House of Commons alone may a Minister introduce financial legislation; in this House are introduced on an average more than four-fifths of the total number of Bills brought before Parlia-

[1] Standing Order 60.   [2] Ibid. 15.
[3] Cf. Standing Orders relative to Local Bills, H.C., 198.

ment; of the seven Ministers who comprise the Cabinet, six are members of the Lower House; of the six Parliamentary Secretaries now in office five are members of the Commons. The sessions of the House of Commons are longer than those of the Senate. Normally the House sits on less than 50 days during the year. Thus in 1933 the House sat on 43 days. The preponderating influence of the democratically elected House is to be found in almost every Legislature in the modern world. It is due, fundamentally, not to legal restrictions upon the power of the Second Chamber, but to the dependence of the Executive upon the vote of the Lower House.

TYPE OF MEMBERS ELECTED

An instructive light is thrown upon the working of the Parliamentary system in Belfast by an analysis of the occupational interests of the members of the democratic House. Obviously the success or failure of local self-government in Northern Ireland depends to no inconsiderable extent upon the type of person actively engaged in the work of government.

ANALYSIS OF OCCUPATIONS AND PROFESSIONS OF THE MEMBERS OF THE HOUSE OF COMMONS (ELECTED 1933)[1]

Occupation or Profession	Number
Titled and Landed Classes	8
H.M. Fighting Services	6
Directors and Business Men	7
Medical and Academic	4
Lawyers and Solicitors	10
Tradesmen	4
Journalists	3
Farmers	2
Engaged in Local Government	21

[1] There is no claim that these figures are precisely accurate since there are obvious difficulties in classification. They are derived from reference books as *Who's Who* and from personal information. I have placed members in a single category, though frequently they have claims to appear in more. Thus a member of the Landed Classes may also be a Director, in which case I have defined his profession in accordance with his principal occupation. In the case of Local Government alone do names reappear which have already appeared under other titles. This is necessary since Local Government work is usually supplementary to some other occupation.

This analysis gives somewhat surprising returns in one or two cases. For example, in a "business man's" Parliament one would have expected more business men. Instead there is a very high percentage of members of the legal profession, which indicates perhaps that business interests like legal representatives. Again one is struck by a distinctly aristocratic tone. This is derived mainly from representatives of rural constituencies; and it would appear that the small farmers still accept the leadership of the landowning classes. It is indeed remarkable that the representatives of a predominantly agricultural province in which just 96 per cent of the total number of holdings[1] are under 100 acres in extent, and in which 83·7 per cent of the holdings are under 50 acres, should return such a very small proportion of farmer-members. This contrast is brought into relief by a consideration of the occupations of Deputies of Dáil Eireann. In the Irish Free State there exists a lesser proportion of small holdings. There 92·2 per cent of the total number of holdings are under 100 acres in size—as against 96 per cent in Northern Ireland —and 76 per cent under 50 acres as against 83·7 per cent. None the less the farmer deputies comprise a large and constant element in the successive Dálà.

ANALYSIS OF THE OCCUPATIONS AND PROFESSIONS OF DEPUTIES OF DÁIL EIREANN (ELECTED 1932)

Occupation or Profession	Number
Business	24
Learned Professions	27
Teachers	8
Tradesmen	18
Journalists	5
Farmers	39
Engaged in Local Government	40

The total membership of Dáil Eireann was 153.[2]

A comparison between these two analyses of occupation

[1] I.e. holdings over 1 acre in size.
[2] These figures are taken from my book the *I.F.S., Its Government and Politics.* See Note on previous page as to the method of classification adopted.

shows that a high proportion of members both of the House of Commons and of the Dáil have acquired political experience in Local Government before contesting a parliamentary election. In both instances such members have held or hold almost without exception unpaid offices in Local Government. In the Free State they are members of a City Corporation, County and Urban District Councillors, whilst in the North a large proportion fill the more ornamental rôle of Justice of the Peace or of Deputy Lieutenant. But in other respects the analyses indicate a very different balance of political power. In the Irish Free State only a small minority of Deputies are drawn from the wealthier classes. For the most part they are shopkeepers or farmers or business men in a small way. In Northern Ireland the majority of members are well-to-do. They are landowners, rentiers, officers of H.M. Services, industrialists and members of the highly paid professions. The Dáil is the more democratic, the House of Commons the more aristocratic assembly. Where about 75 per cent of the members of the former are men of small personal means, about 65 per cent of the members of the latter are drawn from the moneyed classes.

REPRESENTATION AT WESTMINSTER

Walter Bagehot reckoned the function of legislation as third in importance amongst the duties of Parliament. He denied categorically that it was as important as the "executive management of the whole State or the political education given by Parliament to the whole nation."[1] If Bagehot's sense of proportion is just—though to-day his statement is clearly open to challenge—then there would be no anomaly in the fact that representation at Westminster attracts an attention that is quite negligible in comparison with that bestowed upon the Parliament at Stormont. For it is perfectly accurate to state that the Parliament of the United Kingdom exercises but one function

[1] Cf. *English Constitution*, chap. iv.

in the eyes of the inhabitants of Northern Ireland, and that is *legislation*. Thirteen members are returned by Northern Ireland constituencies to Westminster. They are elected by universal suffrage. The elections do not arouse any great interest, and it is usual for at least two-thirds of the members to be returned unopposed. These thirteen members put forward the particular needs of Northern Ireland in matters falling within the field of "reserved legislation," and can place their special knowledge of conditions in the Province at the disposal of the Commons. In all respects save one their status and privileges are similar to those of other members of the House. It is, however, very rare, if not unknown, for a member sitting for a Northern Ireland constituency to catch the Speaker's eye in any debate upon a matter which (so far as concerns Northern Ireland) is transferred. Thus administration of unemployment relief lies within the jurisdiction of the local Parliament. Consequently, the Speaker at Westminster will not permit speeches from Northern Ireland members in a general debate on unemployment at Westminster. It is possible for the same person to sit in the House of Commons both at Stormont and at Westminster and it has been done on several occasions. Such double representation is not satisfactory to the respective constituents since the sessions of the two Houses normally coincide, thus compelling the member to neglect one of his duties. Prior to the Imperial elections in 1929, Lord Craigavon imposed a veto upon dual membership to be applied to all Unionist candidates. Since then no member of this party, with the exception of Captain Dixon, the Government Whip, has held a seat in both Parliaments. For the same reason it is in practice impossible, though in law permissible, for a member of the Northern Ireland Cabinet to sit in the Parliament of the United Kingdom.

The actual time spent exclusively upon a discussion of the affairs of Northern Ireland in the House of Commons is very small. From October 1934 to November 1935—that, is a period of just over a year—only *one* hour and fifty minutes was devoted exclusively to the discussion of the affairs of Northern Ireland, and this appears to be roughly the average time so spent each year. None the less, Northern Ireland is vitally affected by a very large proportion of the legislation of the Parliament of the United Kingdom—to a far greater extent indeed than it is by "transferred legislation." For example, since its foundation, the local Parliament has been anxious to reorganize Agriculture in Ulster. But the limitation of its powers confined its action to matters of detail. Thus from 1923 to 1928, assistance given to the industry was confined to improvement in education, stock-breeding and marketing methods. In 1928 a constitutional amendment enabled the enactment of a code of legislation designed to standardize the methods of grading, packing, and marketing agricultural produce. But the effect of this legislation passed by the Parliament of Northern Ireland is totally insignificant in comparison with the radical changes effected by the Agricultural Marketing Act of 1933 and by the introduction of the various Marketing and Reorganization schemes sponsored by Mr. Walter Elliot, the Minister of Agriculture in the Imperial Parliament. It is because of legislation introduced, debated, and enacted by the Parliament of the United Kingdom that the area under wheat in Northern Ireland increased from 3,035 acres in 1931 to 6,873 in 1936, that is, an increase of over 100 per cent; that the number of pigs has increased in the same period from 216,000 to 521,000, an increase of just 140 per cent, and that the number of cattle has increased in the same period from 672,000 to 769,000, that is, by about 15 per cent.[1] The relative importance of legislation enacted by the respective Parliaments is similar in other spheres of industrial and social life. There is, therefore, no doubt whatever but that the Parliament of the United Kingdom is the more important assembly legislating for Northern Ireland today. But it does not perform the other and, in Bagehot's opinion, more important duties of a Legislature. It is the Parliament and

---

[1] Certain of these increases were facilitated by the imposition of penal tariffs against agricultural produce from the Irish Free State.

Government of Northern Ireland that are responsible for the maintenance of peace and order within her territory; it is from the Parliament of Northern Ireland that Ulstermen receive their political education; and so it is perhaps not without reason that public opinion relegates the Parliament of the United Kingdom to the second place in its political interests.

CHAPTER IX

THE EXECUTIVE

THE GOVERNOR OF NORTHERN IRELAND

A LONG process of historical development in the status of the representative of the Crown in the British Dominions has stamped that office indelibly with certain well-defined characteristics. Even though Northern Ireland—in contrast to the Dominions—is not in any sense a sovereign State, yet the Governor of that province has assumed, partly by law and partly by constitutional convention, all the more significant attributes appertaining elsewhere to the respective Governors-General. The existence of his office is the outward sign of local self-government in Ulster. The Governor himself is the symbol of the permanence both of the authority of the Northern Government and of the union with Great Britain. In his name are performed all the executive functions of the Government of Northern Ireland, whilst at the same time he is the guardian of a royal prerogative exercisable at the will of the Imperial Government. In 1920 it was originally intended that a Lord Lieutenant should act as the representative of the Crown in relation to the Parliaments both of Northern and Southern Ireland. Subsequent to the signature of the Anglo-Irish Treaty it was decided to continue the office, under a changed title, for Northern Ireland alone. Admittedly, the area was somewhat small to support the full dignity of a representative of the Crown, but this disadvantage was outweighed by two important considerations. It was felt that the appointment of a Governor, in adding to the prestige of the new Government, would thereby facilitate its exercise of authority, and further that the very structure of the Cabinet system demanded the existence of some such supreme and permanent symbol of executive authority. In fact, the latter, or purely constitutional, basis for such an appointment was decisive; since in the circumstances any alternative would have necessitated an experimental departure from the familiar practice of the English Constitution. The salary of the Governor is £8,000 per annum. This includes the salaries and allowances of his personal staff. But the greater part of this expenditure is covered by the Exchequer of the United Kingdom, only £2,000 being deducted annually from Northern Ireland's share of reserved revenue.

The first Governor of Northern Ireland was appointed in December 1922. Since the creation of such an office had not been contemplated in 1920, Letters Patent were issued defining his authority and status in the Constitution. The definition is given only in general terms.[1] To the Governor is delegated the exercise of such executive power as had been transferred under the Act of 1920. Within that sphere of authority he fulfils functions similar to those exercised by the Governors-General in the Dominions. The framework of executive government in Ulster is designed in strict accord with the formal structure of government in the Dominions. Thus the statement as to the status of the Governors-General propounded by the Imperial Conference in 1926 may be reckoned applicable in Northern Ireland. The Governor-General, it was then declared, "holds in all respects the same position in relation to the administration of public affairs in the Dominions as is held by H.M. the King in Great Britain."[2] None the less, there are certain points in which the special case of the Governor of Northern Ireland deserves a particular examination. Whilst the rigidity of party politics in Ulster has, in fact, given no occasion for the exercise of the discretionary authority such as his office confers, yet under somewhat different political conditions it might determine issues of wide importance. For this reason it is of interest to note the manner in which the

[1] Cf. Letters Patent of December 9, 1922, and those of April 27, 1921, which constituted the office of Lord Lieutenant of Ireland under the Act of 1920.

[2] Inter-Imperial Relations Committee of the Imperial Conference, 1926.

Governor is appointed, the extent of his power of veto, and his discretion in the event of a dissolution.

The Governor of Northern Ireland is appointed by the Crown acting on the advice of the Government of the United Kingdom. In normal circumstances there is no doubt but that the Government of Northern Ireland is consulted. The appointment would not be made unless that Government assented. But there is no reason whatever to suppose that the Government of Northern Ireland exercises an initiative in the making of the appointment. When the Act of 1920 was passed it was the normal practice that the Government of the Dominion concerned should be consulted before any recommendation was made to the Crown, but that the initiative should lie throughout with the Imperial Government. In 1930, however, the Imperial Conference defined the change that had taken place in the manner of appointment. Six rules were laid down the import of which is that the appointment is made by the King on the advice of the Dominion Cabinet. The King acts on the advice of his responsible Ministers and in this instance "the Ministers who tender and are responsible for such advice are His Majesty's Ministers in the Dominion concerned." Further, the Governments of the Dominions now communicate directly with the Crown. But it seems clear that this change in practice does not apply to Northern Ireland; though there will be a desire to adopt contemporary Dominion procedure when the time comes for a new Governor to be appointed. This may not, however, be achieved, since the Government of Northern Ireland does not enjoy the right of direct access to the Crown. Not much light has been shed in practice upon the mode of appointment, since the Duke of Abercorn has held the office since its inception in 1922. His term has twice been renewed. The third Duke of Abercorn is the head of one of the two most notable Ulster families and enjoys by right of birth the chief place in Ulster society. The Dukedom was conferred upon the second Marquess of Abercorn in 1868. He was twice Lord Lieutenant of Ireland.[1] The family

[1] From 1866 to 1868 and from 1874 to 1876.

is old and distinguished, the present Duke being the heir
male of the House of Hamilton. He is one of the three peers
who enjoy distinct peerages in England, Scotland and Ireland.[1]
The first Earl of Abercorn was created by James I in 1606.
There is no doubt that the acceptance of the office of Governor
by the present Duke relieved both the Governments concerned
of a difficult choice. For the Duke combines to a rare degree
the qualities and the character suitable for a representative
of the Crown in Northern Ireland. There are circumstances—
as, for example, should the office fall vacant whilst a Labour
Government were in office in the United Kingdom and a
Unionist Government in Northern Ireland—when a choice
acceptable to both Cabinets may well prove of exceptional
difficulty.

In his legislative capacity the Governor summons, prorogues
and dissolves Parliament. His liberty of action is restricted
by the rule of annual Parliaments and by the maximum statutory
period of five years fixed for the duration of the House of
Commons.[2] In regard both to the exercise of the veto and the
right of reservation of Bills sent up by the two Houses of Parliament he occupies a position very different from that of the
Governors-General in the Dominions. Unlike them, he is
under the obligation of giving or withholding assent according
to his instructions received from the Imperial Government.
In such circumstances the Imperial Government is represented
by the Secretary of State for Home Affairs. If so instructed,
the Governor must reserve any Bill, which will then lapse
unless assented to within a year.[3] The Imperial Government
has not as yet exercised this power but it is well to remember
that it is thereby enabled to stultify the legislative programme
of the Parliament of Northern Ireland at will. This control
over legislation is analogous to that exercised in Canada by
the Dominion over the provinces,[4] and there is no doubt

---

[1] He is also Duke of Châtellerault in France.
[2] The Act of 1920, s. 11.   [3] Ibid., s. 12.
[4] Cf. Keith, *The Governments of the British Empire*, pp. 366–67.

but that it could be made effective. It is of interest to recall that at the Conference of 1920 it had been proposed as an integral part of a scheme of federal devolution that the power of veto should be used both on legislation of doubtful validity and on matters of policy. Since over a reasonably long period in Northern Ireland no Bill has been "reserved" for the signification of the royal pleasure, a precedent of non-interference in internal affairs has been established by the representative of the Crown. In effect this means no more than that the Governor's veto will not be used by the Government of the United Kingdom as a means of frustrating legislation except on fundamental issues of policy.

The power of dissolution is vested in the Governor acting upon the advice of his Ministers. In accordance with constitutional practice he must act upon the advice tendered by the latter. The proclamation is set out in the following terms.

"Whereas it is provided . . . that the Governor of Northern Ireland shall, in His Majesty's name, summon, prorogue and dissolve the Parliament of Northern Ireland. And whereas it is desirable that the present Parliament of Northern Ireland should be dissolved and that a new Parliament should be called: now therefore, I, James Albert Edward, Duke of Abercorn, Knight of the Most Noble Order of the Garter . . . Governor of Northern Ireland, by this proclamation do publish and declare His Majesty's pleasure, that the said Parliament be, as from the date of this Proclamation dissolved . . ."[1]

Under normal parliamentary conditions in which successive Cabinets were drawn from different parties, the Governor might at times be in a position to exercise a real choice in the appointment of a Prime Minister. But there again the discretionary authority vested in the Governor possesses some potential, but no actual, significance. It would, however, be wrong to suppose that the static political life of Northern Ireland has undermined the power of the Governor in depriving him of all occasion for the exercise of discretionary authority.

[1] Cf. *N.I., Journals of H. of C.*, vol. xvi, 1933–34.

On the contrary, the present holder of the office has exerted considerable influence partly by reason of his intimate knowledge of men and politics in Ulster and partly by his personal as distinct from official standing. In both respects he enjoys advantages not usually possessed by the holders of similar offices in the Dominions.

THE CABINET

The executive powers of Northern Ireland are co-extensive with its legislative powers. All executive authority, in respect of which the Parliament of Northern Ireland has jurisdiction, remains vested in the Crown and is exercised by the Governor through the various departments. The Ministers in charge of the departments are appointed by the Governor. They constitute the Cabinet in Northern Ireland. This body forms the Executive Committee of the Privy Council of Northern Ireland.

Ministers must be members of the Privy Council. Further, a Minister may not hold office for a period longer than six months unless he is, or becomes, a member of one or other Houses of Parliament. This provision does not, however, apply to the Ministers without portfolio. The appointment of such Ministers was specifically allowed in the Constituent Act,[1] but no advantage has yet been taken or indeed is likely to be taken of this privilege. A curious sidelight on constitutional thought is thrown by the acceptance, within a period of two years, of the principle of non-parliamentary Ministers both by the Parliament of the United Kingdom and by the Constituent Assembly of Saorstât Eireann. So far as I am aware,[2] the provisions of the Act of 1920 did not, in any sense whatever, influence either the proposal or the adoption of the principle of "Extern Ministers" in the Irish Free State. There it was introduced on the ground of a supposed differentiation as

---

[1] S. 8.

[2] My information on this point is derived from a personal conversation.

between political and administrative departments. In Northern Ireland the possible appointment of Ministers without portfolio was intended merely to provide a greater constitutional elasticity. In neither instance has the existence of non-parliamentary Ministers been viewed with any sign of favour by the respective Cabinets. This is an indication of the reality of the control of the Legislature.

The number of Ministers in Northern Ireland is small. The present Cabinet consists of seven members, which is the largest in number that has yet been appointed. Each Minister is responsible for one of the departments of State. In the earlier administrations the membership of the Cabinet was smaller owing to the conjunction of two departments under one Minister. In the first Cabinet of Northern Ireland Mr. (now Sir Edward) Archdale was both Minister of Agriculture and Minister of Commerce. Some years later, Mr. J. M. Barbour was appointed to the latter office. The large majority of the Cabinet Ministers are assisted by Parliamentary Secretaries in the exercise of their duties. The Ministers of Agriculture and of Commerce alone do not enjoy the collaboration of a Parliamentary Secretary. The Minister of Finance, on the other hand, is aided by three Parliamentary Secretaries, who hold office under the designation of Parliamentary and Assistant Parliamentary Secretary respectively. It is to be noted, however, that in one instance a Minister acts during his period of office as Parliamentary Secretary to one of his colleagues. Mr. Barbour is Minister of Commerce. He is also Parliamentary and Financial Secretary to Mr. Pollock, the Minister of Finance. Certain Secretaries and the Attorney-General may sit in Parliament without disqualification by reason of their office and without the necessity of seeking re-election on their appointment.

A Minister may sit and speak in either House of Parliament but may vote only in that House of which he is a member. This privilege is freely exercised. All the members of the present Cabinet, with one exception, are members of the House of

Commons. In the earlier Cabinets, a similar practice was followed. Moreover, it is to be noted that the Minister drawn from the Senate even though personally influential has been appointed in each instance to one of the less important Cabinet posts. Thus, in the first Cabinet, Senator the Marquess of Londonderry was Minister of Education[1] and in the present Cabinet Senator the Lord Charlemont holds the same office. The dependence of Ministries upon the vote of the House of Commons in accordance with the practice of the British Constitution renders so inevitable the selection of Ministers from the Lower House as to make comment superfluous. But what is unusual is the remarkable proportion of the total number of M.P.s who hold office under the Crown. In the House of Commons elected in 1933, no fewer than twelve members hold executive office whilst two more elected by majority vote are officers of the House. In all, these include six Cabinet Ministers, five Parliamentary Secretaries, the Attorney-General, the Speaker and the Chairman of Ways and Means. Thus almost one quarter of the members of the House of Commons hold executive office and more than one quarter, to be exact 27 per cent, are in receipt of official salaries. In comparison with the figures for the Dáil and the Imperial House of Commons, this proportion is shown to be very high. In the Dáil elected in 1933, 16 of the total number of Deputies are in receipt of an official salary—that is just over 10 per cent—whilst at Westminster, the number is between 40 and 50, that is only about 8 per cent. The point deserves some emphasis for it reveals the probability of undue executive influence in a small legislature. It is a weakness inherent in every scheme of devolution to a restricted area. Moreover, the high percentage of executive officers means that there will be a corresponding scarcity of back benchers from whose ranks future Ministers may be chosen. The majority of the members of the present Cabinet are now old. The

[1] The resignation of Lord Londonderry in 1926 occasioned considerable surprise.

Unionist Party appears assured of a further prolonged tenure of office. Who is to succeed them? That is a question that is causing genuine anxiety within the Unionist Party today. Since 15 of the members of the Party who sit in the Commons now hold office under the Crown there remain only about 20 members of the House from whom future Ministers may be drawn. This does not present a wide field of selection.

MINISTERIAL SALARIES

It is idle to pretend that Ministerial salaries in Northern Ireland have not occasioned widespread criticism, and that not merely amongst political opponents but also within the ranks of the Unionist Party itself.[1] Since this charge of extravagance has been so freely levelled against the members of the Government of Northern Ireland it is well to give the exact statistical evidence on this point. For purposes of comparison figures are reproduced showing the salaries paid to officers of State fulfilling corresponding duties in the United Kingdom and in the Irish Free State.

The salaries of Ministers were fixed upon the recommendations of a Select Committee which reported to the House of Commons in December 1921.[2] The House agreed to the Report without amendment and an Act fixing the salaries accordingly was passed.[3] Only the salary of the Attorney-General, which is now £4,000 plus fees, has been since changed by legislation.[4] For the period of the world depression, however, the Cabinet salaries have been voluntarily abated by 15 per cent. The reduction is of a temporary character. In the case of the Free State, the salaries of members of the Executive Council are free of Income Tax. Thus there does not exist at the moment so great a disparity in the respective salaries paid in Belfast and in Dublin as the figures suggest, though the former are still decidedly the larger.

[1] Cf. Speech by Sir R. Lynn, *H. of C. Debates,* vol. xi, col. 1182.
[2] Cf. *N.I., Parl. Debates, H. of C.,* vol. i, col. 431 ff.
[3] [N.I.] 12 Geo. V. c. 9. [4] Cf. [N.I.] 13 & 14 Geo. V. c. 18. 51.

Northern Ireland		United Kingdom		Irish Free State	
Office	Salary	Office	Salary	Office	Salary
Prime Minister[1] ..	£ 3,200	Prime Minister and First Lord of the Treasury	£ 5,000	President of the Executive Council	£ 1,500
Minister of Finance ..	2,000	Chancellor of the Exchequer	5,000	Minister for Finance ..	1,000
Minister of Home Affairs ..	2,000	Home Secretary ..	5,000	Minister for Justice ..	1,000
Minister of Labour ..	2,000	Minister of Labour ..	2,000	Minister of Local Govt. and Public Health	1,000
Minister of Education ..	2,000	President of the Board of Education	2,000	Minister for Education	1,000
Minister of Agriculture ..	2,000	Minister of Agriculture..	2,000	Minister for Agriculture	1,000
Minister of Commerce[2]	unpaid	President of the Board of Trade	5,000	Minister for Industry and Commerce	1,000

[1] Together with an allowance of £1,488 "for contingencies of office" and an official residence.
[2] By choice of the Minister, Mr. J. M. Barbour.

The table given opposite is not entirely satisfactory since salaries in the United Kingdom are irrational whilst those in the Free State are unduly low. Nevertheless, it does show beyond question that Ministerial salaries in Northern Ireland were fixed at a disproportionately high level. Thus, for example, the Ministers of Labour, Agriculture and Education at Stormont normally receive salaries identical with those of their counterparts at Whitehall. The other salaries are relatively high, when one remembers that the total revenue from Northern Ireland in 1934 was only one sixty-third, or about 1·5 per cent, of the total revenue of the United Kingdom. Again, it is illogical that the Ministers of a subordinate Government exercising jurisdiction over a population of little more than one-third of that of the Irish Free State, with a revenue in similar proportion, should be entitled to receive larger salaries. Although the salaries in the Free State are admittedly low, yet there is decidedly a lesser volume of work, both parliamentary and administrative, to be accomplished by Ministers in Northern Ireland. Moreover, in the House of Commons of Northern Ireland, criticism has been directed even more against the salaries of Parliamentary Secretaries than against those of the Ministers themselves. The former receive £1,000 per annum in comparison with £1,200 to £1,500 paid in the United Kingdom and £900 in Saorstat Eireann.[1] On the whole, Ministerial salaries in Northern Ireland are criticized so adversely not so much for the actual expenditure involved as for what it represents. These salaries, which are reckoned symptomatic of general extravagance in government, provide an obvious and suitable target for attack.

The Government of Northern Ireland admits that the salaries paid to Cabinet Ministers and their subordinates are large but it denies that they are excessive in the circumstances. The Prime Minister and the Minister of Finance have, at different times,

[1] With the exceptions of the Parliamentary Secretary to the Prime Minister who receives £600 and of Mr. J. M. Barbour, Parliamentary Secretary to the Ministry of Finance, who is unpaid.

thrown an interesting light upon certain particular considerations influencing this scale of remuneration. Lord Craigavon
in 1921 pointed to the danger of minimizing the importance
of the local parliamentary institutions. "There must," he
declared, "be a dignity about our Parliament and that Parliament must be very deeply rooted in Ulster soil, so that no
opponents dare come forward at any time and say of that great
structure . . . 'that it is only a small affair and we can easily
sweep it to one side.' " And so the Prime Minister stated his
desire that the Government, "whilst encouraging and insisting
on economy at every turn, should not go along lines which would
appear to the outside world as though we have in Ulster itself
placed a minor importance upon our Institution, and felt that
a small, trifling, niggardly treatment of the subject was sufficient
for the Ulster people."[1]

The argument used by the Minister of Finance in 1929 in
defending the level of Ministerial salaries was a remarkable
illustration of some of the anomalies created by local self-
government. His speech is of sufficient importance to quote.
Mr. Pollock said:

". . . . The cost of Cabinet Ministers, in fact the cost of the
machinery of this Parliament, would not affect the taxes of
Northern Ireland to the extent of a penny, because the British
Government provide the cost of Parliament caused by the
separation of the two areas of North and South. . . . The
British Government provide the sum of approximately £670,000
a year in order that the cost of our Parliament might be met,
the exact wording of the White Paper being 'because of the
severance of the two areas of North and South.'[2] That money
is provided by the British Government through our Land
Annuities, which would otherwise have to be paid to the British
Government in order to meet the interest on the amounts
necessary to indemnify the landlords. . . . That is why I
say it does not affect the taxes of Northern Ireland to the extent

---

[1] *N.I., Parl. Debates*, vol. i, col. 174.
[2] The reference is to the White Paper, Cmd. 645, 1920.

of a penny whether the cost of our Parliament is £10,000, £20,000 or £30,000 a year."[1]

The moral drawn in the speech by the Minister of Finance has been reiterated by responsible persons on several occasions. It amounts to this. "Within certain limits extravagance is our best policy. Let us pay big salaries, for after all it makes no difference whatever to our taxpayers whether our expenditure in this respect is large or small. And after all, the more money retained in Ulster, the better for the province." The reasoning is incontrovertible. Truly, the children of this world are wiser in their generation than the children of light.

THE FINANCIAL POWER OF THE EXECUTIVE

Mr. Pollock's argument, to which reference has just been made, raises certain points of no little interest in respect of the financial relations between the United Kingdom and Great Britain. More especially how did it arise that increased expenditure on parliamentary salaries would place no extra burden whatever on the Ulster taxpayer? In the Act of 1920 a gift of land purchase annuities, owed in repayment of advances made in respect of agreements entered into before 1920 in Northern and Southern Ireland, was made to the respective Governments. To fulfil the obligation to the beneficiaries from these Annuities the Parliament of the United Kingdom agreed to provide an equal sum and to pay it to the Land Purchase Fund.[2] The interpretation of this provision proved a point of cardinal importance in the dispute that later arose between the British and Free State Governments in respect of the annual annuity payments. In Northern Ireland the control of the Land Purchase system is a reserved service, but the old annuities form a part of the transferred revenue and as such are collected and retained by the Government of Northern Ireland.[3] Mr. Pollock's

---

[1] *N.I., Parl. Debates, H. of C.,* vol. xi, col. 1165–66.
[2] The Act, s. 26.
[3] To be distinguished from the "new Land Annuities" which do not benefit Northern Ireland at all. Vide Chapter x.

argument presumably is based on the fact that the annuities being a gift to the Government of Northern Ireland, expenditure to the amount raised from this source is reckoned as "necessary" expenditure for the purpose of calculating the amount of the Imperial contribution regardless of whether such expenditure fulfils the requisite conditions as laid down by the Colwyn Committee.[1] Consequently, a greater expenditure on the Parliament involves but a corresponding deduction in the amount of the Imperial contribution payable to the United Kingdom. In this way the Northern Ireland taxpayer is only very remotely affected.

Apart from this anomalous instance the general effect of the financial relations between the United Kingdom and Northern Ireland is to render the local executive independent of the local legislature in respect of the greater proportion of its expenditure. This situation arises in consequence of the fact that the "transferred revenue" meets only a small proportion of the "transferred expenditure." The balance is covered in bi-monthly instalments derived from the "Residuary Share of Reserved Taxes" issued from the Consolidated Fund of the United Kingdom and paid into the Exchequer of Northern Ireland.

THE DEPARTMENTS

The distribution of the functions of government amongst the various departments of State has never proved an easy task. The executive in Northern Ireland were faced with the still more difficult problem of creating departments to which all the administrative functions devolved might suitably be assigned. Two features deserve to be recalled. First, since only a portion of the normal executive duties of modern government had been devolved, the departments were to administer a wide but not an all-inclusive field. Secondly, it was necessary, in view of the size of the area to be administered, that the framework of government should involve only a small expenditure.

[1] Cmd. 2389.

Consequently, the number of departments had to be limited with some care. For these reasons Northern Ireland did not present a satisfactory field in which an attempt to rationalize the duties of government along the lines of the then recently published Report upon the Machinery of Government might be made.[1] That Report directed attention to the fact that in Great Britain "there is much overlapping in the functions of the Departments" and suggested certain remedies. There exists no doubt as to the value of the Committee's conclusions. And since in the United Kingdom a gradual evolution of the form of government, in compliance with current needs, had created the existing division of function as between the departments, it would appear at first sight that the newly-established executive in Belfast possessed an admirable opportunity for rationalization. But in Northern Ireland the circumstances to which we have referred compelled a somewhat inconsequent distribution of function. Actually seven departments were established. They were:

1. The Prime Minister's Department and Cabinet Secretariat.
2. The Ministry of Finance.
3. The Ministry of Home Affairs.
4. The Ministry of Labour.
5. The Ministry of Education.
6. The Ministry of Agriculture.
7. The Ministry of Commerce.

These departments were established by the Lord Lieutenant in June 1921.[2] Since this "Assignment of Functions to Departments" certain additional matters of minor importance have come within the authority of local administration and have been distributed amongst the departments in accordance

[1] *Report of the Machinery of Government Committee*, 1918, Cmd. 9230.
[2] Cf. the *Belfast Gazette*, June 7, 1921, for notices dealing with the Establishment and Assignment of Functions to Departments.

with their subject matter. In general the titles of the departments indicate clearly the nature of their duties. The Ministry of Finance enjoys the greatest authority. It exercises a financial control over all departments. It deals both with the settlement of financial questions as between the United Kingdom and Northern Ireland and with the collection of transferred revenue. It determines the salaries and the method of recruitment for the Civil Service. The Prime Minister's Department, though actually the smallest in personnel, is important in that it provides the recognized channel of communication between the Government of Northern Ireland and that of the United Kingdom. The office of the Attorney-General is part of the Ministry of Home Affairs. It is to be noted that the creation of a Ministry of Justice, in accordance with the conclusions of the Haldane Commission, was rendered pointless by the reservation of certain judicial services to the Government of the United Kingdom. The positive contribution of the Ministry of Commerce has proved slight. As in the United Kingdom, the Home Office has become the residuary legatee in all later distribution of functions.

THE CIVIL SERVICE

The Act of 1920 contained elaborate provisions designed to effect a transfer of civil servants employed in the then existing Irish public departments to the new Governments of Northern and Southern Ireland.[1] The emergence of the Irish Free State rendered the greater part of these proposals nugatory; though, in fact, a Committee was appointed on the lines therein suggested and this Committee supervised the transfer of civil servants from departments in Dublin to Belfast in agreed cases. The exact proportion of civil servants transferred from the Imperial departments has not been published, but it was sufficient to provide the nucleus of the civil service of Northern

[1] Act, s. 54 to s. 59.

Ireland. The regulation of the civil service lies within the common law executive power of the Crown and in this instance is exercisable by the Governor. An Order made by the latter in 1923 appointed the Minister of Finance together with two permanent officials to act as Civil Service Commissioners. It is their duty to certify the qualifications of candidates for permanent appointments in the Civil Service. In general, the Ministry of Finance determines the conditions of work, remuneration and recruitment for the service. In the early years of self-government special consideration was shown to ex-servicemen, whilst even now certain posts are reserved exclusively for them. It is officially stated that a "large proportion of male staff consists of ex-servicemen."[1] With this exception, all appointments are filled by open competition. The Opposition claims that the scales are weighted against the selection of Roman Catholic candidates. It is a general charge difficult either to prove or to disprove. It would appear certain, however, that in respect of the higher grades of the civil service, which are recruited by open examination conducted in the same way as the examinations for the Home Civil, that such charges are baseless. On the other hand, the evidence that is available tends to show that discrimination against Catholics is exercised in the lower ranks of the civil service. Certainly there is, in fact, only a small proportion of Catholics at Stormont. The Opposition claims that there should be a proportion in the civil service equal to the relative population strength of members of that creed in Northern Ireland. This pretension is quite unjustifiable in principle. But rightly they claim that no bias whatever should exist against Roman Catholic candidates. In fact, as the speeches of several Ministers have shown, such candidates are not regarded with any great favour. For example, a former Minister of Agriculture, Mr. Archdale, declared at Derrygonelly that out of 109 officials in his department only four were Roman Catholics.[2] Below figures are reproduced showing the total number of the Central Govern-

---

[1] Cf. *Ulster Year Book*, 1935, p. 274.   [2] March 31, 1925.

ment staff and its distribution as between the various departments:

Department	Staff	Men	Women
Houses of Parliament	24	23	1
Cabinet Secretariat	7	4	3
Ministry of Finance	761	628	133
Ministry of Home Affairs	333	277	56
Ministry of Labour	872	604	268
Ministry of Education	132	111	21
Ministry of Agriculture	385	296	89
Ministry of Commerce	50	39	11
Unemployment Assistance Board ..	125	109	16
Exchequer and Audit Office ..	10	9	1
Total	2,699	2,100	599[1]

It will be observed that the Ministry of Labour employs the largest staff.[2] When the Parliament of Northern Ireland assembled in 1921 it was faced with the task of establishing all the departments of State. The Prime Minister then declared his belief that "in this great centre of labour and industry it is absolutely essential to have a Ministry dealing with the problem of labour in all its aspects and that alone. I look upon the Ministry of Labour,"[3] he said, "as one of the most important Ministries in my Government." That, in fact, it has proved to be, and under the able guidance of its Minister, Mr. Andrews, it has done valuable work. The Ministry of Education, on the other hand, has not fulfilled the hopes of the Prime Minister. In 1921, Sir James Craig declared that "it is admitted on all

[1] These figures are published in *Ulster Year Book*.
[2] It is a matter of some interest to observe that very few graduates of the Queen's University are to be found at Stormont. There are a considerable number of graduates of English Universities and a large number from Dublin University. Graduates of the latter University in addition occupy a remarkable proportion of the high offices in the Church, in the Judicature and in the State.
[3] *N.I., H. of C. Debates*, vol. i, cols. 171–74.

sides that our educational system in the North is not one that can be even amended, but one that requires to be rooted out of the soil in order that we may begin to plant a new fabric."[1] It was believed that a local Ministry of Education would prove admirably fitted for the task. Its achievement, though considerable, has been of a superficial rather than of a fundamental character.

THE DISCRETIONARY AUTHORITY OF THE EXECUTIVE[2]

The Ministers, in addition to their political rôle, preside individually over the work of the various administrative departments. Since the sessions of Parliament are comparatively brief and since the Ministerial majority has hitherto survived undefeated over a period of more than fifteen years, the latter has proved their more important task.

Administration in the modern State is creative both in intention and in execution. No longer may the administration be described with accuracy—if indeed it ever could—as a passive instrument carrying out the enactments of the legislature. For in order to apply the law the administration must needs interpret it. In so doing it effects changes, frequently merely of emphasis, but sometimes in actual intention. The positive aspect of modern legislation, more particularly in its concern to organize the life of the people, compels a very real dependence upon the executive departments. This dependence is expressed by a provision inserted in almost every important statute, permitting the Minister to exercise a certain discretion—it may be merely in fixing the "appointed day" or in the adaptation of this Act, but it is to be found also in striking instances of delegated legislation or judicial power. This extension of the functions of the executive over matters formerly thought to be quite outside its scope has become so much an accepted feature of government as to lead constitutional commentators

---

[1] *N.I.*, *H. of C. Debates*, vol. 1, cols. 171–74.

[2] No reference is made here to the Civil Authorities Acts which are exceptional in character and are discussed in Chapter xii.

to over-emphasize the hegemony enjoyed by the executive.[1] The issue is of interest in relation to Northern Ireland, in that it might be expected that a subordinate legislature, exercising restricted powers in a small area, would not find it necessary to delegate any discretionary authority to the executive. Inasmuch as the legislature had delegated such authority it goes far to disprove the contention that the discretionary authority of the executive is due to an insufficiency of time for consideration of detail by the legislature. Authority is delegated in Northern Ireland for two reasons alone: (*a*) because it is convenient for the Parliament to do so; (*b*) because it leads to more satisfactory administration.

The breach effected in the traditional forms of parliamentary government by statutory delegation of legislative and judicial functions is in no sense whatever exceptional to Northern Ireland. A brief statement of its principal features in that province is of interest in giving evidence as to its form of application under somewhat unusual conditions.

In Northern Ireland the annual volume of published statutory rules and orders is large. In the table below are enumerated, for purposes of comparison, the number of Acts, both Public and Private, enacted in any given year, together with the number of rules and orders published by authority of the executive.

Year	Number of Public and General Acts	Number of Local and Private Acts	Number of Statutory Rules and Orders
1923	33	4	64
1925	30	3	113
1928	30	8	86
1930	24	3	123
1932	21	3	83
1934	25	3	106[2]

[1] E.g. W. A. Robson, *Justice and Administrative Law.*

[2] These figures may be taken as inclusive since the Rules Publication Act, 1925.

This statistical table suggests a somewhat larger legislative output than is, in fact, the case. This is due to the numerous amending Acts necessitated by the existence of two Parliaments exercising legislative authority over the same area. But they do indicate also no inconsiderable dependence upon executive discretion—and in this respect they are not misleading. It should, however, be stated at once that such figures *prove* nothing. Significance, not quantity, is the criterion by reference to which a judgment should be framed. But they do establish a prima facie case for a brief consideration of the form of such delegated authority.

It is difficult in practice to draw a precise dividing line between a legislative and a purely administrative act, and a rigid definition is rendered the more difficult by the frequent addition of a quasi-judicial aspect. A general survey, however, of the contemporary extent of executive power in Northern Ireland may be estimated by an examination of the following principal features of its operation:

(*a*) The discretionary powers of Ministers.
(*b*) Delegated legislation by Ministers of the Crown.
(*c*) The Judicial Powers exercised by the Executive.
(*d*) Safeguards.

(*a*) It is impossible to put forward a simple classification of the heterogeneous collection of regulations, rules and orders which are exercised by the executive today. The distinction between the first two categories mentioned above is frankly arbitrary. It was inserted in order to segregate rather less important instances of Ministerial discretion from the wide powers of subordinate legislation conferred in certain statutes. Thus it is usual, though not invariable, that the executive should be granted the power of fixing the "appointed day." In the Motor Vehicles Act, 1930,[1] it is provided "that this Act shall come into operation on such day or days as may be appointed by the Minister of Home Affairs." More frequently

[1] [N.I.] 20 & 21 Geo. V. c. 24, s. 21.

this discretionary power is conferred upon the Privy Council and the day is fixed "as the Governor of Northern Ireland may by Order in Council appoint."[1] In certain cases the date is determined by the Legislature itself when it is stated that this Act "shall come into operation on the appointed day and the appointed day for the purpose of this Act shall be . . ."[2]

(b) Delegated legislation by Ministers of the Crown invariably takes one of two forms:

(1) the statutory Order in Council;
(2) the Departmental regulation.

The former is the traditional authority available to undertake to make rules and regulations, but with the elaboration of the departments of State it has become more usual for the latter to be entrusted with such legislative powers. In Northern Ireland the phrases "the Governor may by Order in Council . . ." and "the Ministry of Finance may by order . . ." occur with similar frequency. The distinction is one of form not of reality. The more valid test is supplied by the Committee on Ministers' Powers. Therein it is stated that the *normal* type of delegated legislation has two distinguishing characteristics, namely:

(i) that the limits of the delegated power are so clearly defined by the Enabling Act as to be made plainly known to Parliament and the Public and to be readily enforceable by the Judiciary;
(ii) that the powers delegated do not confer the authority to legislate on matters of principle, to impose taxation or to amend Acts of Parliament.[3]

Examples of this type of delegated legislation occur frequently in the statutes of Northern Ireland. In the Marketing of Eggs Act, 1926,[4] it is provided that the Ministry of Agriculture

---

[1] Cf. 16 & 17 Geo. V. c. 15, s. 18.   [2] Ibid., c. 30, s. 13.
[3] Cf. *Committee on Ministers' Powers*, p. 29 ff. Cmd. 4060.
[4] 16 & 17 Geo. V. c. 28, s. 4.

may "by rules, made under the principal Act, provide that persons" shall comply with certain clearly defined regulations. In the Agricultural Produce Act, 1930, the Ministry of Agriculture was empowered to "make rules prescribing anything which is to be prescribed and providing for any matter in regard to which rules may be made, under this Act, and generally for carrying this Act into effect. . . ."[1] With the possible exception of the last clause quoted, these powers of subordinate legislation conferred upon Ministers do not in any way infringe, either by intention or by consequence, the actual sovereignty of the Legislature. They are designed to facilitate administration, but in so doing the extent of the powers conferred is delimited with precision by reference to the terms of the Enabling Act. Such a type of subordinate legislation, while frequently used in the statutes of Northern Ireland, does not in any vital respect violate the time-honoured principles of the English Constitution.

There are, however, other, and by contrast, *exceptional* instances of delegated legislative powers, which constitute a recent and remarkable tendency in governmental practice.[2] Here again classification is difficult, but certain examples indicate the extent of such development in Northern Ireland. In numerous statutes the Ministry to which reference is made is empowered to make regulations prescribing anything which is to be prescribed and "*generally for carrying this Act into effect.*"[3] The latter phrase obviously permits of a somewhat elastic interpretation. Sometimes the wording allows a wider latitude, as when it is provided that the Ministry may make rules under the Act and "all such other rules as are necessary or proper for carrying this Act into effect."[4] It would not be easy for a Court of Law to determine precisely what did and what did not come under this description. In the Agricultural Marketing Act (N. Ireland), 1933, no check whatever exists

---

[1] 20 & 21 Geo. V. c. 23, s. 16.

[2] The Civil Authorities Act provides the most extreme instance of delegated authority, Cf. pp. 273-76.

[3] E.g. Milk and Milk Products Act (N.I.), 1934, s. 9.

[4] E.g. Housing Act (N.I.), 1933, s. 9.

upon the discretion conferred upon the Ministry of Agriculture. "The Ministry may," it is provided, "by regulations, make such provision, *as appear to the Ministry to be necessary*, for all or any of the following purposes:

(*a*) for giving full effect to this Act";[1] A somewhat similar discretion was conferred upon the Ministry of Labour in the National Health Insurance Act (N. Ireland), 1930. The Ministry was empowered to make regulations generally for carrying the Act into effect and further "if any difficulty arises in bringing into operation this Act the Ministry with the consent of the Ministry of Finance may, by order, do anything which appears necessary or expedient for bringing this Act into effect."[2] In these circumstances the powers conferred are so wide that it is difficult to know what limits the Legislature did intend to impose. The provisions are of a similar character to those appearing in the statutes of the United Kingdom. It is to be noted, however, that the reservation, by the United Kingdom, of certain fiscal powers, especially the right of imposing import duties, has eliminated the possibility of wide discretionary powers being conferred upon the Minister of Finance, as has been the case in the Irish Free State and in Great Britain.

(*c*) As it is difficult to distinguish with precision in certain cases between a legislative and administrative act, so also is it difficult to draw a clear line between an administrative and a judicial decision. Although the authority to make a purely judicial decision is rarely conferred upon the executive, yet there are frequent occasions when powers are granted, whose exercise involves, at some stage in the procedure, a judicial decision. In such instances the judicial element may loom large in comparison with the administrative, although the final act is administrative.[3] They arise, for example, in the application of the various licensing laws and the decision in such a case is described as quasi-judicial. In respect of such powers, practice in Northern Ireland has developed along lines

[1] S. 14. The italics are mine.   [2] S. 17 and s. 18.
[3] Cf. Committee on Ministers' Powers.

identical with those laid down in the United Kingdom. Judicial or quasi-judicial powers are conferred normally either upon Ministerial tribunals or upon the Ministers themselves. An example of the former practice is to be found in the Arbitration Tribunal established under the Road and Railway Transport Act (N. Ireland), 1935. The Tribunal is appointed by the Governor of Northern Ireland. It has power by summons to cause any persons to appear before it, to examine them upon oath, to inspect documents and to reach a decision which is final, save in that reference may be made to the Supreme Court on a question of law.[1] In the Planning and Housing Act (N. Ireland), 1931, the Ministry as Arbitrator is authorized to determine any matter arising out of certain provisions of the Act.[2] An example of the exercise of a judicial function by a Minister himself is to be found in the Unemployment Insurance Act (N. Ireland), 1922, in which it is provided that he may determine questions of no little importance, e.g. whether an individual has fulfilled the conditions of the Act and so is entitled to benefit under it, and whether an addition ought to be made to the weekly rate of benefit.[3] This involves the performance of a strictly judicial function by an officer of the executive.

The discretionary power of the executive is further increased by rights of enquiry now frequently conferred with the object of facilitating administrative action. Under the Milk and Milk Products (N. Ireland) Act, 1934, any authorized officer is entitled to enter and inspect certain specified premises. Similar provisions have been inserted in numerous Acts. The general effect of the powers conferred upon the administration is to leave a wide discretion in the hands of the executive. This discretion is the more real in that the authority so delegated is permissive in principle. The departments are at liberty, not merely to determine the character of their subordinate legislation, but also to decide whether or no they will exercise the powers that have been delegated.

[1] S. 7.   [2] S. 18.   [3] S. 1.

N

(*d*) What safeguards does the public enjoy against a possible misuse of the wide powers now conferred upon the executive? They may be classified under two headings:

(*a*) Statutory safeguards;
(*b*) Public opinion.

There is no doubt that the second is by far the more important.

In 1925 an Act was passed providing that all statutory rules must be sent to the Government Printer, so that later they might be printed and obtained by the public.[1] This was a very desirable reform, the more especially since its application was inclusive. It ensures that all Ministerial rules and regulations shall be made available to the public. In addition, several Acts prescribe, as the Agricultural Produce Act, 1930, that "all rules made by the Ministry of Agriculture under this Act shall forthwith be laid before both Houses of Parliament" and "if either House, within the statutory period . . . resolves that the rule ought to be annulled the rule shall, after the date of the resolution, be of no effect. . . ."[2] It may be mentioned that the statutory period for the laying of rules before either House was fixed in 1925 as comprising at least five days on which the House has sat.[3] Even though a rule so laid is very rarely annulled by either House, the practice does afford a very valuable safeguard against abuse. A further check on arbitrary action by the executive is also provided by the existence of various consultative committees. The committees are formed with the object of advising the Minister and the persons composing them are usually intimately concerned with the working of the Enabling Act. Such committees have been formed in connection with various Acts dealing with agricultural organization, with Education and National Health Insurance.[4] Normally, the Minister is under no compulsion to accept the advice of

[1] Rules Publication Act (N.I.), 1925.
[2] S. 16. Cf. similar provisions in Superannuation Act, 1935.
[3] Cf. Rules Publication Act, 1925, s. 4.
[4] Cf. Education Act (N.I.), 1930; Pig Marketing Act (N.I.), 1934.

these committees, but at the same time it is unlikely that he will consistently disregard it.

The second and only effective safeguard against the misuse of discretionary authority by the executive is public opinion. In Northern Ireland its validity is the more unquestioned in that it is comparatively easy to secure proper attention for grievances of such a kind in a small self-governing community. The problem, presented by recent developments in the type and extent of Ministerial power, is one of the most distinctive features of modern government. In this brief analysis of its principal aspects in Northern Ireland, it has been impossible to consider the fundamental constitutional issues at stake. But the examination does enable us to draw two conclusions— the one positive, the other negative. It is evident from the provisions of the later statutes of Northern Ireland that there is increasing devolution of function by the Legislature to the administration. It is logical, therefore, to assume that such delegation of authority has proved beneficial in the opinion both of the Legislature and of the executive. The negative conclusion is derived from the fact that in a small partially self-governing unit, in which considerations of time need not affect the deliberations of the Legislature, the practice of delegating powers has none the less been fully accepted. A strong case is thereby advanced for the belief that in general this practice originates, not in any supposed deficiency in parliamentary time, but in the real needs of modern administration.

CHAPTER X

THE FINANCIAL SYSTEM

THE distribution of financial authority as between the central and subordinate Government constitutes the most complex problem of Devolution. The relationship established should not diminish the fiscal resources of the Central Government to any serious degree; whilst at the same time definite financial responsibility should be conferred upon the local executive. How are these apparently contradictory objectives to be achieved? The evidence afforded by experience in Northern Ireland is mainly negative. Admittedly the first condition is fulfilled, for the Act of 1920 leaves the fiscal authority of the Imperial Parliament substantially unimpaired. To this end, however, the proper responsibility of the subordinate executive is sacrificed. The undue limitations imposed upon its financial authority were designed to restrain the Southern Nationalists, but were not amended when the Act ceased to be even legally operative in the South. Moreover, the financial relationship established between Northern Ireland and Great Britain suffers from an additional inherent defect. It is complicated. Neither its intention nor its operation is understood by half the members of the Legislature—not to speak of the general public. The confusion is increased by the secrecy which surrounds the all-important deliberations of the Joint Exchequer Board. The public are informed of the outcome but they are left in ignorance of the reasons for it. This is most undesirable in a democratic State.

THE PROVISIONS OF THE ACT OF 1920

The financial provisions of the Act of 1920 were much criticized in Parliament. The criticisms were substantially just in as much as they were directed against the unwarranted fiscal restrictions imposed upon the subordinate Parliaments in Dublin and in Belfast. Mr. Asquith emphasized the obvious divergence that existed as between the measure of legislative and executive power devolved and that of financial authority. He said:[1]

". . . if in the existing conditions you can safely trust the Irish Legislature and Executive with the powers already given to them by the Act on the Statute Book you may add, without undue risk, to those powers the imposition of Customs and Excise and Income Tax duties." In logic, Mr. Asquith's argument is irrefutable, but in fact such a delegation of fiscal authority was entirely out of harmony with the spirit of the Act of 1920. The transfer of income tax and of customs to the local Parliament had been advocated by the Committee on National Finance in 1912. They recommended, subject to certain reservations in matters of detail, that "the power of levying and imposing all taxation in Ireland should rest with the Irish Government."[2] This conclusion was prompted in part by the conviction that "the experience of the last few years amply confirms the theory that a financial partnership with Great Britain does lead in Ireland to a scale of expenditure beyond the requirements and beyond the resources of the country itself." There was, therefore, no lack of financial evidence to support the contention that a full delegation of fiscal authority was essential for the proper self-government of Ireland. Therefore, criticism of the financial provisions of the Act of 1920 was justified *so long as Ireland remained the unit of self-government.* When Northern Ireland alone accepted the Act then criticisms, as those of Mr. Asquith, were rendered invalid because the issue in question had been materially modified. No longer was there a possibility of Devolution operating in a well-defined political and economic unit; no longer did there remain any hope of reconciling Irish Nationalists by fiscal concessions; but instead self-governing institutions were to function within a six-county area artificially created by the disintegration of Ireland. Consequently, the

[1] *H. of C. Debates*, vol. 127, col. 1117.　　[2] See *Report*, p. 6.

financial system of Northern Ireland was never analysed in the light of its actual sphere of operation. Herein lies the explanation of much that appears inconsequent in the financial relations established between Great Britain and Northern Ireland.

The six counties do not constitute an economic unit. As a result, partition has brought serious financial loss to the smaller tradesmen, manufacturers, and commercial men of the North. Belfast, as Vienna in modern Austria, is left as a city without a background. Even more serious is the plight of Derry, situated on the Border and thereby deprived of normal economic intercourse with the inhabitants of a countryside with whom it has traded for centuries. In this way, the prosperity of Northern Ireland has come to depend on two industries—shipbuilding and linen. The risk of economic slump is thereby exaggerated; for a small area dependent on two industries whose market is governed by purely external trade conditions, is peculiarly liable to suffer acutely in times of international distress. The risk of unemployment is not, as in Great Britain, spread over a wide field of commercial and industrial activity. It is confined to an extent that renders recurrent periods of acute unemployment inevitable. This means heavy expenditure on social services and relief works. How are they to be financed? Certainly not by direct taxation, for the predominance of small farmers and small shopkeepers renders the yield of income tax per head of the population much lower than in Great Britain. In 1929–30 when the standard rate of income tax was 4s., the average of income tax paid per head of the population in Great Britain was £5–6, whereas in Northern Ireland it was only £2–3.[1] The alternatives that remain—since the dependence on external industrial and agricultural markets renders economic self-sufficiency for the six counties impracticable—are either a scale of social services lower than that in Great Britain or an essentially complete fiscal union with Great Britain. The latter alternative is obviously the more attractive

[1] Vide *Ulster Year Book*, 1932, p. 206.

to Northern Ireland. And, in fact, it was established, with certain limitations, by the provisions of the Act of 1920 as amended and supplemented by the Report of the Colwyn Committee. But the terms of the Act were designed expressly to disguise the continued fiscal unity of the British Isles in order to conciliate the Nationalist sentiment by the measure of self-government conceded. In the event, the Nationalists remained frankly unimpressed; yet the product of the design survived. Consequently, these exists today a *veiled* financial unity between Great Britain and Northern Ireland.

The characteristics of the economic life of Northern Ireland entail—if the standards of its social services are to be maintained in parity with those of Great Britain—that an underlying fiscal unity should be preserved. In the circumstances the principle is sound, the more so in that close association with Great Britain is an article in the creed of the predominant political party in the six counties. But the desire to give a semblance of financial authority to the subordinate Government has been permitted both to distort the principle and to render the system obscure. The defects lie not so much in essentials as in interpretation.

THE DISTRIBUTION OF FINANCIAL POWER

The Parliament of Northern Ireland enjoys only a restricted financial authority. An Exchequer was established in Belfast under the terms of the Act,[1] and it controls the administration of public finance in Northern Ireland, in the same manner— subject to the necessary modifications—as does the Exchequer in the United Kingdom. The Minister of Finance prepares the annual budget to be approved by Parliament at Stormont, and that Parliament exercises full control over all expenditure by the local executive. But the greater part of financial authority is, in fact, reserved to the Imperial Parliament.

Certain forms of taxation are excluded from the control

[1] S. 20.

of the Parliament of Northern Ireland. These include customs and certain excise duties, income tax and surtax and any other taxes on profits. In this way the practical fiscal supremacy of the Imperial Parliament is assured since by far the larger portion of the total revenue of Northern Ireland is raised through these taxes. They are collected by the Imperial Revenue officers and are paid direct into the Exchequer of the United Kingdom. The revenue ultimately accruing to Northern Ireland from this source is termed "Reserved Revenue." But the amount that is actually transferred to the Exchequer of Northern Ireland by the United Kingdom Treasury is termed the "Residuary Share of Reserved Taxes." The distinction is necessitated by the existence of the various "Reserved Services." The expenditure on these services is covered in the first instance by the Imperial Exchequer, but the cost is eventually deducted from the Reserved Taxes collected in Northern Ireland. Likewise, the amount of the Imperial contribution and certain other charges are deducted from the Reserved Taxes. The balance of the account then remaining to the credit of Northern Ireland is issued from the Consolidated Fund of the United Kingdom and paid as the residuary share of Reserved Taxes into the Exchequer of Northern Ireland.

In general the distribution of financial power between Great Britain and Northern Ireland means that about four-fifths of the total revenue of the six counties is levied by authority of the Imperial Parliament, whilst about four-fifths of the expenditure is authorized by the subordinate Parliament and incurred by the subordinate executive departments. This may appear incongruous, but in fact it is a necessary, and not harmful, corollary of any partial delegation of financial authority. Responsibility to the local Parliament is as real in the case of reserved as of transferred revenue, for no distinction is drawn between monies emanating from either source.

The Act of 1920 provided that a contribution should be made by the subordinate authority to the central Government in respect of Imperial services. The amount of Northern

Ireland's contribution is fixed by formula. It varies considerably in accordance with changes in economic conditions. The amount to be paid in any given year is determined by the Joint Exchequer Board. Till 1936–37 the Imperial Contribution from Northern Ireland declined rapidly.

The Joint Exchequer Board wields a decisive influence in determining issues relating to the finances of Northern Ireland. The Board consists of two members appointed by the Treasury, one member appointed by the Government of Northern Ireland and a Chairman appointed by the Crown.[1] The Board determines the amount of the reserved revenues and the cost of the reserved services to be attributed to Northern Ireland. Further, they decide, in accordance with the principle laid down by the Colwyn Committee, the amount of the Imperial Contribution, and such other questions affecting the financial relations of the two Governments as may be referred to it. No report of the proceedings of the Exchequer Board is published.

REVENUE

The public revenue of Northern Ireland may be divided into two categories:

(*a*) Transferred Revenue.
(*b*) Reserved Revenue.

An estimate of their relative significance may be formed from the analysis overleaf.[2]

It will be observed that the revenue accruing from Transferred Taxes comprises but a small percentage of the total revenue of Northern Ireland. The taxes within the direct control of the subordinate Parliament are, with the two exceptions of Death Duties and Motor Licence Duties, of very secondary importance. Death Duties on an average yield over half a million each year. They are levied at the same rates and in accordance with the same principles as the similar

[1] The Act, s. 32. [2] Reproduced from *Ulster Year Book*, 1935.

duties in Great Britain. The Act of 1920 made provision[1]
to avoid double payment in Great Britain and Northern Ireland.
No administrative difficulties of undue complexity have arisen,
as anticipated by the Conference on Devolution, by this transfer
of Death Duties to the subordinate Parliament. No new taxes
have been imposed by the Parliament of Northern Ireland
within the sphere of its financial authority. Nor has that Parliament displayed any desire to vary the level of transferred
taxes from that of similar taxes in Great Britain. In Motor
Licence Duties, however, the rate levied in Northern Ireland
is higher than that in Great Britain. Below are given the yields
derived from transferred taxes in the financial year 1934–35.[2]

REVENUE—TRANSFERRED TAXES

	£	s.	d.
Death Duties, etc.	527,000	0	0
Stamp Duties	244,000	0	0
Mineral Rights Duty	200	0	0
Excise	130,000	0	0
Motor Vehicles duties—Licences, etc. ..	634,498	11	11
Total Transferred Tax Revenue ..	£1,535,698	11	11

This revenue is supplemented by the transferred non-tax
revenue, which includes interest on various Government loans,
Church Temporalities and the Land Purchase Annuities.
The latter item is the most considerable. In 1934–35 receipts
from this source amounted to £658,000. The position regarding
Land Annuity payments as a whole is somewhat involved.
The control and administration of the Land Purchase System
is a reserved service. The terminable annuities payable by
tenants in repayment of advances made under agreements
to purchase entered into before 1920[3] were transferred to the
Government of Northern Ireland as a "free gift . . . to meet
the additional expense incidental to the severance of the two
Irish Governments from Great Britain and from one another."[4]

[1] S. 28.   [2] Vide *Finance Accounts for the Year* 1934–35, H.C. 350.
[3] The actual day being December 23rd.
[4] Vide *Outline of Financial Proposals of the Government of Ireland
Bill*, 1920, Cmd. 645.

Type of Revenue	1931–32		1932–33		1933–34	
	£	%	£	%	£	%
Transferred Revenue:						
Tax	1,555,191	17	1,469,865	13	1,453,309	13
Non-Tax	964,414	9	928,387	8	929,835	9
Total	2,519,605	23	2,398,252	21	2,383,144	22
Reserved Revenue:						
Tax	7,489,630	67	7,917,383	70	7,604,323	69
Non-Tax	891,402	8	978,950	9	1,006,231	9
Total	8,381,032	75	8,896,333	79	8,610,554	78
Unemployment Fund: Equalization Payment— Contribution from Imperial Exchequer	200,852	2	—	—	8,885	—
	£11,101,489	100	£11,294,585	100	£11,002,583	100

They are collected and retained in Belfast. Since these annuities are terminable the Northern Government is provided thereby only with a temporary source of income. The Minister of Finance has accordingly instituted a Sinking Fund designed to provide an income in perpetuity equivalent to the amount now received from the Land Annuities.[1] On the other hand, the new Land Purchase Annuities derived from agreements entered into after 1920, although collected by the Government of Northern Ireland, do not benefit her revenue since a deduction equivalent to the amount to be collected is made from the Residuary Share of Reserved Taxes.

RESERVED REVENUE

All taxes other than those expressly reserved lie within the authority of the Parliament of Northern Ireland, but the over-riding importance of the actual reserved taxes is clear. They include Customs and Excise Duties, Income Tax and Surtax, Excess Profits Duty and Corporation Profits Tax. The two latter taxes have been abolished—Excess Profits Duty in 1921 and the Corporation Profits Tax in 1924. This means that Reserved Revenue is derived from two all-important sources—Customs and Excise and Income Tax. The revenue on Customs and Excise Duties is attributed to Northern Ireland on the basis of the consumption of dutiable goods within its area. This consumption is calculated by adding to the net collection of duty in Northern Ireland the amount of the duty attributable to goods imported from Great Britain and deducting the duty attributable to goods exported to Great Britain. The net amount of the duties finally attributed to Northern Ireland is credited to the yield of reserved taxes.[2] A similar principle is applied in the case of income, though obvious difficulties have been encountered in determining the precise amount of the tax to be credited to Northern Ireland. In general, the

[1] The Minister has not explained how this end is to be achieved·
[2] Vide *Year Book*, 1935.

revenue derived from income tax is attributed according to the area in which the taxpayer resides. All issues arising out of the relative proportion of reserved revenue to be attributed to Northern Ireland are decided by the Joint Exchequer Board.

The following figures for the years 1931–32 and 1933–34 show the yield of the various reserved taxes.[1]

Source of Revenue	1931-32		1933-34	
	£	%	£	%
Customs and Excise ..	3,948,316	51	4,744,455	55
Income	2,462,471	32	2,492,615	29
Super-tax	403,559	5	359,927	4
Corporations Profits Tax	24,423	1	322	—
Excess Profits Duty ..	15,492	—	7,004	—
Non-Tax Post Office ..	839,175	11	919,614	12
Total Reserved Revenue	7,704,652[2]	100	8,523,937	100

EXPENDITURE

The general principle of the Act of 1920 is that all expenditure on Northern Ireland, other than such as is definitely Imperial, is to be met from the revenue of Northern Ireland whether the expenditure be on a transferred service administered from Stormont or on a reserved service administered by the Imperial authorities.[3] In contrast to the distribution of authority for revenue purposes the similar division between reserved and transferred expenditure is made so as to place the major responsibility for expenditure in the hands of the Government of Northern Ireland. An analysis of expenditure in two financial years is given in the following table:

[1] Derived from the Finance Accounts, H.C. 150.
[2] Included in total £11,216 derived from Fees, etc.
[3] Vide White Paper, Cmd. 645.

Head	1928–29		1933–34	
	£	%	£	%
Transferred Services:				
Consolidated Fund Services	1,096,572	10	998,157	9
Supply Services ..	6,708,631	62	8,734,748	75
Reserved Services ..	1,797,347	17	1,751,750	15
Imperial Contribution ..	1,175,000	11	76,000	1
Total Expenditure ..	10,777,550	100	11,560,655	100

In 1933–34 transferred expenditure amounted to 84 per cent of the total expenditure of Northern Ireland. It is divided, in accordance with English financial practice, between the Consolidated Fund Services and Supply Services. The former represents various fixed charges upon the Exchequer as statutory salaries, sinking and Reserve Funds and the Road Fund. The expenditure on Supply Services, on the other hand, is authorized annually by the Parliament of Northern Ireland. The estimates are prepared by the various administrative Departments and approved by the Ministry of Finance. No distinction is drawn between revenue derived from reserved and transferred taxation. The Minister frames his budget according to his own estimate of the yield of transferred taxes and according to the British Exchequer's estimate of the yield of reserved taxes. The total then estimated from these sources is the amount at the disposal of the Minister of Finance for expenditure in any given year. It is evident, of course, that the total available is determined in large measure by agencies outside the control of the Minister. A drop of sixpence in income tax as decreed by the Chancellor of the Exchequer in 1934 materially diminishes the residuary share of reserved taxes available for Northern Ireland. Similarly a rise in income tax of 3d. in the pound, as imposed in April 1936, increases the revenue of Northern Ireland, even though the higher rate was imposed to meet additional expenditure on armaments.

Likewise in indirect taxation the taxable capacity of Northern Ireland is not in many respects comparable to that of Great Britain. But the Chancellor of the Exchequer in the preparation of his budget is in no position to take count of particular circumstances prevalent in Northern Ireland. For example, in 1928–29 Customs and Excise produced 51 per cent of the total reserved revenue. Of that 51 per cent just one half was produced from taxes on Beer, Wine and Spirits. In 1933–34 Customs and Excise produced 55 per cent of the total reserved revenue. But less than one-third of this amount was produced from the taxes on Beer, Wine, and Spirits. The yield from this source had dropped by almost half a million pounds in five years and by a million in a decade. The reason does not lie in any variation in the rate of duty, but in the fact that the consumption of alcoholic drink in Northern Ireland is diminishing to a marked extent. Thus in 1929–30 the average yield per head of the estimated population of Northern Ireland from the duty on Beer, Wine and Spirits was £1 10s., whereas in Great Britain the same rate of taxation yielded £2 15s. per head of the population. The decline in the amount of drink consumed in Northern Ireland is due partly to social distress but more largely to the strength of the temperance movement. On the other hand, the consumption of tea in Northern Ireland appears almost as great per head of the population as that in Great Britain. Consequently the imposition of 2d. a pound extra duty on tea by the Chancellor in 1936 should yield the same amount proportionate to population in Northern Ireland as in Great Britain. These examples—though perhaps not of great significance in themselves—do illustrate the difficulties with which the Minister of Finance inevitably must be faced from time to time. The major portion of taxation in Northern Ireland is imposed by the Imperial Parliament. The reasons which guide its imposition are determined by general considerations upon the taxable capacity of the United Kingdom as a whole. It may well happen, however, that the yield of any particular

tax in Northern Ireland is low in comparison with its yield
in Great Britain. In such a case the Minister of Finance is
placed in a dilemma through no decision of his own. Either
he must impose a higher rate of transferred taxes or he must
reduce the standard of various public services in order to make
good the deficiency. The former alternative is limited in scope
and obvious difficulties arise in its application. The latter was
adopted in the case of cuts in teachers' salaries, which were
not restored in full in 1936, but in general, its application is
not possible in Northern Ireland since the Government have
made it a cardinal point of policy that the social services in
Northern Ireland should be maintained at the same level as
the corresponding services in England. Consequently a budget
at times may be balanced—as it has been for the last three years
—by drawing upon the Reserve Fund.

The following table shows the character of the expenditure
on Supply Services in the year 1934–35.[1]

Head	Amounts £
The Ministry of Finance—	
Houses of Parliament and Cabinet Offices	29,800
Public Works and Buildings	143,263
Other Services	259,282
Ministry of Home Affairs—	
Constabulary	718,902
Grants to Local Authorities	1,411,949
Other Services	113,076
Ministry of Labour—	
Unemployment Insurance and Employment Services	1,984,180
Old Age Pensions	1,364,750
Other Services	596,682
Ministry of Education	1,961,000
Ministry of Agriculture	166,174
Ministry of Commerce	38,027
Total Supply Services	8,787,085

Expenditure on reserved services comprises a comparatively
small proportion of the total expenditure of Northern Ireland.

[1] From the Finance Accounts, H.C. 150.

The monies required to cover this expenditure are deducted from the reserved taxes paid into the Exchequer of the United Kingdom. Neither the Parliament nor Government of Northern Ireland exercises any control over these services. The expenditure on them is authorized by the Parliament of the United Kingdom and services administered by the Imperial departments. The actual cost of the administration properly chargeable to Northern Ireland is certified annually by the Joint Exchequer Board. The principal items of expenditure on the reserved services are shown below.

Head	1933-34	
	£	%
Revenue Departments ..	172,097	9·8
Post Office	915,996	52·3
Land Purchase	280,542	16·0
Justice and Police Pensions ..	272,680	15·6
Miscellaneous	110,435	6·3
Total	1,751,750	100·0

THE IMPERIAL CONTRIBUTION

Since Northern Ireland remains an integral part of the United Kingdom she must contribute towards the cost of the various Imperial services. These include the Army, Navy, Air Force, Foreign Relations, the National Debt and various other services. The expenditure on these items is very large. In 1920, it was intended that Ireland's contribution to the Imperial Services should be fixed, after a preliminary period, by the Joint Exchequer Board at such proportion of the total Imperial liabilities and expenditure as the Board "having regard to the relative taxable capacities of Ireland and the United Kingdom" might determine to be just. During the preliminary financial period the contribution was fixed at £18,000,000, of which 56 per cent or £10,080,000 was to be paid by Southern Ireland and 44 per cent or £7,920,000 by Northern Ireland. This sum, it was stated,[1] represented the estimated amount which was being contributed by Ireland during the then current financial year. It was, however, apparent, once self-government began to function in Northern Ireland, that a contribution of £7,920,000 was beyond the capacity of the province to pay. The Memorandum issued with the Government of Ireland Bill might point out that if Ireland as a whole contributed £18,000,000 then Great Britain would be required to contribute at least £600,000,000. On these assumptions the respective contributions per head of the population would be £4 2s. in Ireland and £14 13s. 8d. in Great Britain. On paper this appears a handsome concession to Ireland, but in fact it was nothing of the kind. For it is the wealth of an area not its population that provides the proper criterion of taxable capacity. This was at once apparent so far as Northern Ireland was concerned; and in 1923 the Colwyn Committee was appointed to reconsider the whole question of the amount of the Imperial contribution to be paid by Northern Ireland. The Final Report of this Committee was published in 1925.[2] Its recommendations have been accepted as providing a proper test of the contribution due from Northern Ireland in each financial year.

The Colwyn Committee, having observed that taxation common to Great Britain and Ireland is in itself to a certain extent a measure of relative gross taxable capacity, and further, that the satisfaction of certain basic needs of local administration is essential before taxable capacity in an appropriate sense can be effective, recommended that due regard would be paid to relative taxable capacities were the proportion to be contributed based on the following lines:

"The extent to which the total revenue exceeds the actual and necessary expenditure in Northern Ireland shall be taken as the basic sum for determining the contribution, but only

---

[1] Cf. *Outline of Financial Provisions*, Cmd. 645, and the *Further Memorandum on Financial Provisions*, Cmd. 707.

[2] *Final Report of the Northern Ireland Special Arbitration Committee*, 1925. The first *Report* was dated 1923. Cmd. 2073.

after a full consideration by the Joint Exchequer Board of the result of the application of the formula referred to below to the facts of the year under consideration, and so that the contribution shall be such basic sum modified and adjusted as the Joint Exchequer Board may consider just and proper having regard to that result.

"In determining the necessary expenditure there shall be eliminated:

(a) all expenditure on any service in existence in both Northern Ireland and Great Britain incurred in providing Northern Ireland with a higher average standard of service than exists in Great Britain;

(b) such expenditure on any service in existence in both Northern Ireland and Great Britain as is incurred in providing an average standard of service, which, while not higher than the average standard of service in Great Britain, is in excess of the strict necessities of the case in Northern Ireland having regard to any lower general level of prices, of wages, or of standards of comfort or social amenity which may exist in Northern Ireland as compared with Great Britain;

(c) all expenditure undertaken by the Government of Northern Ireland on services which do not exist in Great Britain."

The formula to which reference is made rests on the assumption that changes in rates of taxation in Great Britain and Northern Ireland should be almost identical, and that similar social services will be undertaken in both areas. The financial year 1923–24 was taken as the standard year for the purpose of fixing a normal yield of revenue and expenditure in both areas. Differences in Great Britain from the standard thus established are translated into equivalent figures for Northern Ireland, due regard being paid to changes in population and in the relative yield of taxation.

The Colwyn Committee considered that the principles of

the Report should not necessarily be applied for a period longer than five years without specific reconsideration of the problem. In fact, the results of its application have evidently proved satisfactory to both Governments, since they have been continued to the present day. Unquestionably, the Colwyn Committee Report was favourable to Northern Ireland. Its contribution is reckoned, not in accordance with the measure of Imperial needs, but in accordance with its capacity to pay in any given financial year. Northern Ireland has the amount of its contribution determined by the excess of its total revenue over its actual and necessary expenditure. In this way, a low productivity of taxes in times of economic slump results, so far as Northern Ireland is concerned, in an automatic reduction of the Imperial Contribution. In similar circumstances the United Kingdom as a whole is compelled to increase taxation. Northern Ireland is secure from any such drastic remedy so long as her expenditure on particular services is not higher than that of Great Britain. The point is illustrated by the amounts contributed in the last decade.

Year				Amount of Imperial Contribution £
1926–27	..	..	..	1,350,000
1927–28	..	..	..	1,450,000
1928–29	..	..	..	1,175,000
1929–30	..	..	..	855,000
1930–31	..	..	..	545,000
1931–32	..	..	..	298,000
1932–33	..	..	..	75,000
1933–34	..	..	..	76,000
1934–35	..	..	..	10,000
1935–36	..	..	..	10,000
1936–37	..	..	..	400,000[1]

It is clear that the severity of the economic slump in Northern Ireland, coinciding as it did with an increased expenditure on social services in the United Kingdom as a whole, reduced the Imperial contribution to a negligible figure. The fixing of a sliding scale on the principle adopted by the Colwyn

[1] As Estimated by the Minister of Finance in April 1936.

Committee renders this possible—perhaps even probable—
in an area as Northern Ireland which is peculiarly liable to
suffer in times of depression. In fact, the Colwyn award would
have broken down in 1935–36 had not a new Unemployment
Insurance Agreement been reached with the Imperial Government some little time before the close of the financial year.
As it was, the Imperial Contribution had been reduced to
vanishing point, and the Government of Northern Ireland may
well consider themselves fortunate in being able to transfer
the consequences of their economic difficulties on to the more
ample shoulders of the Imperial Exchequer.

It is to be noted that the amount of the Imperial Contribution
is determined by the Joint Exchequer Board. In so doing
it has full power to modify and adjust the "basic sum" having
due regard to the result of the application of the special formula.
The deliberations of the Board are private and no report of
its proceedings is published. Obviously it must exercise a
very wide discretion in the framing of its annual award. Indeed,
in a very real sense it wields a greater authority in regard to
the finances of Northern Ireland than does the Parliament
of Northern Ireland itself. While it may be to the convenience
of the Governments concerned that its discussions should
not be made public, yet from a wider aspect this secrecy
creates a precedent seriously at variance with the traditional
conduct of public finance in a democratic State.

THE UNEMPLOYMENT FUND

The Colwyn Arbitration Committee fixed the principle that
Northern Ireland was entitled—so long as it maintained
taxation approximately on the same scale as in Great Britain—
to enjoy an equal standard of social services. In practice the
principle has been endangered by the extent of Northern
Ireland's liabilities in Unemployment Insurance. Not only
has the percentage of unemployment in the six counties been
considerably higher than that in Great Britain during the last

decade, but further an actual increase in the standard of social services has been necessary in Northern Ireland in order to keep in parity with similar services in the remainder of the United Kingdom. In 1922–23 Northern Ireland's expenditure on social services amounted to 3½ million pounds; in 1927–28 it was almost 5 million; in 1933–34 it had jumped to almost 7½ million. This rapid increase in expenditure presented a problem of real complexity in a small, partially self-governing area. As the Minister of Finance remarked in the House of Commons[1] . . . "our province is not a Dominion responsible for its entire finances. No less than 89 per cent of our total revenue is collected by the Imperial authorities on a scale settled at Westminster in accordance with the needs of the Kingdom as a whole, and moreover even the remaining 11 per cent within our purview does not admit of much variation."

The issue was first brought to the front by the scale of unemployment expenditure in Northern Ireland. Accordingly, in 1926 an Agreement was arranged with the Imperial Exchequer "with a view to assimilating the burdens on the respective Exchequers in respect of Unemployment Insurance."[2] This object was to be achieved by providing that the Unemployment Funds of the two parts of the United Kingdom might from 1925 onwards be kept in a state of parity on the basis of insured populations by means of additional Exchequer grants to the poorer fund, and that a substantial part of the extra burden so placed upon the Exchequer of the area to which the poorer fund belongs should be spread over the taxpayers of the United Kingdom as a whole. The Agreement was, therefore, in form reciprocal, but in fact, it redounded, as anticipated, only to the benefit of Northern Ireland. A check on extravagance was imposed by providing that the payment from one Exchequer to the other was to be the equivalent of *three-quarters* of the sum required to equalize per head of the total population

[1] *N.I., H. of C. Debates*, March, 1936.
[2] Unemployment Insurance (N.I.) Agreement Act, 1926, 16 Geo. V. c. 4.

the payments out of the two Exchequers into their respective Unemployment Funds.[1]

This Act, and a supplementary Act passed in 1929, were rendered necessary by the disproportionately heavy burden of unemployment in Northern Ireland. Accordingly, some such equalization payment was essential, unless the rates of contributions and of benefits in Northern Ireland were to be fixed at a level different from that in Great Britain. The latter alternative was clearly undesirable both for social and industrial reasons. The figures below show the mean percentages of the insured persons recorded as unemployed in Great Britain and Northern Ireland in various years since 1925.

Year	Percentage of Insured Persons Unemployed in Great Britain	Percentage of Insured Persons Unemployed in Northern Ireland	Total Payment from Exchequer of the United Kingdom to that of Northern Ireland under the Agreement
			£
1926	12·3	23·2	879,591
1927	9·6	13·2	296,356
1929	10·3	14·8	346,566
1930	15·8	23·8	541,416
1931	21·1	27·9	165,437
1932	21·9	27·4	Nil
1933	19·8	26·6	Nil
1934	16·6	23·4	Nil
1935 (Provisional)	15·3	25·0	—[2]

It will be observed at once that under the 1926 Agreement Northern Ireland received no grant from the Imperial Exchequer from 1932 onwards. That was so because the Agreement reckoned that the relative burden of unemployment should be borne *per head of the general population.* The operation

[1] Vide Memorandum on the Financial Resolution of the Bill, Cmd. 2588 of 1926.

[2] These figures are taken from White Paper on the Act of 1936. Cmd. 5081.

of the Agreement was explained clearly by the Comptroller and Auditor-General to the Public Accounts Committee in 1934. He said:[1]

"To state the figures in another way, the Exchequer payments per head of the insured population in Great Britain amounted to £6 7s. 2d. in 1932–33 and the corresponding figure for Northern Ireland was £7 4s. 8d. You see the payments per head of the insured population were higher in Northern Ireland. When you give the payments per head of the general population, it is reversed simply because the relation between the insured population and the general population is different in Great Britain from what it is here in Northern Ireland. There is a bigger general population in proportion to the insured population here.[2] The Exchequer payment per head of the general population in Great Britain for 1932–33 was £1 15s. 2d. and in Northern Ireland £1 10s. 2d. For 1933–34 the Exchequer payments per head of the insured population in Great Britain was £5 15s. 6d. and in Northern Ireland £7 3s. 4d. The figures per head of the general population are, Great Britain £1 11s. 10d., Northern Ireland £1 9s. 8d. That is why we got nothing."

The statistical diagram on the opposite page shows the inadequacy—from the point of view of Northern Ireland—of the 1926 Agreement.

The particular basis of the 1926 Agreement undoubtedly operated against the interests of Northern Ireland. Since the cessation of the payments from the Imperial Exchequer in 1932, her financial position has been unsound. In May 1931 the Leslie Committee reported[3] that "the limit of taxable capacity in Northern Ireland has been exceeded." This should not be taken too seriously since taxation has been increased very considerably since that date. But none the less, expenditure

[1] Vide. *Report of Select Committee on Public Accounts for* 1933–34, pp. 46–7. H.C. 348.
[2] Since it is an agricultural area.
[3] *Committee on Financial Relations*, Cmd. 131, p. 76.

UNEMPLOYMENT INSURANCE[1]

STATEMENT SHOWING EFFECT OF REINSURANCE AGREEMENT

		General Population	Insured Population	Insured Population Proportion of General Population	Exchequer Payments to Unemployment Funds and Transitional Payments	Exchequer Payments Per Head of General Population (£ s. d.)	Exchequer Payments Per Head of Insured Population (£ s. d.)	Equalization Payment in respect of Period (included in Column 6)	Payments by British Exchequer to N.I. Exchequer
				%	£			£	£
1929–30	G.B.	44,470,000	11,700,000	26·31	19,411,386	0 8 9	1 13 2		346,566
	N.I.	1,250,000	258,400	20·67	1,018,658	0 16 4	3 18 10	596,300	
1930–31	G.B.	44,652,000	12,000,000	26·87	35,148,336	0 15 9	2 18 7		547,416
	N.I.	1,244,000	266,000	21·38	1,729,452	1 7 10	6 10 0	919,406	
1931–32	G.B.	44,831,000	12,360,000	27·57	49,612,532	1 2 2	4 0 3		165,437
	N.I.	1,251,000	270,000	21·58	1,611,167	1 5 9	5 19 4	736,386	
1932–33	G.B.	45,084,000	12,400,000	27·50	79,331,282	1 15 2	6 7 11		Nil
	N.I.	1,262,000	265,000	21·00	1,901,903	1 10 2	7 3 6	508,319	
1933–34	G.B.	45,262,000	12,473,000	27·55	71,931,770	1 11 9	5 15 4		Nil
	N.I.	1,271,000	263,000	20·69	1,879,336	1 9 7	7 2 11	463,450	
1934–35 Provisional	G.B.	45,446,000	12,540,000	27·59	66,850,000	1 9 5	5 6 7		Nil
	N.I.	1,280,000	268,000	20·94	1,864,000	1 9 2	6 19 1	664,211	

[1] *Report of Public Accounts Committee, 1933–34, Appendix 2.*

on unemployment has proved severe and the Government have been unable to meet it in full out of revenue. Consequently, monies have had to be taken from the Reserve Fund—to the amount of £150,000 each year since 1933–34—in order to balance the budget. The financial position would have been very serious indeed at the end of the financial year 1935–36 had not a new Unemployment Insurance Agreement[1] been enacted a few days before its close. Under the new Agreement the payment from the one Exchequer to the other is the equivalent of three-quarters of the sum required to equalise the payments out of each Exchequer into their respective Unemployment Funds in proportion to the *population insured against Unemployment*. In addition the new Agreement covers Unemployment Assistance. Under the Act of 1936, the contribution from the Exchequer of the United Kingdom amounts to £722,000 in 1935–36 as compared with £275,000 which would have been required under the Agreements of 1926 and 1929.[2] The Minister of Finance said:[3]

"The real outcome of the new arrangement was that, in years of depression, they would pay little Imperial contribution, and would receive a considerable sum for unemployment expenditure. In normal years they would receive less for unemployment and pay more Imperial contribution while in prosperity they would receive nothing for unemployment and pay a still larger Imperial contribution."

In intention the new Agreement is equitable. Northern Ireland as a part of the United Kingdom has a right to claim equal social services for the industrial workers in her area. But it also emphasizes the disadvantage of self-governing institutions within an area small in size which does not compose even in a general sense an economic unit.

[1] 26 Geo. V. & 1 Ed. VIII. c. 3.
[2] Vide White Paper, Cmd. 5081.
[3] *N.I., H. of C. Debates*, March 1936.

THE COST OF DEVOLUTION

It was the intention of the Act of 1920 that Northern Ireland should contribute a substantial sum towards the cost of the Imperial Services. The amount originally fixed was rightly criticized as excessive but no question has arisen as to the justice of the contribution in itself. So long as Northern Ireland remains part of the United Kingdom it is bound to pay its proper share, however determined, of the various Imperial Services. But in recent years the Imperial Contribution has been reduced to vanishing-point. Is Northern Ireland thereby tacitly evading her obligations? At first sight such indeed would appear to be the case. But on looking closer one finds particular circumstances which provide in large measure a warrant for her action, more especially in the financial difficulties in which she has been involved owing to the prevalence of unemployment. But it is well to state the number of the subventions or grants received by Northern Ireland from the Central Exchequer. They are three in number, namely, the Unemployment Fund Equalization Payment, the Milk Industry Assistance Grant, and the Fat Cattle subsidy. In 1935–36 the unemployment contribution from the Imperial Exchequer is estimated at £722,000, the Milk Industry Assistance Grant may not amount to more than £200,000 per annum, and on an average about £150,000 is paid to the Northern Ireland Exchequer, whilst payments to farmers in Northern Ireland under the fat cattle subsidy scheme amounted to £216,809 from September 1934 to August 1935.[1] The latter payment is made direct to the farmers selling fat cattle. The other payments are made to the Exchequer of Northern Ireland. Thus, in the financial year 1935–36, Northern Ireland has received in grants and subsidies over one million pounds. Against this must be offset the amount of the Imperial Contribution, which is £10,000 together with certain "concealed

[1] It has amounted to £353,000 from September 1934 to February 1936

contributions." It is claimed, for example, that Northern Ireland received no benefit from the recent War Loan Conversion although her citizens contributed to its success. This is regarded in Northern Ireland as a concealed contribution.[1] A more valid counter-claim is to be found in Northern Ireland's contribution to the Wheat Fund. In the six counties wheat is grown only to a very small extent. Consequently, Northern Ireland contributes far more to the Wheat Fund than is received back by farmers in deficiency payments. The actual figures for the cereal years 1932–33 and 1933–34 are of sufficient importance to quote. Northern Ireland's gross contribution to the Wheat Fund consists of:

(a) Quota payments made in respect of flour milled in Northern Ireland and
(b) Quota payments in respect of flour imported and retained for consumption in Northern Ireland.

The amounts are as follows:[2]

	1932–33	1933–34	1934–35
(a)	£53,516	£119,104	£130,000
(b)	£104,636	£116,600	£92,000
Total Contribution	£158,152	£235,704	£222,000

Deficiency payments received by farmers in Northern Ireland in 1932–33 amounted to £6,413, in 1933–34 to £19,245, and in 1934–35 to £31,000. Northern Ireland therefore made a net contribution of £151,689 to the Wheat Fund in 1932–33, of £216,459 in 1933–34, and of £191,000 in 1934–35. It is essential therefore that this concealed

---

[1] Any such concealed contribution would be covered by special grants from the Imperial Exchequer as that made for the building of Stormont and a later grant of £300,000 to be expended on relief works in Belfast.

[2] Derived from the Wheat Commission figures and from imports into N.I. of wheat and wheat flour. Imports of wheat are converted into flour on the assumption that 28 per cent of wheat is offal.

contribution should be offset against the grants received from the Imperial Exchequer.

There is a widespread illusion in Northern Ireland that the six counties are paying far more than their proper share of Imperial expenditure. This, of course, is far from true. The balance of evidence, after allowing for the impossibility of reckoning the exact fiscal productivity of the two parts of the United Kingdom, shows quite decisively that in recent years the contribution of Northern Ireland to the cost of the Imperial Services is considerably outweighed by the grants from the Imperial Government to Northern Ireland. It is unlikely that the balance will be redressed in future years, for although the contribution to the Unemployment Insurance Fund is exceptionally high at the moment yet the cattle subsidy, now part of a long-term policy, will no doubt tend to increase. Thus the present financial relationship though it be, to say the least, surprising in character, is likely to continue.

GENERAL SURVEY

The first impression derived from a survey of the financial system in Northern Ireland is that a minimum of final responsibility has been delegated. A consideration of the Revenue and Expenditure of Northern Ireland indicates the small measure of ultimate financial responsibility transferred.

This lack of local responsibility has, in fact, rendered grants from the Central Government inevitable since there exist no other means whereby extra revenue may be raised. So far the cracks that have appeared in the financial relationship established between Great Britain and Northern Ireland have been papered over by supplementary agreements involving subventions to Northern Ireland. Thereby the financial system has been rendered unsatisfactory. The extent of unemployment does justify the Unemployment Reinsurance Agreement; it is possible that the extent of local claims accounts satisfactorily for the decline in the Imperial Contribution. After all, though the percentage of insured persons unemployed in Northern Ireland is 9 per cent higher than that in Great Britain yet it is well to remember that other parts of the British Isles show a percentage higher than that of Northern Ireland. In February 1936 the percentage of insured persons unemployed in Great Britain might be only 15·4 per cent as against 24 per cent in Northern

Revenue 1935-36	£	Expenditure 1935-36	£
Transferred Revenue:		Transferred Services:	
Tax	1,625,000	Consolidated Fund	
Non-Tax	1,000,000	Service ..	1,028,000
		Supply Services ..	9,203,000
Reserved Revenue:		Reserved Services	1,908,000
Tax ..	7,630,000		
Non-Tax	1,104,000		
Unemployment Rein-		Other Expenditure ..	365,000
surance Agreement	643,000		
Reserve Fund ..	150,000	Provision for Im-	
		perial Contribution	
		and Surplus ..	13,000
Amounts collected for			
the Government of			
the U.K.	365,000		
Total	12,517,000	Total	12,517,000

Ireland. But in Scotland it was 21·4 per cent and in Wales 32·3 per cent. Therefore, were Devolution extended to Scotland and Wales, they would be faced with difficulties similar to those of Northern Ireland. But even though one allows the economic problems of the six counties to be naturally greater in intensity than those of Great Britain as a whole, that does not justify the present financial relationship. For it is its weakness that in its day to day application it adheres to no clearly-defined principle; and that it carries no conviction of an ability to secure a just distribution of financial burdens.

The Imperial Government has displayed no little anxiety lest any public discussion on any aspect of the relationship between Great Britain and Northern Ireland should reopen the Irish Question as a whole. This anxiety is shared by the Government of Northern Ireland. Yet a critical analysis of the financial system now in force is needed either to restore public confidence in its equity or to confirm public suspicion of its inherent incapacity to secure a proper distribution of revenue and expenditure as between the two parts of the United Kingdom. Moreover, the present system labours under two particular disadvantages. On the one hand its operation is totally incomprehensible to the general public; on the other, the widest discretion in determining all outstanding questions is vested in a non-democratic body whose deliberations and whose proceedings are secret.

CHAPTER XI

POLITICAL PARTIES

ADMIRATION for the party system is general at those times when party conflict is waged on behalf of some great principle of government; contempt for political parties is common when men believe that the issues which divide them bear no vital relation to the realities of contemporary political and economic life. At its best, a political party, in Mr. Lowell's words, acts as a broker of ideas; at its worst it distorts divisions which it has itself accentuated. On the whole the English people—as a consequence of a prolonged experience of party government—have concluded that its virtues outweigh its vices. A study of the working of the party system in Northern Ireland endorses, though from a negative view point, the validity of this opinion. For although more than a reasonable proportion of the vices of the party system are exhibited in the political life of Northern Ireland at the present day, yet that system remains indispensable to the survival of democratic government. After all the party alone provides a means whereby public opinion may be focussed effectively upon clearly-defined issues. What, at least, is certain, Professor Laski has written,[1] is that without parties there would be no means available to us of enlisting the popular decision in such a way as to secure solutions capable of being interpreted as politically satisfactory. It is this all-important contribution of the party system to democratic government that more than counterbalances its defects even when—as in Northern Ireland—the latter are by no means insignificant or obscure. Parties in Ulster emphasize traditional religious and racial antagonisms in order to exact a rigid loyalty from their supporters. They intensify a sectarian bitterness which civilized opinion deplores; and in so doing they force the judgment of the electors into the service of their prejudices. Needless

[1] Cf. *Grammar of Politics*, pp. 312–13 (George Allen & Unwin Ltd.).

to say, the parties have done no more than derive the fullest possible advantage from an existing situation. In every society there is a conflict of wills. The parties exist for the purpose of securing a decision between them. The main criticism, therefore, that one would direct against the operation of the party system in Northern Ireland is not that it fails to permit of nice shades of distinction in public opinion—for that were outside its function—nor yet that it fosters a bellicose spirit, though indeed the pugnacity of the respective parties might, with advantage, be restrained—but that it subordinates every vital issue, whether of social or economic policy, to the dead hand of sectarian strife.

A simple analysis of a political situation is invariably popular. It should always be sought for. But it cannot always be found. Thus, there exists an ever-present temptation to explain the very complex forces which mould the political life of Ulster in terms of false simplicity. It is not merely that the obvious contemporary party conflict is regarded as the ultimate expression of the political character of Ulster; but also that the successive stages in the historical development of the province are ignored in so far as they do not lend themselves to a particular interpretation—be it Unionist or Nationalist. As a result we find on the one hand that the attitude adopted by the majority in the six counties as a protest against Home Rule has become crystallized into an enduring political dogma; on the other that outside observers have discounted overmuch the peculiar qualities that have coalesced in the making of modern Ulster. Of the former one must remark that the negation of a policy is bound to provide no more than an ephemeral basis for political action, of the latter that it is a misfortune which has befallen the rest of Ireland in common with Ulster. An instructive illustration of this misunderstanding is given in a Resolution drafted by Karl Marx in 1869. He wrote:

"If England is the fortress of European Landlordism and Capitalism, then the point at which a strong blow can be struck at official England is *Ireland*. . . .

"In this way the viewpoint of the International Working Men's Association on the Irish Question is very clear. Its first task is the speeding on of the social revolution in England. For this end the decisive blow must be struck in Ireland.

"The essential preliminary condition of the Emancipation of the English Working Class is the turning of the present compulsory Union, that is slavery, of Ireland with England into an *equal and free union*, if that is possible, or into *full separation* if that is inevitable."[1]

Today the Irish landlords are but a memory in the land whose destinies they once controlled, their system of government has been replaced by a national government enjoying a political freedom as wide as that which Marx envisaged; and yet the time of social revolution in England does not appear to have been hastened or delayed in any material respect by these events in Irish history. In what way then was the analysis of Marx mistaken? His most serious mistake was his underestimation of the strength of Irish Nationalism. While he recognized that "the revolutionary fire of the Celtic workers does not harmonize with the restrained force but slowness of the Anglo-Saxons" he did believe that the pressure of economic forces would compel them to unite. But, in fact, Irish labour has proved a staunch ally to Irish Nationalism in the most vital crises of its history. It is comparatively easy to give reasons as to why workers should accept the message of the Communist Manifesto "Proletarians of all nations, unite!" but it is very difficult, if not impossible, to secure any such union. In addition, by the very precepts of his philosophy of history, Marx was impelled to ignore the rôle which Ulster was destined to play. He disregarded her racial and religious inheritance. As a consequence, he was mistaken in his anticipations. Any possibility that Irish Nationalism might be diverted to a struggle for economic power was eliminated by the emergence of the

---

[1] Quoted in *Handbook of Marxism*, ed. by Emile Burns. Kuno Mayer in his biography of Engels has an interesting chapter on the latter's estimate of economic forces at work in Irish politics.

Ulster Question. It is true that there was a distinct economic motive force behind Ulster's resistance to Home Rule, but this only emphasizes the fact that Marx was at fault in regarding economic conflicts as being always conflicts between classes, whereas frequently, as in this instance, they are between nations or political groups. The economic causation of political events in pre-War Ireland operated within its limited sphere of influence, as a force dividing the nation, not horizontally into classes as the disciple of dialectical materialism would expect, but vertically, into groups. The importance attached to fiscal independence at the National Convention in 1917 shows that at certain periods economic jealousy between North and South did play a distinct part in the evolution of Irish history. But it was never a directing force; for in the event political claims proved stronger than economic. In discussing parties in Northern Ireland today it is vital to remember that though there was, and still is, an *external* economic conflict of limited dimensions, there is not, and there has not been, an internal class conflict of such importance as might tend to override the traditional sectarian strife. In the well-known passage in which Engels defined the Materialist Conception of History he wrote: " . . . the final causes of all social changes and political revolutions are to be sought, not in men's brains, not in man's better insight into the principles of eternal truth and justice, but in changes in the modes of production and exchange. They are to be sought, not in the *philosophy*, but in the *economics* of each particular epoch." It is instructive to observe to what extent the history of Ulster fails to correspond with the law laid down in this too rigid generalization.

STATISTICAL SURVEY OF NORTHERN IRELAND

The aims and programmes of political parties in the modern State are necessarily framed, where universal suffrage is in force, to meet the needs of the citizens as a whole. It is well, therefore, to preface our examination of party politics in Ulster by a brief statistical summary of the principal features of the economy of the six counties. By such a preliminary survey we shall be able the better to understand certain realities affecting political action.

The area of Northern Ireland is 5,237 square miles—that is, approximately one-sixth of the total land area of Ireland. Its population is 1,256,561 persons whilst the population of the Free State is 2,971,992 persons. Thus population of Northern Ireland is 29·7 per cent of the total population of Ireland.[1] The changes of population during the last century are of interest. In 1821, the population of the six-county area was 1,380,451; in 1841, the maximum figure of 1,641,464 was reached; from 1841 to 1891 the population decreased by about 25 per cent, almost one half of this loss occurring in the first ten years of the period. The lowest figure was actually recorded in 1891 with a population of 1,236,056. Since then a small but steady increase has been recorded. It is significant, however, that the population today is 300,000 less than a century ago.

The density of population in Northern Ireland, while greater than that of predominantly agricultural countries, yet falls far short of that of highly industrialized communities as Great Britain or Belgium. The following table gives the relevant statistics for purposes of comparison.

Country	Year of Estimate	Population	Area in Square Miles	Average Number of Persons per Square Mile
Northern Ireland ..	1934	1,279,000	5,200	246
England and Wales	1934	40,467,000	58,300	694
Irish Free State ..	1934	3,013,000	26,600	113
Scotland	1934	4,934,000	29,800	166
Belgium	1933	8,248,000	11,600	711
New Zealand ..	1933	1,546,000	103,500	15
Denmark	1933	3,623,000	17,100	212

[1] These figures are taken from the Census of 1926.

So much has been said and written emphasizing the contrast between the industrial North and the pastoral South that it is a little surprising to notice the importance of the rôle played by agriculture in Northern Ireland. Within its boundaries 50·8 per cent of the population live in urban, 49·2 per cent in rural, areas. The principal "gainful" occupations of its citizens are set out below.

Industry	Persons		Males		Females	
	Number	%	Number	%	Number	%
Manufacturing and Building ..	221,505	22·9	126,806	27·6	94,699	18·7
Agriculture ..	147,514	15·3	131,544	28·6	15,970	3·1
Commerce and Finance ..	69,686	7·2	50,636	11·0	19,050	3·8
Personal Service	48,155	5·0	12,959	2·8	35,196	7·0
Administration and Defence ..	29,726	3·1	25,843	5·6	3,883	0·8
Transport and Communications	21,817	2·3	21,321	4·6	496	0·1
Professions ..	19,210	2·0	9,283	2·0	9,927	2·0
Others	13,093	1·3	11,893	2·6	1,200	0·2
Total gainfully occupied ..	570,706	59·1	390,285	84·8	180,421	35·7
Total not gainfully occupied ..	394,539	40·9	69,916	15·2	324,623	64·3
Total persons aged 12 and over ..	965,245	100·0	460,201	100·0	505,044	100·0

It will be observed from the above figures that while agriculture is the second most general occupation for the people as a whole, it is the most general by a considerable margin for men.

Lastly, in view of the political significance attached to membership of the various Churches, we give below particulars of the religious professions of the population.

Religious Professions	1901		1911		1926	
	Persons	%	Persons	%	Persons	%
Roman Catholics ..	430,390	34·8	430,161	34·4	420,428	33·5
Presbyterians	396,562	32·0	395,039	31·6	393,374	31·3
Church of Ireland ..	316,825	25·6	327,076	26·1	338,724	27·0
Methodist ..	44,134	3·6	45,942	3·7	49,554	3·9
Others ..	49,041	4·0	52,313	4·2	54,481	4·3
Totals ..	1,236,952	100·0	1,250,531	100·0	1,256,561	100·0

Vide *Ulster Year Book*, 1935.

It will be seen from this table that about two-thirds of the population belong to Churches of the various Protestant denominations and the remaining one-third to the Roman Catholic Church.

THE UNIONIST PARTY AND ITS LEADERS

At the close of the nineteenth century, Lord Salisbury remarked that Mr. Gladstone in struggling for Home Rule had "awakened the slumbering genius of Imperialism." No more profound diagnosis has been made of the reaction which defeated Mr. Gladstone's policy. For it is clearly no mere chronological chance which marks out the Imperialism of the *fin de siècle* as the immediate successor to Home Rule. Elsewhere the term that was set to British rule in Ireland after the War marked the close of this epoch in Anglo-Irish relations. But in loyalist Ulster, the menace of Nationalist government seemed no less real in the days that have followed December 21, 1921, than it did when the Covenant was signed. The rigid supremacy of nineteenth-century Imperialism in Ulster is the mark of the reaction against Home Rule and is not the product of native philosophy. Fanaticism will one day be killed by radicalism in Ulster, wrote M. Paul-Dubois in 1908,[1] but the struggle is not yet near its end. Certainly it is not; and the later course of the Home Rule conflict did much to harden Ulstermen against the inevitable reaction. For that struggle impressed upon the Unionist Party in Ulster a belief in Imperialism that was coupled with a contempt for Democracy. Such an outlook represents in its negative aspect a reaction against Nationalism, but its actual supremacy was fixed by the influence of one man. A life-size statue of Lord Carson is placed outside the new Parliament at Stormont. It is fitting that this should be so. For the building of Stormont crowns the achievement of Lord Carson's life. It symbolizes the permanence of self-government in Northern Ireland. It carries the threat of a divided Ireland far into the future.

Lord Carson did not originate the idea of resistance to Home Rule in Ulster. Lord Carson was not the first to organize volunteers, to arrange for the importation of arms. Lord Carson was not the earliest to cry "Ulster will fight!" His contribution lay rather in the fusing of various elements, Conservative and Liberal, Anglican and Presbyterian, into a united whole. His achievement—and it was decisive—was the organization of a coherent movement commanding a disciplined force; for by this means he secured the support of the English Conservative Party. It is beside our purpose to decide to what extent the history of Ulster's opposition to Home Rule was shaped by Lord Carson, for it is now only idle to speculate what might have happened had the *Fanny* never landed her cargo of arms at Larne, had a provisional Government never been formed. Lord Carson was endowed with a remarkable courage and an unquestioned sincerity; qualities which made him an inspiring leader for the Ulster Unionists. In Northern Ireland he is honoured as the founder of a Government; and since this honour is truly earned he must bear in Ireland his responsibility as the chief architect of Partition. For he pursued a policy in such a way as to accentuate in every corner of Ireland the

[1] *Contemporary Ireland.*

inherited division between Nationalist and Unionist and in addition so as to split the Unionist Party itself in two. On his death in October 1935 it was the leading Unionist paper in the South which remarked in its editorial: "Edward Carson's career was one of the tragedies of Irish history. . . . He has died at the age of eighty-one, after a life crammed with great achievements, and yet strangely barren of great results."[1] This opinion, coming from such a source, throws into relief the extremist character of Ulster Unionism. There are many men in the Southern provinces who, though not professing Nationalists, find a truth—it is often an unwelcome truth— in the words of Mr. George Bernard Shaw,[2] "When the Orange-man sacrifices his nationality to his hatred of the priest and fights against his own country for its conqueror he is doing something for which, no matter how bravely he fights, history and humanity will never forgive him: English history and humanity, to their credit be it said, least of all."

The Settlement left the Southern Unionists to make what terms they might with the Dublin Parliament. They had been encouraged to resist Home Rule by the Orange leaders but the latter showed little intention of standing by them when the crisis came. "You are cutting off three or four hundred thousand people who agree with you in faith," said the Rev. J. B. Armour. "It has been said again and again 'you are throwing us to the dogs.' Now I cannot abide the like of that. If the cause is right then stand by it to the last."

When the Act of 1920 was passed Sir Edward Carson resigned his leadership and took no office in the new Government in Belfast. But his reputation remained and proved even more valuable than himself. He had led the Ulster Unionists in perhaps the most decisive years of their history, and so it is not surprising that the Government whose existence he had done so much to make possible was permeated with his own outlook. In its extreme opposition to compromise, in the well-

[1] Cf. *The Irish Times,* October 23, 1935.
[2] Preface to *John Bull's Other Island.*

nigh religious fervour of its Unionism, in its thinly disguised contempt for the niceties of constitutional government, it reflected Carson's own political creed. And inasmuch as the violent political atmosphere of pre-War years has exercised a decisive formative influence on the character of present-day Ulster Unionism, so the task of establishing a genuinely popular democratic system of government in the North has proved impossible of fulfilment.

Sir James Craig (now Lord Craigavon) became the first Prime Minister of Northern Ireland on the retirement of Lord Carson. For more than fifteen years he has remained the chosen leader of a large parliamentary majority. He has fought four General Elections without appreciable loss. Though this continued support be derived rather from the ice-bound polity of the Northern State than from the personality of the Prime Minister, yet Lord Craigavon has contributed to it by the skill with which he extracts the fullest advantage from every move in party warfare. For this reason he fills his office to the admiration of the older Unionists. His courage—notably displayed in the Dublin visit of May 1921—is unquestioned. His heavy, immobile features betray a stubborn will and a complete self-assurance. It must be many years since Lord Craigavon doubted any article in his political creed. By temperament he is pessimistic; and in his countenance there is a look of lowering strain not uncommon amongst politicians who swayed the destinies of Ireland in the anxious post-War years.

Lord Craigavon's parliamentary gifts are in no way remarkable. As a speaker he is lucid but unimaginative. He is not given to rhetoric. His speeches at critical moments are forceful; at other times discursive. He rarely neglects—no matter how remote the opportunity or how inappropriate the occasion—to refer to the "loyalty of Ulster," the British Empire, and the Union Jack. In addition, he possesses a remarkable capacity for reiterating the rigid negatives of Unionist policy with a conviction undiminished by the passage of time. He is more at home in dealing with personalities than with political principles. In him, the ferment of political ideas in post-War England awakened no response. Together with the majority of his Cabinet he is completely out of sympathy, not merely with the whole trend of progressive political thought, but also with all moderate elements within the Conservative Party. By circumstance and by predilection he is an extreme Tory. Politics, to his mind, are a fore-ordained diarchy between right and wrong, between capitalism and socialism, between Orangemen and Sinn Feiners. Consequently, his opinion on all questions is decided.

The source of Lord Craigavon's power is extra-parliamentary. He is a leader such as delights the heart of a party manager. He is deferential to the party caucus; he humours the "odd perverse antipathies" of the Orange Lodges, even when experience must suggest to him that his speech is unwise. His outlook is provincial. He has achieved a commanding position, not because he is original but because he is representative of the Unionism of the Covenant. His record, though remarkable for an unflinching consistency of purpose, allows of no claim to statesmanship. But he is a good party leader and an astute manager of men.

The first Cabinet of Northern Ireland was composed as follows:

Prime Minister—Sir James Craig.
Minister of Finance—Mr. H. M. Pollock.
Minister of Home Affairs—Sir A. D. Bates.
Minister of Labour—Mr. J. M. Andrews.
Minister of Education—The Marquess of Londonderry.
Minister of Agriculture and Minister of Commerce—Mr.
    E. M. Archdale.

Since then the Cabinet has been enlarged by the appointment of separate Ministers for Agriculture and Commerce. Its personnel underwent remarkably few changes in a period of fifteen years; in itself a tribute to the quality of Lord Craigavon's leadership. Lord Charlemont succeeded Lord

Londonderry as Minister of Education, Sir Basil Brooke is now Minister of Agriculture and Mr. J. M. Barbour is Minister of Commerce. The static character of the Ministry has certain attractions. It carries a guarantee of settled policy and of continuity of control. But it possesses possibly greater disadvantages. It is discouraging to the younger members of the party, it deadens the party policy and it destroys the benefit of change in departmental administration. Moreover, there are few persons who can enjoy so prolonged a term of office without either a slackening of vitality or a surrender to bureaucratic control.

ITS POLICY

A general impression of the policy of the Unionist Government in Northern Ireland may be given by a survey of three aspects of its programme: (1) its policy in respect of the Constitution of Northern Ireland, (2) its attitude towards the minority, (3) its social and economic policy.

(i) Sir Edward Carson and his party took no part in the divisions in the House of Commons during the passage of the Government of Ireland Bill in 1920 but they moved many amendments in Committee, the majority of which were accepted. But the Bill was not well received in the North. Captain Redmond was quite accurate when he remarked a little later that the Act of 1920 "was condemned in every corner of Ireland and had not the support of a single member whether he came from the North or the South."[1] The objection of the Ulster Unionists is succinctly stated in one of Sir James Craig's letters to the Prime Minister. "It has always been," he wrote, "the desire of Northern Ireland to remain in the closest possible union with Great Britain and the Empire, which Ulstermen have helped to build up and to which they are proud to belong."[2] And since self-government involved a certain loosening of the tie with Great Britain it was accepted

[1] *H. of C. Debates*, vol. 161, col. 1508.
[2] Letter of November 11, 1921.

by Northern Ireland, although not asked for by her representatives, "as final settlement and supreme sacrifice in the interests of peace."[1] The general reason for this "sacrifice" given by the Prime Minister was the hope that it would provide the solution "of the long outstanding difficulty with which Great Britain had been confronted."[2] On the whole, however, the Ulster Unionists were, very naturally, less concerned with solving the difficulties of the Coalition Cabinet than with safeguarding their own future. And to the Ulster Unionist the future could hold no more unwelcome prospect than the establishment of an all-Ireland Parliament. "The Government of Northern Ireland consider it their duty to say," wrote Sir James Craig to the Prime Minister, "that their inability to accept an all-Ireland Parliament does not depend merely on the question of safeguards. . . . They are certain that no paper safeguards could protect them against maladministration. The feelings of the loyal population of Ulster are so pronounced and so universal on this point that no Government representing that population could enter into any Conference where this point is open to discussion."[3] So it was, lest worse befall them, that the Unionists decided to work the Act of 1920.

With the passing of time, the Unionist Government spoke less of "supreme sacrifice" and more of the "final settlement" of 1920. The Prime Minister continued to speak of the "preposterous proposal"[4] of an all-Ireland Government, but he also spoke of the necessity of retaining their self-governing institutions in the North.[5] Even before the building of Stormont it was evident that the Government was extremely averse to considering any proposal which might involve the reabsorption of Northern Ireland under direct government from Whitehall. That attitude is crystallized today. "History would vindicate, and has already vindicated," declared the Ulster

[1] Letter of November 11, 1921.
[2] Cf. *N.I., H. of C. Debates*, vol. i, col. 48.
[3] Letter to the P.M. Cmd. 1561.
[4] *N.I., H. of C. Debates*, vol. i, col. 294.
[5] Ibid. Cf. vol. ii, col. 953.

Unionist Council Report in 1936,[1] "the action of Ulster's leaders taken under memorable circumstances in 1921. . . . The Government set up for the six counties has functioned with courage . . . and surmounted almost insuperable difficulties. The cry 'Back to Westminster' is a subtle move fraught with great danger. Had we refused to accept a Parliament for Northern Ireland and remained at Westminster there can be little doubt but that now we would be either inside the Free State or fighting desperately against incorporation. Northern Ireland without a Parliament of her own would be a standing temptation to certain British politicians to make another bid for a final settlement with Irish Republicans." Mr. J. M. Andrews, the Minister of Labour, has also recently underlined the attitude of his Government. "Irish Free State people know in their hearts," he said, "that they can never reach the goal of an all-Ireland Republic, because Ulster blocks the way. We shall never have a boundary between ourselves and Great Britain and *we are determined, come what may, to hold what we have got. We are determined to maintain our Parliament.*"[2]

The changed opinion of the Unionist Government as to the value of self-governing institutions in Northern Ireland is a fact of cardinal importance. It was caused partly by a belief that self-government had undoubtedly conferred certain administrative benefits upon Northern Ireland and partly by a conviction that such a form of government gave the most explicit guarantee possible in a world of changing political forces of permanent supremacy to the Unionist Party. The former influence is of considerable interest to students of constitutional reform, and we have attempted elsewhere to estimate the reality of the progress made in Northern Ireland since 1921. The latter or party interest is, however, a far more potent factor in deciding the political aims of the Government. After all, it is obviously in the immediate interest of the Unionist

[1] *Report of the Standing Committee of the Unionist Councils*, February 11, 1936.
[2] Cf. report in *Irish Times*, February 9, 1936. The italics are mine.

238 The Government of Northern Ireland

Party to prolong this experiment in self-government regardless of whether or no the experiment has justified itself on constitutional or economic grounds. In 1920, there were three alternative possibilities as to the government of Northern Ireland. Now there are only two. The possibility of absorption in an all-Ireland Parliament may for the moment be eliminated. The Unionist Party are faced, therefore, either with a continuation of self-government in the six counties or with direct government from London. The former is now the official Government policy. The latter is viewed as the most subtle menace to the present balance of political forces. Not only would it remove the influence and patronage, that is attached to every Government, from the control of the local party leaders but further, it is considered, with some reason, that a reversion to government from Whitehall would prove a step on the road to the political unity of Ireland. As a consequence the Unionist Party, whilst retaining in full measure its hostility to a United Ireland, has further defined its position by stating its unqualified opposition to reabsorption in the United Kingdom. Thus the building of Stormont was not, as its critics claimed, an act of wanton extravagance but rather the full expression of a new political faith.

(ii) It were idle to deny that the new Government was faced with a problem of exceptional difficulty in that it had no prospect of reconciling one-third of its citizens to its rule. None the less, it is also undeniable that the record of the Government in their treatment of the minority has been unfortunate. A Cabinet, independent of day-to-day fluctuations of opinion in the Legislature, is in a position to perform its executive functions regardless of extremist opinion within its own party. But the Government of Northern Ireland has shown itself deficient in those very qualities which its independence should encourage. It has made no consistent attempt to break down the traditional hostility between the respective creeds; it has not possessed either the wish or the courage to ignore the demands of the Orange extremists; it has not given that positive leadership which is so needed if a spirit of common citizenship is to be established. Admittedly, a Unionist Government is in power; but Ministers would be well advised to remember that Unionist is the adjective and Government the noun.

The periodic riots in Belfast are uniformly held to be the product of sectarian feeling. But in fact the political motive would appear to be the stronger. When Lord Carson attended the unveiling of his statue at Stormont in 1934, he referred to the Ulster Volunteers, remarking, "I admit we were rebels. We were rebels to those who were rebels to the King." Lord Carson's party now compose the Government, but they have been unable to forget their bitter strife with the supporters of the policy of His Majesty's Government whom they were pleased to designate " rebels to the King." At the same time the Nationalists have shown no respect towards the Government of the day. The violence of party feeling is accentuated by the close identification of the Unionist Party and the Northern State.

The abolition of Proportional Representation first in Local Government and later in the parliamentary elections aroused more feeling than any other action of the Government. This was due, not to the mere fact of a reform in electoral law, but to a feeling that the destruction of a cherished privilege of the minority implied at the least an indifference, at the most a hostility, to the rights of that minority. It was believed that constitutional reforms were being made to serve political motives. Certainly these debates on the abolition of P.R. did reveal one interesting aspect of Unionist policy. At the Orange Celebrations on July 12, 1927, Lord Craigavon coupled his announcement of the forthcoming abolition of P.R. with a statement that he desired to eliminate all minorities except the Nationalist Party.[1] This aim was later elaborated in the House of Commons. And it has been achieved in large measure by the reintroduction of the simple majority system. The policy of the Unionist Party on this issue was dictated by a

[1] Cf. *Irish News*, July 13, 1927.

belief that P.R., in facilitating the growth of a multiplicity of parties, would thereby break down the traditional politico-religious division. In this way, the assured supremacy of the Unionist Party would ultimately be threatened. No doubt this was sound party reasoning. For under existing conditions political opinions in Northern Ireland never change. There is no swing of the pendulum at an election. There is no floating vote. There is no appeal to a new standard of judgment, for in the last analysis the memory of old political conflicts has always proved stronger than an appeal to new political ideals.

In view of the fierceness of political passions, especially in the large industrial towns of Northern Ireland, the language of those in authority needs to be studiously moderate in tone. The record of the Northern Ministry in this respect does not bear too close an examination. Some members of the Cabinet, indeed, have made statements such as no responsible Minister should utter. For example, Sir Basil Brooke, the Minister of Agriculture, said on July 12, 1933:[1] "Many in the audience employ Catholics, but I have not one about my place. Catholics are out to destroy Ulster with all their might and power. They want to nullify the Protestant vote, take all they can out of Ulster and then see it go to hell." Later, Sir Basil justified this language by pointing out that, since "97 per cent" of the Roman Catholics in the North were Nationalists and therefore "disloyalists," he was right in recommending people not to employ them.[2] This entirely inadequate explanation throws a very real light on the failure of the Government to reconcile the minority in any respect to its rule. Speeches of other Ministers, including the Prime Minister, have been equally calculated to intensify sectarian strife. The Prime Minister said in 1932: "Ours is a Protestant Government and I am an Orangeman."[3] And later he said: "I do not care a snap of my fingers so long as I have a staunch, loyal and Protestant

[1] At Newtown Butler.
[2] *N.I., H. of C. Debates*, vol. xvi, col. 1118 seq.
[3] At Dumbanagher, July 12th.

majority at my back."[1] In the House of Commons the Prime Minister said: "I am very proud indeed to be Grand Master of the Orange Institution of the loyal County of Down. I have filled that office for many years and I prize that far more than I do being Prime Minister. I have always said I am an Orangeman first and a Member of this Parliament afterwards . . ."[2] Since every citizen in the North is fully aware of the extreme political outlook of the Orange Lodges, language such as this, used by the head of the Government, can have no consequence other than that of alienating the minority.

It is most emphatically not the language proper to the head of a democratic State. Mr. Donnelly was quite accurate in stating that people as the Prime Minister and the Minister of Agriculture, who make speeches of such a kind in an area with a history of sectarian feeling such as Belfast, were guilty of "indescribable folly." It is pleasant to record Mr. Healy, the Nationalist leader's declaration that: "We have assurances from many Protestants that they abhor such a policy and have not any intention of paying the least heed to it."[3] It is certain that the large majority of Northern Protestants detest this policy all too frequently encouraged by their political leaders.

(iii) Elsewhere we have remarked upon the final control that is exercised by the Imperial Government upon social and economic policy in Northern Ireland. The positive contribution of the Unionist Government is therefore not fundamental in character. None the less, the party has a well-defined attitude towards economic policy. It is based upon the essential individualism of the Ulsterman. His sympathies lie, not with the modern industrial "planning," not with the ever-increasing social services of the modern State, but rather with the economic radicalism of English nineteenth-century thought. This attitude was happily defined by Mr. J. W. Good in writing of the manufacturing North:[4]

---

[1] At Belfast, September 3, 1932.
[2] *N.I., H. of C. Debates*, vol. xvi, col. 1091.
[3] Ibid., col. 1085.   [4] *Ulster Unionism*, p. 228.

"Its main industries—textiles and shipbuilding—not only import their raw materials, but export their finished products, with the result that those who control those industries have, in their everyday life, no intimate relationship with the mass of their fellow-countrymen, and not unnaturally come to feel themselves in Ireland rather than of it. Economically, their outlook has not advanced beyond that of the later Victorians, and remains a curious blend of the arrogant individualism of the Manchester School combined with a belief, of which nowadays Mr. Horatio Bottomley is the high priest, that the world will be saved only in so far as it places dictatorial powers in the hands of the 'business man.' "

This criticism was published in 1920, and since then circumstances have in fact modified the economic outlook of the Unionist Party. That party draws a large measure of its strength from industrial workers. In times of depression, therefore, party opinion is naturally favourable to the extension of the social services. In 1930 the Prime Minister of the Northern Unionist Government announced his intention of proceeding "step by step" with the English Socialist Government in the provision of social services. In addition economic nationalism within the six-county area has become apparent in recent years. The official exhortations to buy Ulster goods are symptomatic of a slowly-moving change in economic thought. The peculiar financial relationship that exists between the Northern and Imperial Governments facilitates the acceptance of English social policy, in that the Northern Ireland social services are not supported in their entirety by the taxpayers in that area. The ever declining figure of the Imperial contribution—it decreased from £3,175,000 to £10,000 in the decade ending 1935—has provided a source of revenue which inflicts no taxation on the citizens of Northern Ireland.

ITS COMPOSITION

It is not entirely true to state that political are synonymous with religious divisions in Northern Ireland. But as a general rule it is remarkably accurate. A Protestant who is a Nationalist, or a Catholic who is a Unionist, is reckoned by his co-religionists in their kinder moods as a phenomenon, and on more ordinary occasions as one who has betrayed his faith. The predominance of such feelings results in a situation in which the relative strength of the parties may at all times be calculated by reference to the latest Census returns.

The Unionist Party commands the allegiance of approximately two-thirds of the Northern Ireland electorate. Of this number somewhat more than 50 per cent are Presbyterians, and rather less than 50 per cent Church of Ireland Episcopalians. There is only a small percentage of Wesleyans. It is to be observed that while the number of the Church of Ireland Episcopalians has increased by about 22,000 since the beginning of the century, that of the Presbyterians has declined by 3,000.

The parliamentary strength of the Unionist Party has varied very little since 1921. The following are the electoral returns for the North Ireland House of Commons:

Year					Number of Unionist Members returned
1921	..	..	..	..	40
1925	..	..	..	..	37
1929	..	..	..	..	40
1933	..	..	..	..	39

These figures include the Independent Unionists whose representation varies between two and four members. Their existence is of importance, in that they are elected generally for constituencies in Belfast. In certain instances their outlook is radical and their criticism of the Government unsparing. But owing to the supremacy of the constitutional issue they must be enrolled amongst its supporters since they prefer self-government to an all-Ireland Parliament. These independent Unionists may be considered either as the heirs of eighteenth-century radicalism or as the heralds of the political creed of the future.

The Unionist Party almost monopolize representation at Westminster. On occasion indeed, they have returned the whole thirteen members. In the normal course the present representation of 11 Unionists and 2 Nationalists or Republicans appears destined to endure so long as the constituencies remain unchanged. In the Tyrone-Fermanagh constituency—which has nearly one hundred thousand voters on the registers and which returns two members to Westminster—the Unionists are in a distinct minority of about 6,000 and so fail to elect a member. Elsewhere their majority is secure; in certain instances so secure as to render a contest futile.

In opposition to the minority the Unionist party is firmly united. But on other subjects this union is uneasy. There is a very real difference in political outlook between the two component forces in the party—between the Church of Ireland Episcopalians led by a landed aristocracy, possessing a clergy drawn from the older Universities, and the more severe Presbyterians led by City business men with ministers drawn from the middle class. The Presbyterians were firm supporters of Mr. Gladstone's ecclesiastical legislation, particularly in respect of the disestablishment of the Church of Ireland; they formed the backbone of radical discontent against the privileges of the established order in Ireland; they suffered under the penal laws of an earlier age. The Church of Ireland, on the other hand, was the Church of the privileged. Prior to Disestablishment Episcopalians enjoyed a monopoly of power in Unionist Ireland. But towards the close of the century the controlling power in Northern Unionism was passing out of the hands of the landed proprietors into those of the manufacturers of Belfast. The landlords of the old régime were making way for the Presbyterian capitalists of the new. None the less, even as late as the election of 1906 the majority of candidates returned for Orange constituencies were in a very real sense representatives of the landed class.[1] But by 1920 the challenge of labour in every country had brought forward the capitalists as the natural defenders of the *status quo*. So it was that the Northern Presbyterians came to take the leadership in the

[1] Cf. J. W. Good, op. cit., pp. 226–27.

struggle, nominally against nationalism alone, but also in fact against a possible growth of the Labour movement. Circumstances compelled a very close co-operation with the Northern Episcopalians, but it is noticeable that the Belfast Presbyterians had almost as little contact with the Southern Unionist as they did with the Southern Nationalist. The area of the new Northern State fixed the supremacy of the manufacturing class. One of the arguments most effectively used behind the scene to reconcile opinion to the exclusion of the six counties instead of the whole province was that the smaller enclave would possess not merely a Protestant but a Presbyterian majority.[1] It is to be noted, however, that this recommendation did not satisfy Lord Carson. Its adoption has, in fact, meant Presbyterian-Capitalist rule in Northern Ireland. The Cabinet is a Government of business men ornamented by a landed aristocracy. Since his accession to office, Lord Craigavon has had altogether seven Cabinet Ministers serving under his leadership. Of these, three were past Presidents of the Belfast Chamber of Commerce, one a partner in a large well-known firm of solicitors, one an industrialist and director of companies, one a peer and one the titled owner of one of the largest estates in the North. These Ministers belonged in almost equal number to the Presbyterians and Episcopalian Church, but it is not entirely without significance that the office of Prime Minister was held by the former. The submergence of Liberalism in Ulster is now complete. An attempt was made in 1928 by Sir Herbert Samuel to revive the Liberal Party in the six counties. The task proved hopeless. Only one candidate went forward at the election in the following year and he was heavily defeated. The disappearance of this party from the political life of Ulster has meant more than the loss of a particular party organization. It has involved also—what is more serious—the elimination of a liberal outlook on politics. The life of Armour of Ballymoney shows the invaluable contribution that liberalism might have made to Ulster's

[1] Cf. J. W. Good, op. cit.

political life today. But both the party and the outlook which it represented were doomed to extinction when Home Rule became the dominant issue in Ulster's politics. Liberals became Liberal-Unionist and later as the conflict hardened were absorbed completely in the Unionist Party. At times, their distinct identity reappeared as in 1902 when Mr. T. W. Russell, a former Liberal, advocated compulsory Land Purchase and succeeded in returning one of his candidates at a by-election in East Down, then, as now, one of the firmest Unionist strongholds. But the bitterness that characterized party warfare from 1911–14 created in Ulster a definite and enduring hostility to the Liberal Party. The triumph of the Unionists in 1920 made it certain that Liberalism in Ulster would disappear for many years to come. So it is that in the once radical city of Belfast, a survival of its former political creed—as the motto of the Northern Whig *"pro rege saepe, pro patria semper"*— is regarded with unsympathetic curiosity.

The Orange Lodges have confirmed the extreme character of Ulster Unionism. Their organization is efficient, their membership considerable, and many of the officers hold prominent positions in the Northern Cabinet. Thus the Lodges are in a position to influence policy to no little extent. In fact, in Ulster itself it is widely believed that they exercised a decisive control. This is not entirely accurate, since the Government have on occasion taken steps unwelcome to the Orange Order. The most notable was the Nixon case in 1924. District Inspector Nixon of the R.U.C. was dismissed for making a political speech at a Orange Lodge contrary to the disciplinary regulations of the force. A Court of Inquiry was summoned to investigate the charges against him, but found that it had no power to compel the attendance of witnesses. District Inspector Nixon was then dismissed by administrative order, despite vigorous protests from the Orange institution. This provides an instance of determined action on the part of the Government. On the other hand, it was unduly subservient to the Orange Order in a guarantee publicly given that the provisions of the Civil Authorities Act should not be used against any of its members. Moreover, the speeches made by Ministers, with the intention of gratifying opinion in the Orange Lodges on July 12th, reflect little credit upon the Government.

It is a common criticism of the Unionist leaders to say that they pay overmuch attention to the clamour of their extremist supporters. The speeches made at the various Orange celebrations certainly give foundation to the charge. In the North the violent extremists as elsewhere are vocal but not numerous. But they do appear to influence policy out of proportion to their significance. A quotation perhaps gives the most vivid account of the language of the extreme Right. In the autumn of 1935 a meeting was held in Belfast under the auspices of the Maiden City Protestant League. The first resolution passed amid applause was as follows:[1]

"That the loyalists of Belfast, assembled in the Ulster Hall, wish to protest against the speech of Lord Craigavon, made at Bessbrook, promising protection to the minority whom we consider rebels to the British Throne, the British Flag, and to Protestant Ulster."

It would give a very wrong impression if such a resolution were taken to imply that similar sentiments animated the vast majority of Ulster "Loyalists," but it does reflect the virulence of extreme party feeling in Belfast only too accurately.

In more sober-minded quarters the Government has not escaped criticism from among its own supporters. Its apparent inability to cope with the recurrent riots each July has provoked unfavourable comment. The Belfast Corporation, which is called upon to compensate for malicious injuries and damage within the city, has protested strongly against Government inactivity. The sporadic rioting that persisted from the Jubilee in May till the end of July in 1935 provided very real grounds for criticism. The members of the Corporation claimed that had the law been administered with greater firmness much of

[1] Cf. *Irish Times*, October 16, 1935.

the rioting would not have occurred. Alderman Pierce voiced the general feeling in remarking that "he held, as a loyal Ulsterman, that those who administered the country should pay the bill. If they were not able to administer the country then they should get out."[1] Such dissatisfaction within the party is fairly widespread, but it is unlikely to lead to definite action. For a party split always holds out the possibility of a Nationalist triumph.

THE NATIONALIST PARTY

In the Irish Free State national sentiment has achieved a virtually complete independence from any form of external control. In Northern Ireland the Nationalist is still the "rebel" of tradition. This diversity in fortune has sharpened the bitterness of the Ulster Nationalist. Once he was the companion of his fellow-countrymen in a heroic conflict for national liberty; now he is left becalmed in the Sargasso Sea of Ulster politics, watching the high tide of a national movement sweep past him. And the fact that he is no longer in complete sympathy with the direction of national policy does nothing to diminish his disappointment.

The policy of the Nationalist Party in Northern Ireland is directed towards one end—reunion with the rest of Ireland. Everything else is subordinated to this sentiment. Thus from the point of view of the Northern Government their policy is entirely negative; in that its avowed objective is the termination of the existence of self-government. As a party they have no positive contribution to make to a State whose authority they do not recognize. As Mr. Healy said in the House of Commons: "We will not allow ourselves to become an official Opposition in this House. We will only intervene when we feel that we can expose injustice. But we reserve the right to come in or stay outside as and when our people may decide."[2] To the Nationalist Partition is the supreme tragedy.

[1] Cf. report of meeting, November 1935.
[2] *N.I., H. of C. Debates*, vol. xvi, col. 1084.

The electoral record of the Nationalist Party in the North has not been as consistent as that of its opponents owing to the periodic intervention of the Republican Party. In 1921 the Nationalists returned 6 members, the Republicans also 6; in 1925 the Nationalists returned 10, the Republicans 2; in 1929 the Nationalists returned 11, Republicans none; and in 1933 the Nationalists returned 9, the Republicans 2. From these figures it is clear that there exists a consistent bloc of Nationalist-Republican opposition to the Unionist Government, even though the relative strength of its component forces may vary considerably.

Both the Nationalist and Republican parties have the same immediate objective, namely, the destruction of the Northern Government and the end of Partition. But they differ profoundly as to the best means by which this goal may be attained. The Nationalists at the present day believe that the longest way round may well prove the shortest way home; they advocate a return to direct government from London in preference to a continuation of self-government; and they hope that a United Ireland may yet be achieved by constitutional means. The Republicans, on the other hand, are far less averse to the use of force; they have no faith in constitutional forms so long as a Partition Government is in power; they are uncompromising in their refusal to recognize the "alien" legislature in Belfast. These differences in policy indicate a fundamental difference in outlook. The Nationalists, apart from their desire to end Partition, are conservative by temperament. They emphasize the importance of home life, they believe in the benefits derived from the private ownership of property, their plan of social reform is inspired by Papal Encyclicals and not by Socialist thought; they are devoted members of the Catholic Church. The Republicans, on the other hand, are more radical. They state their Irish claim to national self-determination in its extreme logical form. They call on all Irishmen to unite for the purpose of ending Partition— by force if necessary. Their inspiration is to be found in the

Declaration of Independence of 1919, and they are in closer sympathy with continental Socialism. They show no great deference to the Catholic Church. They are rigid and uncompromising and have displayed a remarkable consistency in the pursuit of their ideals. They have much in common with the "idealogues" of the French Revolution. They are revolutionaries by temperament whereas the Nationalists are revolutionaries by circumstance.

The Nationalists are the most powerful Opposition party. For a period after the establishment of the Northern Government, the members of this party decided to abstain from the legislature. This created a situation in which the Opposition were unrepresented in either House of Parliament, and so were unable to state their grievances. After the collapse of the Boundary Commission in 1925, Mr. Devlin and a few of his colleagues took their seats. But it was not till 1928 that the Nationalist Party formed a definite party organization. And even then, though the second largest party in the House, they declined to constitute an official Opposition. The Republicans have remained rigid abstentionists throughout. Since, for better or for worse, the Northern Government is the established authority in the six counties, the former party has taken the wiser course, but its action was not accepted by the Government as a gesture of conciliation. The Nationalists have as yet been unable to influence in any way any legislation proposed by the Government.

The basis of Nationalist policy is clearly defined. One recent electoral declaration states:[1]

"The Nationalists press onward to the definite objectives of an unpartitioned Ireland, the defence and advancement of the minority, the furtherance of a world-wide propaganda of enlightenment upon the disabilities imposed on the minority, whose interests they will promote to the utmost of their ability. Our struggle is to help those humble homes, irrespective of creed, where bare tables, ragged clothing, odds and ends

[1] Cf. *Report of West Belfast Nationalist Convention*, November 1935.

of furniture, and cold hearthstones speak of misery which
should be swept away."

It is instructive to contrast this appeal with a contemporary
Republican manifesto, which states:[1]

"Notwithstanding the decisive repudiation of English rule
and of the English Parliament in 1918, disloyal sections of
our people have continued to send representatives to this
alien legislature. By doing so they are attempting to give it
a semblance of authority to legislate for the people of North-
East Ulster . . .

"Our national faith is based on the Proclamation of the
Republic of 1916, which declared Ireland to be a sovereign
and independent State, the right of the Irish people to the
unfettered control of Irish destinies to be sovereign and
indefeasible, and which guaranteed civil and religious liberty,
and equal rights and opportunities to all its citizens.

"We ask you to declare your allegiance to the sovereign
Republic and to the principles enshrined in that Proclamation,
and to elect us to a Parliament of the Republic of Ireland."

Needless to say this division of opinion in the ranks of the
Opposition is a source of strength to the Unionist Party, both
because it enables them to hold the Opposition as a whole
responsible for the utterances of its extremists, and because
it tends to split the anti-Unionist vote at elections. The
first point was emphasized in the Report of the Standing
Committee of the Ulster Unionist Council in 1936.[2] From a
survey of the contests in the 1935 November election to the
Imperial Parliament the Committee concluded: "the moral
for loyalists is clear beyond misapprehension." "Hitherto,"
it declares, "a distinction has been drawn between constitutional
Nationalists and the extremists, who boldly call themselves
Republicans. That deception will serve no longer." And the
Report goes on to instance the special case of West Belfast,

[1] Republican Election Manifesto, November 1935.
[2] Cf. *Report of Standing Committee of Unionist Council*, February 10,
1936.

where in 1931 a Nationalist polled 22,006 votes and where in 1935 "an out-and-out Republican, while domiciled in a Free State prison, procured almost as many, despite the show of indignation with which the advent of Republican candidates was received in official Nationalist quarters." This process of reasoning is based on the fact that whereas on former occasions Nationalists abstained from voting in constituencies in which the Opposition candidate was a professed Republican, now they poll almost full strength in favour of such a candidate. The Unionists like to believe that this support given to the Republicans implies a fundamental unanimity in outlook between members of the two parties. In fact, however, it indicates no more than a preference for an anti-Unionist to a Unionist candidate in any circumstances. After all, an out-and-out Republican, even though "domiciled in a Free State prison," is more likely to work for an unpartitioned Ireland than an Orangeman. But the mere fact that Republicans and Nationalists agree as to the kind of State they would like to establish does not in any degree minimize the reality of their disagreement as to the best means by which this common goal may be reached. In 1935 the intervention of six Republican candidates in the elections for the Imperial Parliament emphasized the differences between the two sections of the Opposition. In Down, Derry, Armagh, and West Belfast, the Republican candidates had no chance of success. Indeed the party admitted as much, but declared that the "elections must be regarded as a plebiscite against British rule and domination and against the claims of the British Parliament to legislate for the Irish people." But a different position arose in the large two-member constituency of Fermanagh-Tyrone. The seats were held at the dissolution by two Nationalist members. The nomination of Republican candidates threatened to split the Anti-Unionist vote and thereby enable two Unionists to be returned to Westminster. The Nationalists, who spend about £700 a year in nursing the constituency and in keeping the register up to date, suggested a compromise. But the Republicans were rigid in

their determination to nominate two "abstentionist" candidates;
and so the retiring Nationalist members, Mr. Cahir Healy and
Mr. Stewart, decided to withdraw. In the event both the
Republican candidates were successful. The incident is instructive. In the early days of subordinate government in Belfast,
the Nationalists were numerically far stronger than the
Republicans. Nationalist opinion was definitely pro-Treaty.
It resented Republican intervention. In the first election to
the Imperial Parliament in Fermanagh-Tyrone, the Nationalists polled roughly 44,000 votes. In 1924, however, the
Republicans nominated two candidates. The Nationalists decided to abstain. The Republicans polled only 6,800 votes and
two Unionists were returned. But the Republicans are in a far
stronger position to-day as a consequence of one fundamental
political mistake by the Nationalists and of the continued
verbal aggression of the Unionist Party. When Mr. Devlin
and his colleagues organized a Parliamentary Nationalist
Party in 1928 Mr. Devlin said, "There is not, and there is
not going to be, any attempt of any kind, much less a conspiracy,
to force the people of Northern Ireland into a Dublin or any
other Parliament." This was a very proper pronouncement
of policy from the leader of a parliamentary party, and had
it been supplemented by a positive appeal to all liberal and
progressive political elements in Ulster then the record of
the Nationalist Party would not have been so unsatisfactory. But instead the Nationalists have chosen to regard
themselves as the representatives of a particular creed. Since
Roman Catholics are in a minority in the six counties a narrow
sectarian appeal of this kind dooms the party to a rôle of
ineffective opposition when it might have become the rallying
ground for all who would like to awaken a new spirit in
Ulster politics. This, the cardinal mistake of the Nationalist
Party, has been accentuated by the complete disregard of
amendments proposed or of suggestions made by Nationalist
members in the House. In this way the Unionists have reinforced the argument for abstention and so weakened the Nation-

alists to the profit of the Republicans. The latter party has the wider appeal; and it is significant that the younger generation even in the University are members of the Republican rather than of the Nationalist Party. In a sense, therefore, the gulf that divides the majority from the minority in Northern Ireland is growing wider. But this process does nothing to further a reconciliation between the two Opposition parties. The Nationalist Convention of West Belfast declared before the recent election:

"It is now our duty to refer to our attitude to the I.R.A., a body which aims at the overthrow of the Free State Government by force if necessary. . . . We refuse to share the title of Irish Nationalists with any element which is ready to fight against their fellow-countrymen. If the paramount consideration for the Free State is the reunion of Ireland, why should we by our support strengthen its internal enemies? Why should we countenance a policy which may lead innocent victims to the shambles?"

The Republican manifesto stated:

"It is particularly deplorable that citizens styling themselves Irish Nationalists should sit in defiance of the wishes of the Irish Nation in the Parliament of the conqueror. Representation in this Parliament is the symbol of Ireland's subjection and slavery."

These internal denunciations show that Nationalists as a whole are strangely forgetful of the moral so fittingly drawn in the well-known lines to the Memory of the Men of Ninety-Eight.

> Then here's their memory—may it be
> For us a guiding light
> To cheer our strife for liberty
> And teach us to unite————[1]

Quite apart from this division in the ranks of the Opposition, the position of the Nationalists is fraught with difficulties. They

[1] From the poem *To the Memory of the Dead*, by John Kells Ingram.

constitute a minority which can, under no conceivable circumstances, become a majority for many years to come. As a
consequence there exists an ever-present temptation to turn
from constitutional to unconstitutional opposition. Nationalists
throughout the whole of Ireland place a major responsibility
for Partition upon the British Government, for they claim
that self-determination for Ireland as *a whole* should have been
the guiding principle of the post-War settlement. Partition
was imposed by a Act of Parliament and not by the will of the
Irish people. This belief does not encourage a willing acceptance
of the authority of either the Northern or Imperial Legislature.
Further, statistical evidence suggests that the Nationalists
need not anticipate any future increase in the number of their
supporters. On the contrary the figures show that the number
of Roman Catholics in Northern Ireland has declined at
every Census since the beginning of the century.[1] In 1901
they comprised 34·8 per cent of the population, in 1926 33·5
per cent. In Belfast this decrease has been most remarkable.
In 1861 Roman Catholics numbered 33⅓ per cent of the population; now they are said to number 23 per cent. "Our people will
have to fight almost with the energy of despair," declared the
Nationalist Convention, "to keep the ground from slipping away
from under our feet. To-day they have to face odds which are
enormous. They see practically every avenue of public employment and almost every avenue of remunerative private employment closed against them and their children. Only by organizing
and holding together as a body, and by hard work and iron
sacrifice as individuals, can they hope to arrest the exodus of
their best intellects and best workers."

---

[1] The number and percentage of marriages according to the various
modes of celebration show over a period of seven years (1928–34)
that the number of Catholic marriages is somewhat less than those of
the Church of Ireland, but greater than the number of Presbyterian
marriages. On the other hand it is claimed that the number of
Roman Catholic children is increasing. There appears to be no decisive evidence on this point. But if it is true the increase is very
slight.

THE LABOUR PARTY

The numerical strength of the Labour Party is very small. In 1920 it returned no representatives to Stormont; in 1925—3; in 1929—1; in 1933—2. Labour Party candidates have not polled more than 25,000 votes out of a total of 290,000 votes cast at any one election.[1] The strength of the party is dependent almost entirely on the votes in the Belfast constituencies, and even in the industrialized areas of the city its hold on the loyalty of its supporters is not so secure as that of the older parties. The party programme is, in all essentials, a replica of that of the Labour Party in Great Britain. Since its chance of adoption by the electorate may be disregarded, the more valuable work of the party's few representatives is accomplished in bringing specific grievances to the attention of Parliament and of certain Local Government authorities.

Outside Northern Ireland there is a widespread belief that the Labour Party is the party of the future. Admittedly it has been vouchsafed no support by electors in the past nor does it enjoy any great influence at the present time, but none the less it is felt that the pressure of economic and social forces will create in the process of time a strong working-class movement. Now, though speculations regarding the politics of the future do not concern us here, it is well to account for the contemporary insignificance of the Labour Party in Northern Ireland. In the first place it is necessary to dispel the common illusion that Ulster is an industrial area. In fact, just half of its total population live on the land, and of the 59 per cent of its population who are "gainfully employed" only one quarter, at most, may be termed industrial workers.[2] Thus the material from which a strong national Labour movement is almost invariably derived simply does not exist. In addition the strength of the agricultural vote suggests a strong anti-socialist bloc, for neither in Great Britain nor in Saorstat Eireann have the

[1] This maximum reached in 1929.
[2] I am including transport workers, etc., in this category.

Labour Party achieved any success in rural constituencies. It is of first importance to notice that the percentage of small farms in Northern Ireland is greater than that either in the Free State or in England and Wales. In 1934 Northern Ireland contained 96,520 holdings over one acre in area, of which 87·7 per cent were *less than* 50 acres in extent. And the percentage of large holdings—that is, holdings of over 100 acres in extent—in Northern Ireland is only 4·1 of the total number, whereas in the Free State it is 8·8 and in England and Wales 20·3 per cent. Since Land Purchase is now generally completed this means that there are a very large proportion of peasant proprietors in Northern Ireland. Their existence is a serious obstacle to the growth of a Socialist Party. Further, there exists a psychological opposition to Socialism. The Irish people, whether of North or South, are intensely individualist. They may reject the economics of *laissez-faire* capitalism; they may recognize a need for the substitution of public for private interest in the organization of industry; they may demand a wide extension of the social services; but they will not surrender their political or individual liberties. They will not be content to replace the heritage of their past by a purely "proletarian" culture. And because of this outlook one finds that the Labour Party in Ireland has hitherto achieved no substantial measure of success. In the Irish Free State its representation has dropped from 22 in the third Dáil elected in 1927 to 8 at the present day.[1] In Northern Ireland its failure has been equally remarkable. In the latter case the most obvious reason for this weakness of the Labour Party lies in the pre-dominance of the politico-sectarian party strife. In 1907 an upheaval in the ranks of unskilled labour, organized by James Larkin, tended for a brief period to override the old religious divisions. But the intensification of Home Rule politics quickly dissolved any such co-operation.[2] Since the post-War strike of 1919, the emergence of a strong Labour Party has always appeared a very remote possibility. In general, social-radicalism

[1] Total membership 153.   [2] Cf. J. W. Good, op. cit., p. 226.

R

is more likely to secure acceptance in the North than the more rigid creed of continental Socialism.

The larger proportion of the industrial workers are Unionists and the Labour Party itself, though somewhat divided, would probably vote Unionist on any vital constitutional issue. Within the Unionist Party there is a Labour branch. It is well organized and composed entirely of industrial workers. The solidarity of the Unionist Party as a whole is illustrated by the fact that Mr. Andrews was, in the same year, Minister of Labour at Stormont, Chairman of the Belfast Chamber of Commerce, and President of the Unionist Labour organization.

THE CHURCHES AND THE FUTURE

In Ulster the Churches exercise a very real influence on political life. To no inconsiderable extent their outlook determines the character of the party programmes. So it is to their leadership that the people look for guidance. Hitherto the authority of the Roman Catholic and Protestant Churches has been lessened by their intervention in current political controversies. The hierarchy of the Roman Catholic Church intervened on several occasions—not always with political wisdom—during the struggle for national independence; the leaders of the Protestant Churches—with a few notable exceptions—were unwise in signing the Covenant. Now that political passions are no longer so violent it should be possible for the Churches to exercise an authority independent of the political party to which they are bound by a natural sympathy. Indeed the attitude publicly adopted by their leaders during the riots of 1935 shows a realization of the all-important rôle that the Churches should play in removing causes of mistrust, in reconciling the divided. Dr. MacNeice,[1] Bishop of Down and Connor and Dromore, has striven very courageously in the past few years to

[1] He was previously Bishop of Cashel and Emly and Waterford and was elected to the Northern Diocese in 1934.

restore a spirit of moderation. His admirable words spoken in
St. Anne's Cathedral, Belfast, during the rioting in July 1935
deserve to be quoted:

"Our real differences may have their own importance. I
have no wish to minimize them but something is now at stake
which is incalculably more serious. If that something is lost
then the terms 'Protestant' and 'Roman Catholic,' 'Unionist'
and 'Nationalist' will be but empty names. But, thank God,
we have good reason for the prediction that all is not lost . . .
God may be calling us—I think He is—through the agonies
of these depressing days to a venture of faith. . . . We have
neither the right nor the wish to dictate to Christian men and
women what their political party should be. As far as our Church
is concerned her members may belong to any party. But what
we have a right to say to those who, with us, acknowledge the
supremacy of Christ is this: 'Make sure that your loyalty to
your party does not mean disloyalty to your Lord.' "

Two and a half centuries ago the Lord Mayor of London
inscribed on the walls of the house in Pudding Lane where
the Great Fire broke out—"Here by the permission of Heaven
Hell broke loose upon this Protestant City from the malicious
hearts of barbarous papists." Something of this virulent
bigotry survives to this day in Ulster, and for that the various
Churches cannot be held entirely free of responsibility. Like
the wandering Oisin of legend these Churches too have
known three centuries . . .

Of dalliance with a demon thing.

None the less, in spite of the past, and not because of it,
the future yet lies with the Churches in Ulster. By teaching
and still more by example their leaders can instil a
spirit of tolerance and co-operation in the North. The task
may not be easy. But that is no reason why it should not be
attempted by Christian Churches. It is a great occasion for
valuable service—and now is an opportunity such as may not
recur.

CONCLUSION

The success or failure of the experiment in Devolution now in force in Northern Ireland will depend on the actual political forces at work in Ulster more than on any other single factor. Consequently full count must be taken of the party system as it exists there to-day. It provides the dynamic motive power which gives life to a complex constitutional organism. The conclusions one is compelled to submit provide in themselves no great hope for the future.

It is commonly held by English critics that a two-party system is essential to the proper working of parliamentary Democracy. It is true that two parties exist in Ulster but they do not fulfil the needs of the system, for one party constitutes an apparently permanent Government whilst the other appears destined to be an equally permanent Opposition. The unfortunate constitutional consequences of this frozen political state are emphasized by a disagreement between the two parties on fundamentals. There is no residue of political beliefs—as in Great Britain and the Free State—acceptable to both parties. The gulf dividing them is widened by a sectarian strife so bitter as to eliminate all sober discussion of desirable reforms.

In a democratic State it has been said the only right of a minority is the right to convince the majority. This right involves also the obligation to accept the decision of that majority. There is a right to protest; there is a duty to obey. In Northern Ireland the minority have exercised their right to protest; they have not always remembered their duty to obey. The majority have the right to rule; but it is their duty to exercise this authority for the good of the whole community. In Northern Ireland the majority, in the enjoyment of their right, have been, at times, unmindful of their obligation to those citizens who differ from them in race and creed.

Divisions in Ulster lie deep. No Nationalist can forgive Partition, no Unionist can overcome his fears of a United

Ireland. Yet it is misleading to conclude that these sections of one community cannot live in friendship or co-operate for the welfare of a common State. In the Irish Free State a responsible leader of the small Unionist minority declared after fifteen years of self-government: "I am very much concerned that we should allow ourselves to think of ourselves or encourage others to think of us as an alien minority. We belong to this country. It is for us to take our part in its work . . . it is our business to amalgamate ourselves with the country, to take our part in its life, and make others think of us, not as a separate body, but as belonging to the integral life of the community."[1] This speech by the Protestant Archbishop of Dublin shows that the divisions of former years are losing their bitterness in the South. In the North they still survive in all of their former intensity. As a result of the tension that prevails members of either party are easily frightened, though impossible to intimidate. There the political leaders

> . . . must to keep their certainty accuse
> All that are different of a base intent.

Political discord is fanned each year by the July celebrations, which are the outward symbol of internal mistrust. "The very name of Orangemen," said Archbishop Whately, the last of all men to be a friend of the Roman Catholic Church, "is a sign chosen on purpose to keep up the memory of a civil war which every friend of humanity would wish to bury in oblivion. It is doing what among the heathen was reckoned an accursed thing—keeping a trophy in repair." But Ulster remains greater by far than the loyalties within which her most fervent patriots seek to confine her.

[1] Cf. Report in the *Irish Times*, February 11, 1936, and cf. also reference by Vice-President of the Executive Council. *Debates Seanad Eireann*, February 12, 1936.

CHAPTER XII

THE JUDICATURE, THE LAW AND LOCAL GOVERNMENT

THE main features of subordinate government, in the form in which it has been established in Northern Ireland, present a striking example of the practical operation of Devolution under the parliamentary system. Public attention has been directed, as always, almost exclusively upon the activities of the executive and the legislature. But there exist other instruments of government, which fill a rôle of an equally essential, though less constructive, character. In Northern Ireland the latter deserve attention, not so much because of the functions they perform as because of the manner in which they perform them. British procedure has been followed in all important respects in the exercise of judicial functions, in the administration of law and in the organization of local government. Interest lies, therefore, not in the extent of the departure from earlier practice, but rather in the problems of administration raised by a grant of Devolution. We may find no great originality in practice but we will discover a distinctive significance in the adaptations which self-government rendered essential. In this way we are continually reminded of the very important fact that the self-governing institutions in Northern Ireland are the product of a legislative enactment, and not the consequence of constitutional evolution.

(a) *The Judicature*

The Government of Northern Ireland is responsible for "peace, order and good government" within the six counties. None the less, all matters relating to the Superior Courts of Northern Ireland remain under the jurisdiction of the Parliament of the United Kingdom "until after the date of Irish Union."[1]

[1] The Act, s. 47.

The Judges of these Courts are appointed by the Crown and are removable only on an address from both Houses of the Parliament of the United Kingdom. In respect of appointment the Crown acts in accordance with the advice given by the Imperial Cabinet. The cost of the administration of the Superior Courts is borne by the Exchequer of the United Kingdom; and the salaries and pensions of the Judges are paid out of the Consolidated Fund. The expenditure thus involved is deducted from the "Reserved Taxes."

(i) *The Superior Courts*

The Superior Courts in Northern Ireland comprise the Supreme Court of the Judicature, the Court of Criminal Appeal, the Railway and Canal Commission, and the Land Purchase Commission. The two Commissions are of limited interest. The Railway and Canal Commission is not separate to Northern Ireland, but its jurisdiction as defined in 1888 for the United Kingdom, as a whole, has been continued in respect of matters within that jurisdiction arising in Northern Ireland. No cases relating to the work of the Commission in Northern Ireland have been heard since 1921.[1] The Land Purchase Commission, on the other hand, has carried out services of notable value in fulfilling the intention of the various Land Purchase Acts. It was established for the dual purpose of determining the rights of landowners and other persons interested in the proceeds of land sold under the Land Acts; and of facilitating by financial assistance the acquisition of land by tenants. The Commission in Northern Ireland was established under the Act of 1920 in order that the work begun by the Irish Land Commission might be completed. The Land Commission will shortly be dissolved and questions arising out of its work will be transferred to the ordinary Courts of Law.

The Supreme Court of Judicature of Northern Ireland consists of two divisions—the High Court of Justice and the Court of Appeal. The former consists of three Judges under

[1] Vide *Ulster Year Book*, 1935, p. 183.

the Presidency of the Lord Chief Justice. It is the Superior Court of First Instance and exercises the jurisdiction formerly exercised by the High Court of Justice in Ireland. The Court of Appeal is the Appellate Tribunal and consists of the Lord Chief Justice, who is its President, and two ordinary Justices known as Lord Justices of Appeal. The Lord Chief Justice may request any Judge of the High Court to attend for the purpose of constituting an additional Judge of the Court of Appeal.

The Judges of the High Court receive special Commissions at stated times of the year to hold assizes in each county town in Northern Ireland. Such assizes are held annually in the spring and autumn, whilst a winter assize is held for the whole of Northern Ireland, except the county borough of Belfast. In Belfast the Criminal Jurisdiction of the Assize Court is now exercised by a Judge of the Supreme Court sitting four times a year by virtue of a Commission of Oyer and Terminer and General Gaol Delivery.

An appeal from the High Court lies to the Court of Appeal. It is the final Appellate Tribunal in Northern Ireland. An appeal from its decisions lies only to the House of Lords. It is empowered to review cases involving the validity of legislation enacted by the Parliament of Northern Ireland. In such instances an appeal lies, by leave of the Court, to the House of Lords. In practice, the existence of an alternative, though more costly, means of testing the validity of legislation by a reference to the Judicial Committee of the Privy Council has deprived the Court of Appeal of the hearing of the most important case involving an issue of this kind. Hitherto only one case concerning the validity of legislation has come before the Court of Appeal. This case questioned the legality of certain regulations imposed by the Milk Act on milk produced in the Irish Free State. On appeal it was taken to the House of Lords. On the other hand appeals from the High Court are numerous. In 1930 there were 22; in 1932—18; in 1934—38. On occasion a large proportion of these appeals is pending

at the end of the year[1] but normally they are nearly all disposed
of earlier. Appeals from the Assize Courts are less numerous,
whilst those from the Land Commission have averaged little
more than two per annum over the last four or five years.

The following diagram, reproduced from the *Ulster Year
Book*,[2] indicates in outline the organization of the Supreme
Court:

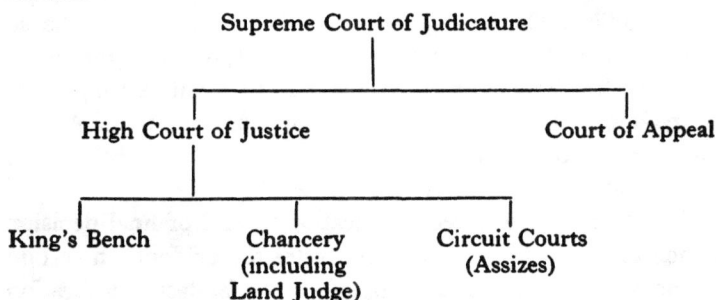

Supreme Court of Judicature

High Court of Justice | Court of Appeal

King's Bench | Chancery (including Land Judge) | Circuit Courts (Assizes)

The salaries of the Judges of Northern Ireland are charged
upon the Consolidated Fund of the United Kingdom. They are
not insubstantial. The Lord Chief Justice receives £5,000 per
annum, the two Lord Justices of Appeal receive £4,000 per
annum, the Justices of the High Court £3,500 and £3,000
per annum respectively.

In 1930 a Court of Criminal Appeal was established in
Northern Ireland by legislation of the Imperial Parliament.[3]
The Court consists of all the Judges of the Supreme Court of
Judicature. Appeal to this Court is allowed to persons convicted
on indictment, either on a point of law, or, with leave of the
Court, on a question of fact or other sufficient ground. An
appeal against the sentence, if it is not fixed by law, is allowed
with leave of the Court.

(ii) *The Judicial Committee of the Privy Council*

The validity of legislation enacted by the Parliament of
Northern Ireland may be tested in the Courts. In that event

[1] E.g. Ten in 1932.   [2] 1935.   [3] 20 & 21 Geo. V. c. 45.

an appeal lies from the Court of Appeal to the House of Lords. But in addition there exists a more direct means whereby the validity of legislation may be finally determined. The actual procedure has been described in an earlier chapter.[1] In general, Ministers or members of the Joint Exchequer Board may refer —should they consider it in the public interest to do so—any issues arising out of the dubious validity of certain legislation to the Judicial Committee of the Privy Council. If it is so decided, then the Judicial Committee may hear the issue involved. In the hearing the Judicial Committee may allow any persons who are interested to appear and to be heard. The decision of the Judicial Committee as to the validity of any legislation is conclusive.

The advantages of direct application to and of final decision of such cases by the Judicial Committee are evident. In certain instances, as in that of the Appeal of the Belfast Corporation against the Education Levy imposed by the Government of Northern Ireland, a satisfactory decision by a local Court might not be possible. The case indeed provides an interesting illustration of the value of this method of determining such issues. In 1934 the Minister of Finance was faced with an estimated total deficit of £284,000. To meet it he decided, amongst other things, to impose the equivalent of a sixpenny rate on local authorities for the purpose of covering part of the expenditure on educational services. This Levy was to be raised in a full year to one shilling in the pound, and was expected to yield nearly £90,000. The levy was imposed in 1934, but the Corporation of the City of Belfast declined to shoulder the cost on the ground that the imposition of a rate by the Central Government was *ultra vires*. In consequence of this refusal to pay, the Government has deducted sums from the grants normally payable to the Corporation. The appeal was delayed, and when the hearing eventually took place before the Judicial Committee early in 1936 the amount of the Levy outstanding, less deductions, was £225,000. Consequently the hearing

---

[1] Vide pp. 152–159.

aroused considerable interest among the ratepayers in Belfast. Before the Judicial Committee of the Privy Council, Mr. Simonds, on behalf of the Corporation, argued that the Levy had all the character of tax and was directly comparable with income tax. He declared that the Levy constituted a contribution towards a State service. The money derived from it was paid into the Exchequer, went into the Consolidated Fund for Northern Ireland, and was available in fact for any purpose, even though publicly designated an Education Levy. Thus it had the character of a tax and not a rate. On behalf of the Government, the Attorney-General, Mr. Babington, pointed out that, contrary to the practice in Great Britain, local authorities in Northern Ireland were not in full control of educational expenditure. Public elementary education was largely a State service since teachers' salaries were borne by the State and the Exchequer annually paid out in grants in aid of education a sum which exceeded the amount of the disputed Education Levy. Where Mr. Simonds maintained that a rate was a local charge by a local authority for strictly local uses, and that the Government was using the machinery of rating to raise a tax, the Attorney-General argued that the Levy could not be described as a tax since it involved no more than a readjustment of the incidence of educational cost. Judgment was given in favour of the Government. The hearing of this case gave the public in Northern Ireland a first opportunity of estimating the value of this alternative means of testing the validity of legislation. The finality of a judgment by the Judicial Committee is certainly attractive but, on the other hand, there was a long delay before the date of hearing was fixed. Moreover, there seems little reason for the existence of two means of deciding similar cases. Reference to the Judicial Committee was intended in 1920 to provide a suitable means of deciding issues arising out of the relations—particularly the financial relations—established between the three Governments of Northern and of Southern Ireland and of the United Kingdom. Even now its value would be unquestioned were a dispute on the interpretation of financial legislation to arise between the Government of Northern Ireland and that of the United Kingdom, which the latter Government was prepared to submit to arbitration. But on more general issues legal opinion in Northern Ireland is somewhat unfavourable to reference to this tribunal largely on account of the expense involved. The public, on the other hand, having complete confidence in the judgments of the Judicial Committee, believe that there are certain cases, as that involving the legality of the Education Levy, which should be referred to it for decision.

(iii) *The Jury System*

No alteration in principle has been made in the jury system since 1921, but certain substantial alterations in detail were introduced in 1926. In accordance with the recommendations of the Report of a Committee appointed to enquire into the system in 1924,[1] legislation was enacted providing for a more equitable basis of jury qualification. The list of persons exempted from serving was substantially altered and provision was made for the remuneration of jurors in civil trials. In addition grand juries at Courts of Quarter Sessions were abolished, since they fulfilled no essential function in judicial procedure.[2]

(iv) *Constitutional Amendments affecting the Judiciary*

Save in one minor respect it has not been found necessary to amend the judicial provisions of the Act of 1920. That Act provided that "all matters relating to the Supreme Court" were reserved matters.[3] The general terms of this reservation created a certain doubt as to the authority of the Parliament of Northern Ireland. While it was recognized that legislation by that Parliament would be enforced by the Supreme Court, it was not clear whether a statute of Northern Ireland could validly designate, for the exercise of jurisdiction, some particular

---

[1] Vide *Report of Committee on Jury System*, Cmd. 25.
[2] Jury Laws Amendment (N. Ireland) Act, 1926.   [3] S. 47.

division or Judge of the Court or could confer jurisdictions
of a new or special kind upon the Supreme Courts. These
and similar issues arising out of the application of the judicial
provisions of the Act of 1920 were decided in an interpreting
Act passed in 1928.[1] By its terms the reservation contained
in Article 47 was interpreted in a restrictive sense; and by
precise statement it was declared that the Parliament of Northern
Ireland was not precluded from conferring authority of this
kind upon the Supreme Court.

(v) *The Inferior Courts*

The Inferior Courts and the magistracy are, in distinction
to the Superior Courts, under the jurisdiction of the Parliament
of Northern Ireland. The Inferior Courts comprise the Courts
of Quarter Sessions, the County Courts and the Courts of
Summary Jurisdiction. The structure and jurisdictions of
the subordinate Courts has not, save in one instance, been
modified substantially by the Parliament of Northern Ireland.
The Court of Quarter Sessions is held in each county, once
in every quarter of the year, before the County Court Judge.
Its jurisdiction in criminal matters is substantially the same
as that of the Judges of Assize. In practice cases triable at
both Courts are returned to the Court where the speediest
trial may be held.[2] There are 29 Quarter Sessions towns in
Northern Ireland. The County Courts enjoy "civil bill"
jurisdiction, and in addition decide a wide variety of land and
equity cases. Appeal from the County Court Judge may be
made to the Judge of Assize, and thence, with special leave on
questions of law, only to the Court of Appeal. There are five
County Court Judges. Two of them, namely, the County
Court Judge of Antrim and of Londonderry, also are entitled
the Recorder of Belfast and of Londonderry respectively.

The jurisdiction of the Courts of Summary Jurisdiction is
derived principally from statute. It includes the power to hear

[1] Miscellaneous Provisions Act, 1928.
[2] Vide *Ulster Year Book*, 1935.

and determine summarily minor criminal and quasi-criminal cases. These Courts also enjoy jurisdiction in civil cases involving small isssues. In 1934 a Summary Jurisdiction Bill was introduced which proposed to transfer the judicial administration of the Justices of the Peace to Resident Magistrates. Under its provisions J.P.s were no longer to adjudicate at Petty Sessions or Quarter Sessions, although they might still adjudicate in a few minor matters "out of Petty Sessions." Petty Sessions would henceforward be conducted by Resident Magistrates appointed by the Governor on the recommendations of the Minister of Home Affairs, whilst the Justices of the Peace would continue merely to conduct the preliminary investigation of indictable offences. The Bill aroused considerable controversy and encountered, not surprisingly, a vigorous opposition from Justices of the Peace generally. None the less, it was carried through Parliament by substantial majorities and enacted the following year. The reform was rendered desirable partly by the need for legally qualified persons to preside at Courts of Summary Jurisdiction, but more particularly because of the laxity of Justices of the Peace in the application of certain statutory regulations. Certainly, the fines they imposed for a breach of the betting laws did not convey an impression of unsympathetic severity, whilst the Ministry of Agriculture was evidently dissatisfied with their enforcement of Marketing Regulations since their duty in this respect had been transferred some time earlier to the Magistrates by explicit statutory provision.

(b) *The Law*

The existence of two Parliaments legislating for the one area necessarily demands a precise definition of their respective spheres of influence. The authority of the local legislature is limited by the provisions of the Constituent Act; that of the Imperial legislature remains by the terms of the same Act "unaffected and undiminished over all persons, matters and things in Northern Ireland and every part thereof."[1]

[1] S. 75.

So it is that sovereignty is explicity reserved to the Parliament of the United Kingdom. In practice, this means that, whereas the validity of statutes enacted by the Parliament of Northern Ireland may be tested in the Courts by reference to the terms of the Act, the validity of those of the Parliament of the United Kingdom may not be questioned. Consequently there exists no legal prohibition whatever of legislation upon transferred matters by the Parliament of the United Kingdom. Obviously, however, it would be absurd to create a local Parliament, and then interfere with it. But the power to override is clear; and no Imperial Act can be questioned because it deals with subject matter within the competence of the local legislature.

(i) *Adaptation of Law*

All existing laws remained in force in Northern Ireland under the provisions of the Act, subject to such modifications as were necessary to adapt them to the Act and subject to repeal and alteration by the Parliament of Northern Ireland in so far as they concerned matters within its powers.[1] Thus in order to determine the application to Northern Ireland of a statute passed by Parliament of the United Kingdom at any time before the transfer of powers, the actual text of the enactment must be read together with the Government of Ireland Act, the Order in Council made under the Act and any repealing or amending enactments of the Parliament of Northern Ireland.[2] The existing laws of the United Kingdom have been considerably modified to meet the special conditions of Northern Ireland. A typical instance of such a form of amendment is to be found in the Uniformity of Laws Act (N.I.), 1922, which enacts appropriate modifications in several scheduled Acts of the Imperial Parliament.[3] The legislature at Stormont does not enjoy the power of altering the Act of 1920 and Amending Acts, save where it is expressly permitted to do so.

The phrase "existing laws" means all laws existing at the

---

[1] S. 61.   [2] Cf. Quekett, op. cit., vol. i, p. 54.
[3] 13 & 14 Geo. V. c. 20.

appointed day for the application of the terms of the Act. The 3rd May, 1921, was fixed as the appointed day for the general purposes of the Act, including the establishment of the legislature. The transfer of the existing administration did not take place till some time later. In a like manner the effect of the Act was to continue all existing taxation. In the magisterial case of Commissioners of Customs and Excise in 1930 a penalty was obtained for wholesale dealing in spirits, without a licence, subject to a tax imposed by a statute of 1910[1] on the ground that this was an "existing" tax.

In legislation affecting subjects of some complexity, different aspects of which are normally the concern both of the Parliament of the United Kingdom and of the Parliament of Northern Ireland, it is usual for the latter legislature to insert a clause indicating the overriding authority of the former. In the Workmen's Compensation Act (N.I.), 1923, it is stated:[2]

"Nothing in this Act shall be construed as making provision with regard to any matter in respect of which the Parliament of Northern Ireland have not power to make laws."

Ten years later an interesting example of the dependence of the local legislature arose in relation to the application of the new agricultural legislation. The Parliament of Northern Ireland provided in its Agricultural Marketing Act:[3]

"In the event of any amendment being made, after the passing of this Act, in the Bill for the United Kingdom Act with such effect as to render any provision of this Act inconsistent with the United Kingdom Act as passed, then in that event the Governor of Northern Ireland may by Order in Privy Council . . . modify the provisions of this Act so far as may appear . . . necessary for making those provisions consistent with the United Kingdom Act."

The legislative output of the Parliament of Northern Ireland has been very considerable. From the meeting of the first

[1] 10 Edw. VII. and 1 Geo. V. c. 8.
[2] 13 & 14 Geo. V. c. 33.   [3] 23 & 24 Geo. V. c. 22.

legislature on June 7, 1921, to the adjournment for the summer recess on July 16, 1935, 380 Public and General Acts, and 55 Local and Private Acts, had been passed. Thus in a period of almost exactly 14 years the average output of public legislation was 27 statutes per annum.

(ii) *Emergency Legislation*

In other countries the introduction of emergency laws is held to mark the existence of abnormal conditions which render government impracticable, unless the executive be endowed with exceptional powers for the suppression of disorder; in Ireland it has become a habit. Where the Irish Free State has her Public Safety Act, Northern Ireland has her Civil Authorities Act. The history that explains them, the motives that caused their enactment, the influence they will carry into the future are in both instances identical. For generations English statesmen responded to Irish disorder with repressive legislation. It is tragic that Irishmen in their first experience of self-government should tread the self-same primrose path and yet hope to escape the same penalty. It would be idle to pretend that the Northern Government were confronted with a simple task in 1921; and many impartial observers are prepared to justify the first Civil Authorities Act. The very existence of the Northern State was threatened, a large proportion of the opposition declined to recognize the authority of the new Government; disorder was rampant until the close of 1922; there were terrible murders followed by equally terrible reprisals. Only two alternatives faced the new Cabinet: to resign or to restore order. They chose the latter, and they achieved their purpose by repressive legislation. In the circumstances there would appear to have been no alternative method, but the form of its application rightly provoked the most severe criticism.

The Civil Authorities Act, 1922,[1] was comprehensive in the powers which it delegated to the Minister of Home Affairs,

[1] 12 & 13 Geo. V. (N.I.), 1922.

S

who was designated the civil authority for the purposes of
the Act. Almost no limit of any kind was imposed upon his
power to suppress disorder, save that "the ordinary course
of law and avocations of life and the enjoyment of property
shall be interfered with as little as may be permitted by the
exigencies of the steps required."[1] The Minister was authorized
to delegate all or any of the exceptional powers conferred
to any officer of police as he saw fit. Further, the Minister had
power to make regulations:

    (a) for making further provision for the preservation of
        peace and the maintenance of order, and
    (b) for varying or revoking any provision of the regulations
        prescribed in the Act.[2]

In the exercise of these frankly despotic powers no check
whatever was imposed on the Minister save that such regulations
must be laid on the table of both Houses of Parliament "as
soon as may be after they are made." Since the Minister was
empowered to alter the regulations at will their actual provisions
were of no great significance. But they were drastic. The
civil power had full right of entry and of search, it might
detain suspects at will. Heavy penalties were imposed upon
persons found to be members of unlawful associations, flogging
was prescribed for a series of crimes connected with a breach
of the various Firearms Acts, the death penalty was imposed
for breaches of the Explosive Substances Act. In addition,
the civil authority might by notice prohibit the circulation
of any newspaper, and—a truly remarkable provision—"no
person may by word of mouth or in writing or in a newspaper
or book,

    (a) spread false reports or make false statements or
    (b) spread reports likely to cause disaffection to His Majesty,
        or

[1] S. 1.   [2] Ibid.

(c) spread reports likely to prejudice the recruiting of persons to serve in the police or any other force employed for the preservation of peace in Northern Ireland."

At the end of this Act one safeguard was provided for the public. The Act was to continue for one year "and no longer, unless Parliament otherwise determines." The Act was passed in 1922. It was renewed by Parliament every year till 1933. Then even this meagre safeguard was discarded, for it was decided that "the Act of 1922 shall continue in force until Parliament *otherwise* determines."[1] It is difficult to find any justification whatever for the permanent adoption of this extreme type of emergency legislation. Till 1922, the conditions in Belfast provided a very weighty argument for the introduction of this Act, even though, as we think, they did not afford a complete justification. But all the arguments that were adduced for the enactment of such legislation in 1922 are arguments for its repeal in 1936—unless indeed one is prepared to say that the Government of Northern Ireland functions in a state of perpetual emergency. There is a very real danger in accustoming citizens to a belief that the rule of law must always be suspended. Moreover, a layman inexperienced in the art of government would have supposed that an executive armed with such powers would have been able to cope effectively with the sporadic rioting that occurred in Belfast in 1935, whereas, in fact, the disorder continued for three months. The *raison d'être* for legislation in the category of the Civil Authorities Act disappears when it ceases to be effective.

A Report of a Commission of Enquiry appointed by the National Council of Civil Liberties to examine the purpose and effect of this Act afforded specific evidence of the injustices— and the stupidities—that such legislation is bound to produce. The Government, who regarded the enquiry as a hostile act, fulminated in general terms against its conclusions, denounced the persons who were responsible for the publi-

---

[1] 23 & 24 Geo. V. (N.I.), 1933, S. 2.

cation, but neglected to answer the particular points at issue.

The executive in Northern Ireland was endowed with wide powers of a different type in 1926. Influenced by the General Strike in the United Kingdom the Unionist Government passed an Emergency Powers Act, which authorizes the Governor to proclaim a state of emergency in the event of any action being taken by any body of persons which, by interfering with the distribution of food, water, fuel or light, or with the means of locomotion, might deprive the community of the essentials of life. Whilst such a state of emergency continues the executive is entitled to make such regulations as it thinks fit for the preservation of public order and for securing the essentials of life to the community. The powers thus conferred upon the executive are in addition to those which it already enjoyed under the Civil Authorities Act. The Act was vigorously opposed by the Labour and the Nationalist Parties on the ground that it was restriction upon the rights of Labour, which was the more unjustifiable in that the General Strike—since it did not extend to Northern Ireland—provided no ground for its adoption. The Government supporters, on the other hand, claimed that the Bill was as essential in Northern Ireland as was the Bill incorporating similar proposals sponsored by the Conservative Government in the United Kingdom, since the vast majority of Trade Unions in Northern Ireland were controlled from the other side of the Channel.

(c) *Local Government*

The grant of Devolution to Northern Ireland has involved no innovations in the field of Local Government. The whole structure of local administration in Ireland was reorganized by the Local Government Act of 1898. Its provisions were modelled on those of the Act of 1888, which had reformed Local Government in England. It is interesting to recollect that the system of Local Government then established in Ireland gave to the Irish people their first experience of democratic self-government. Save in respect of educational administration, no alteration has been made by the local Parliament in the actual framework then established.

(i) *The Local Councils*

In Northern Ireland there are 6 counties, 2 county boroughs, 2 boroughs, 30 urban districts, and 32 rural districts. Their duties correspond with the duties of similar local authorities in the United Kingdom. Of these Local Government bodies the County Councils exercise the widest functions, and since 1922 there has been a distinct tendency to extend their powers. They are rating authorities in rural areas. In distinction to English practice, the County Council is the authority for making, levying and collecting the rates; not only for its own purposes but also for the purposes of Rural District Councils and Boards of Guardians. It is also the medium through which Government grants are paid to these bodies. Apart from the exercise of their financial powers, the authority of the County Councils has been extended by the placing of various public health services within their control. In addition they have been granted by legislation of the local Parliament a more complete control of roads administration, and have been invested with comprehensive duties relating to education and drainage.

There are 2 County Borough Councils, 1 for Belfast and the other for Londonderry. The County Boroughs amalgamate the duties of the County Council and the Urban District Council.[1] It will be noticed that among the less important

---

[1] In Belfast the affairs of the City Corporation have given rise to a periodic demand for its reform. The appointment of Commissioners on the Free State model to administer the affairs of the city received some public support a few years ago. In 1926 a Commission was appointed to investigate charges of corrupt dealings in relation to Housing. The Report of this—the Megaw—Commission found that the majority of the Housing Committee had acted improperly in showing undue favour to certain contractors. Further they found that the timber supplied was bad. Public confidence in the management of the affairs of the capital has not yet been fully restored.

units in Local Government administration Boards of Guardians are continued. Their abolition has been recommended by the Report of the Departmental Commission on Local Government in 1927. Parishes, in contrast to English practice, do not exist. It need perhaps scarcely be added—since it is now inevitable in Ireland—that the police force, known as the Royal Ulster Constabulary, is controlled by the Central Government.

(ii) *Education*

The Education Act of 1923[1] aroused so much controversy in respect of its proposals for religious teaching that the changes it effected in educational administration tended to be obscured. Yet in fact it enacts some of the most important administrative reforms that have been carried through by the subordinate legislature. From the aspect of Local Government the essential features of the Education Act are to be found in the new responsibility vested in the County and County Borough Councils. The Council of each County and County Borough has been made the education authority for its area. It exercises general powers of administration in all educational matters through the medium of specially appointed regional and borough education committees. The mode for appointment of these committees is settled under the scheme. In the case of the County Boroughs the Education Committee consists of 21 members, a minority of whom may be non-members of the Council. By these reforms educational administration in Northern Ireland has been decentralized. Popular control has been established to a considerable extent, even though the Ministry of Education retains the power to supervise and control the work of the local authorities, especially with reference to the organization, curriculum and the working of the public elementary schools. An amusing illustration of the authority of the Minister in this respect is supplied by the protest of various Unionist Senators to Lord Charlemont against the use in schools of Mr. D. C. Somervell's *History*

[1] 13 & 14 Geo. V. c. 21.

of Great Britain, on the ground that the book contained disparaging references to the achievements and policy of the Ulster Unionists. Lord Charlemont was asked to remove it from the curriculum. This has since been done.[1] In general, the transfer of responsibility for education to local authorities has been real and has, in fact, promoted considerable local interest in educational matters. The local authorities have done something to improve school accommodation by a policy of amalgamation and by the provision of central schools. From 1923 to 1931, 260 small or defective schools were closed, whilst 55 large centrally situated public elementary schools were built at a capital cost of about £544,000. As the latest report of the Ministry of Education remarks:[2] "The tendency towards the consolidation of our schools into larger units is proceeding steadily, and with gratifying effects in increased efficiency and greater economy in cost." But the cost of education in Northern Ireland, though below the corresponding level of similar expenditure in the United Kingdom, falls almost entirely upon the central Exchequer. The education levy of 1934, whose legality was questioned, was designed to recoup the central Exchequer for part of the expenditure on Education paid to local authorities through grants-in-aid. There will be little opportunity, as the Report of the Ministry remarks,[3] for further expansion in present circumstances unless the local authorities can be induced to bear a greater share of the cost of educational services.

(iii) *Franchise and Electoral System*

The franchise for Local Government electors is identical with that in the United Kingdom save for certain necessary modifications with regard to residential qualifications. Thus a qualified Local Government elector must be over 21 years of age, must be in occupation of property of at least £5 valuation, must be ordinarily resident in Northern Ireland for six months of the

---

[1] *Senate Debates*, March 1936.
[2] 1934–35, N.I., H.C. 349.   [3] Ibid.

year. In addition the husband or wife of a Local Government elector is *ipso facto* also a Local Government elector. The existence of this property franchise in Local Government naturally excludes a considerable number of parliamentary electors from exercising a vote in local elections. The respective figures provide an interesting comparison:

County or County Borough	Number of Parliamentary Electors	Number of Local Government Electors
Antrim County	132,990	83,933
Armagh County	68,582	44,157
Belfast County Borough	266,265	189,009
Down County	134,467	88,316
Fermanagh County	34,249	21,869
Tyrone County	84,073	54,316
Londonderry County	52,963	32,848
Londonderry County Borough ..	32,181	20,071
Queen's University	3,792	—
Total	809,562	534,519

Thus about 40 per cent of the total number of parliamentary electors do not enjoy a vote in Local Government elections.

In 1919 Proportional Representation was introduced for all Local Government elections in Ireland but its abolition in 1922 was one of the first acts of the Unionist Government in Belfast. Elections of members of the various local authorities are in some cases triennial and in others, as the County Borough of Belfast, a proportion of the members retire each year. No members of local authorities hold office for a period of more than three years. The elections arouse but slight interest. Since the abolition of Proportional Representation there has been a distinct tendency for a considerable percentage of the seats to be uncontested.[1] No doubt this tendency is accentuated by the rather large number of persons required to serve on

[1] Vide figures in Chapter vii.

the various Local Government bodies. For example, the smallest membership of any of the 6 County Councils in Northern Ireland is 25, whilst the largest, that of Tyrone, is 35. The County Borough Council of Londonderry comprises 40 members, that of Belfast 60. In addition persons must be found to serve on the Urban and Rural District Councils. The citizen of Northern Ireland who is a Local Government elector is thus asked to interest himself in the work of three quite distinct aspects of government. He is expected to record a vote in elections for the Parliament of the United Kingdom, for the Parliament at Stormont, and for the local Councils. In addition, there must be found amongst the whole body of electors a sufficient number of persons prepared to put themselves forward as candidates at these various elections. In the circumstances it is not surprising either that little interest is shown in the work of Local Government, or that there is a distinct scarcity of suitable candidates in local as well as in parliamentary elections.

(d) *Local Government Finance*

The importance of Local Government finance tends to be underestimated since little variation occurs either in the means of raising revenue or in the objects of expenditure. None the less, the actual sums handled by the local authorities are almost as large as those passing through the central Exchequer. The figures printed overleaf are instructive.[1] In calculating the total receipts and expenditure shown in this table money received by one authority and transferred to another has been accounted for as income and expenditure once only.

It will be noticed that the local authorities are becoming more and more dependent upon subventions from the Central Government. Even though the revenue from rates is increasing it no longer yields, as it did in 1930, an amount approximately equal to the amount derived from Government grants-in-aid. In 1933–34, 16 per cent of the total revenue derived from Local

[1] Reprinted from the *Ulster Year Book*, 1935.

and Central Government taxation was levied by local authorities. For the purpose of remedying injustices in the valuation of hereditaments a General Revaluation of Northern Ireland was ordered under an Act of 1932. It took about three years to complete and the new valuations for rating purposes came

	1930	1931	1932	1933	1934
	£	£	£	£	£
Receipts from Rates ..	1,656,520	1,614,242	1,632,882	1,636,523	1,777,939
Government Grants ..	1,582,156	1,988,935	1,924,537	2,122,147	2,275,587
Miscellaneous Receipts ..	2,908,667	2,925,744	2,936,068	2,850,384	2,899,827
Capital Receipts .. (from Loans)	2,283,514	1,549,289	1,222,194	1,536,538	2,446,759
Total Receipts	8,430,857	8,078,210	7,715,681	8,145,592	9,400,112
Expenditure from Revenue	6,029,833	6,246,496	6,307,911	6,579,521	6,828,938
Capital Payments ..	1,966,333	1,809,078	1,773,371	1,532,391	2,172,403
Total Expenditure ..	7,996,166	8,055,574	8,081,282	8,111,912	9,001,341
Capital Indebtedness	18,511,736	18,719,757	19,255,623	19,732,800	20,282,726

into force in April 1936. Previously no revaluation had taken place for seventy years. In 1929 the Government of Northern Ireland followed that of the United Kingdom in giving total relief from rates on agricultural land and partial relief for industry and transport.[1] This derating had, as the Committee on Financial Relations remarked, a serious effect upon Local Government finances.[2] Earlier in 1928 a Committee had been set up to consider the application to Northern Ireland

[1] Local Government (Rating and Finance) Act (N.I.), 1929.
[2] Report of Committee on Financial Relations between the State and Local Authorities, 1931. Cmd. 131, p. 77.

of a scheme for the relief of rates, but in the words of the acid comment of the Committee on Financial Relations, "we note that the functions of this Committee were confined to questions of machinery and elucidation, seeing that within about a fortnight of its establishment the Government announced its intention of giving the Northern Ireland farmer the same treatment as the British farmer was to receive. There was not, therefore, any independent enquiry into the necessity of derating or its consequences."[1] The deficiency in the local revenue caused by derating has been made good by a Government grant-in-aid. This grant since 1930–31 has amounted to over one million pounds a year. The grants-in-aid are normally made for a specified object. Thus in 1933–34 a grant of £666,258 was given towards the cost of maintaining roads and bridges.[2] In the same year £244,160 was given for education. The principle of these grants has been challenged, but the Committee on Financial Relations reported "that any drastic change in the making of grants is unnecessary in Northern Ireland."[3] The Committee pointed out that the extent of the relief to the Exchequer which would be afforded by wholly abolishing all existing grants-in-aid, other than the derating grant, would amount to less than 9 per cent of the total State expenditure; and that the injury thereby occasioned to the services involved would be out of all proportion to the Exchequer relief. On this particular point the argument of the Committee is unanswerable. The need in Northern Ireland is not, however, for retrenchment of the various social services but for increased expenditure, particularly on education. This, however, is not probable for some time since the Committee on Financial Relations reported that "the limit of taxable capacity in Northern Ireland has been exceeded and as regards its rateable capacity, the margin available is narrow."[4]

[1] Report of Committee on Financial Relations between the State and Local Authorities, 1931. Cmd. 131, p. 46.
[2] Including grants from the Road Fund.
[3] Cmd. 131, p. 76.   [4] Ibid.

The expenditure of the local authorities covers a wide field. The largest individual item in the expenditure from revenue is Education, which has increased from £107,820 in 1929–30 to £276,943 in 1933–34. In the latter year Technical Instruction and Agriculture absorbed £139,587 whilst Road Works cost £889,866. Poor Relief cost £643,486, whilst Electric Lighting and Gas Works[1] amounted to more than £1,200,000. Under the title of capital payments appear Unemployment Relief Works, Housing, Roads and Water Supply. The expenditure upon Relief Work has increased rapidly from £196,287 in 1929–30 to £523,446 in 1933–34, thus reflecting the severity of the slump from which Northern Ireland is now emerging.

[1] Including payments in respect of borrowed money.

PART IV

THE MERITS AND DEFECTS OF DEVOLUTION IN THE LIGHT OF EXPERIENCE IN NORTHERN IRELAND

"Mieux l'Etat est constitué, plus les affaires publiques l'emportant sur les privées, dans l'esprit des citoyens."

"Sitôt que quelqu'un dit des affaires de l'Etat: *que m'importe?* on doit compter que l'Etat est perdu."

JEAN JACQUES ROUSSEAU

CHAPTER XIII

THE CONSEQUENCES OF GOVERNMENT
BY DEVOLUTION

THE constitutional structure of the Government in Northern Ireland was determined by legislation of the Imperial Parliament. As we have seen, that Constitution contained no radical deviation from the traditional conventions of the English parliamentary system. The originality of the experiment lay therefore not in the type of the self-governing institutions, but in their creation. In an age remarkable for an ever-increasing centralization of government there had been granted to a province an effective measure of Devolution. The very conception of delegation was opposed to the dominant school of political thought, and ran entirely contrary to the popular belief that the future lay with the progressive unification of all functions under a supreme central authority. For this reason the actual consequences of this grant of Devolution provide a most interesting field of enquiry. Where the Conference on Devolution could only conjecture we, today, are in a position to frame a judgment based upon experience of the operation of such a system of government over a period of sixteen years. In the course of this study the development of subordinate government, the functioning of its machinery, the relationship established between local and central authority, the reaction of the respective political parties have been analysed. It remains to suggest the actual difference in government experienced by the people of Northern Ireland as a result of this grant of Devolution. After all, the advocates of Devolution claim as its principal virtue that it enables local needs to be answered more quickly and more effectively than would be possible under centralized government. How far does the experience of Northern Ireland confirm this pretension?

IN EXECUTIVE GOVERNMENT

There is no doubt but that the machinery of government for Northern Ireland has been decentralized. Previous to 1920 Ireland used to be administered through a separate department of State—the Chief Secretary's Office. Now the affairs of Northern Ireland—so far as the Central Government is concerned—are administered in the ordinary course by the departments of the United Kingdom. No separate department exists for Northern Ireland. The official channel of communication with the Central Government lies through the Home Office. In that department there is a small branch dealing with the affairs of Northern Ireland. Its history is of some interest. Till March 1926 the Council of Ireland survived in law though not in fact. Consequently till the date of its formal abolition the administrative powers destined to be transferred to the Council remained (with certain exceptions) in the hands of the Secretary of State for Home Affairs, who was represented in Belfast by an "Imperial Secretary to the Governor." The anomaly of a Council of Ireland ceased in 1926 under the terms of the Act[1] endorsing the agreement reached on the Boundary Question. These powers of the Council were transferred to the Government of Northern Ireland, the Imperial Secretary's Office ceased to exist and a branch in the Home Office was established on April 1, 1926, to deal with the affairs of Northern Ireland. At its inception this branch of the Home Office contained several members of the former Chief Secretary's Office. Now only one remains. Sir John Anderson[2] was in charge in the initial period of its existence and exercised no little influence upon the nature of the relations established with Belfast. These relations, more especially since the settlement of the Boundary Question, have been uniformly cordial.

[1] 15 & 16 Geo. V. c. 77.
[2] Joint Under-Secretary to Lord Lieutenant of Ireland, 1920, Under-Secretary at the Home Office 1922-32. Since 1932 Governor of Bengal.

It is of particular interest to notice that the volume of work to be accomplished by the special branch of the Home Office has been steadily diminishing; thus showing that Devolution once firmly established does lighten in real measure the work of the Central Government.

The administration of the transferred services is performed by the various departments at Stormont. The creation of some such departments is a necessary feature in any system of subordinate self-government. In the following table are shown the names of the departments, the numbers of persons employed in them and their respective cost to the subordinate Government in any given year.

Department	Staff	Expenditure in 1934–35
		£
Houses of Parliament	24	21,308
Cabinet Offices	7	9,827
Ministry of Finance	761	147,852
Ministry of Home Affairs ..	333	67,010
Ministry of Labour	872	262,910
Ministry of Education	132	66,609
Ministry of Agriculture ..	385	94,137
Ministry of Commerce	50	21,663
Unemployment Assistance Board	125	9,462
Exchequer and Audit Office ..	10	4,700
Total	2,699	705,478

These figures[1] suggest that the organization of the subordinate Government is somewhat elaborate for the area under its jurisdiction. But they also indicate that local self-government is a reality; that it has at its disposal an administration well-organized and fully competent to undertake the duties devolved upon it. In the normal course, the people of Northern Ireland are far more conscious of the existence of the subordinate than of the central administration. Indeed they rarely come

[1] Derived from the Appropriation and Consolidated Fund Services Accounts, 1934–35. H.C. 361.

T

into direct contact with the latter save only in the payment
of taxes. In certain instances it has been found desirable to
effect an interchange of officials. Thus, for example, the Imperial
administration in the exercise of its fiscal authority levies
customs duties on the Irish Free State frontier. The collection
of these duties is not always easy. So the Imperial Government
has arranged for the policing of the land frontier by members
of the R.U.C. The Minister of Home Affairs is compensated
for permitting these services to be rendered. Similar inter-
changes of executive officers take place between the two
Governments as frequently as is demanded by administrative
convenience.

IN LEGISLATION

Statutes of the Imperial Parliament affecting Northern Ireland
are listed annually and rendered available to the public through
the Belfast Stationery Office. By a self-imposed limitation the
Central Parliament does not legislate on "transferred matters."
Considerable care is needed—and is exercised at Stormont—
to ensure that Acts of the local Parliament do not infringe
upon matters reserved to the jurisdiction of the Imperial
Parliament. In fact no confusion has arisen hitherto as a
consequence of two legislatures legislating for the same area,
even though the output of legislation by both Parliaments
has been large during the past fifteen years. From June 1921
to July 1935, the subordinate legislature passed 380 public
and general Acts. This is unquestionably a heavy dose even
when one allows for the fact that many of the statutes merely
adjusted technical points of law. Of the remainder a very
substantial proportion has been supplementary in character
to that passed by the Imperial Parliament. It is rare for the
local Parliament to legislate on principle; and well-nigh
impossible for it to introduce laws involving innovations of
wide application even where it is constitutionally competent
to do so. This practical restriction is imposed by considerations
of administrative convenience. In general, therefore, the positive

legislative contribution of the subordinate Parliament is to be found in its adaptation of Acts of the United Kingdom, so as to render them more suitable to the particular conditions of Northern Ireland, and in legislation on matters of secondary, but none the less real, importance within the six-county area. The value of this contribution as a whole may best be gauged by a selective examination of its effects in the administration of the various social services and in the organization of industrial life. The most profitable fields of enquiry for this purpose are supplied by Agricultural legislation, by the reforms in Education and by the treatment of Unemployment. It is the purpose of this analysis to estimate the practical value of Devolution to the people of Northern Ireland and for this reason it is essential to distinguish with some care as between the consequences of central and subordinate legislation.

IN AGRICULTURE

The industrial distribution of the people of Northern Ireland, as ascertained by the Census of 1926, shows that over one quarter of the total number of persons "gainfully occupied" are engaged in agriculture. Indeed outside Belfast and Londonderry, industrialization is almost negligible. About 90 per cent of the total area of the six counties is devoted to agriculture. The fact is of importance in that it shows that the place of agriculture in the economic life of Northern Ireland is far more important than in any other part of the United Kingdom. In addition, both the system of land tenure and the type of farming most general in Northern Ireland differ from those in practice in the United Kingdom. In Northern Ireland, 84 per cent of the farms are less than 50 acres, whereas in England only 64 per cent are less than 50 acres in extent. Northern Ireland is essentially a land of small holdings. And as a result of land legislation the majority of these farmers are either owners, or about to be owners, of their holdings. This means, if one assumes that holdings of 10 acres and upwards receive

the wholetime care and attention of their occupiers, that
there is in Northern Ireland a body of roughly 70,000 holders
with farms of from 10 to 100 acres in extent, cultivating with
the aid of their families and some 20,000 permanent agricultural
labourers almost 80 per cent of the total cultivated land in
the province.[1] The distinction is of no little importance, for it
means that there exists a prima facie case for the modification
of Imperial legislation on agricultural matters in order to
suit the special conditions prevalent in Northern Ireland.
In turn this would seem to provide an admirable test of the
practical value of this form of local self-government.

A countryside of small holdings suggests mixed farming.
Such is the case in Northern Ireland. Live-stock farming in
one form or another is the more general. Its products account
for nearly 80 per cent of the total agricultural output of the province. Of this a large proportion is made up in cattle and dairy
farming. The annual value of the output of cattle in Northern
Ireland is about £2,000,000 whilst the production of milk
and butter is valued at slightly less than £3,000,000. There
if a rapidly growing output in pigs and a reasonable trade in
sheep. But the most important individual item in the agriculture
of Northern Ireland is poultry and eggs. The annual value
of its production is about £3,000,000 a year and Northern
Ireland has now a higher number of poultry per thousand
acres of crops and pasture than that obtaining in any other part
of the British Isles. The amount of land under the plough
has diminished considerably since 1922 owing partly to
the decline in the demand for flax. Almost the whole of
the agricultural exports of Northern Ireland are sold in the
British market. These are not so large as one might expect
owing to the survival of subsistence husbandry on many of
the small farms. Purely commercial agriculture does exist
on a considerable scale, but the larger proportion of the
agricultural produce of Northern Ireland is consumed on the
farms.

[1] Vide *Ulster Year Book*, 1932, pp. xiv, xv.

Such in brief outline was the foundation upon which the Northern Ministry of Agriculture has had to work. The period at which it began to function made it certain that its task would not be easy. During the War the farmer of Northern Ireland found an unrestricted market for all his surplus agricultural produce in the United Kingdom. In every way he was encouraged to increase production. Then some little time after the War came a sharp reaction which was accentuated by the increasing imports of agricultural produce to Great Britain from the Dominions and foreign States. Thus the Northern Ireland farmer was compelled both to restrict his output and to compete with overseas rivals. The latter he was not well equipped to do, for agricultural methods in Northern Ireland were backward and the manner of export slovenly. The position therefore was serious. What action was taken to remedy it by the subordinate Government? Well, it must be remembered that the now popular panacea of a heavy protective tariff or of actual exclusion of foreign produce could not be adopted, since the necessary authority did not lie within the powers devolved to the Northern Government. It was explicitly precluded from passing legislation interfering with external trade in any form. Thus the Government was confined to remedies within the area of its jurisdiction. In these circumstances attention was directed to four principal aspects of the problem—to agricultural education and research, to the improvement of live stock, to financial assistance to farmers and—later—to the standardization of exports. Valuable work on a limited scale has been accomplished in agricultural education and research. The number of students has increased from about 300 in 1922 to about 700 at the present day. Likewise the parliamentary expenditure has risen from £809 in 1922 to £38,000. One of the most notable developments of this policy has been the creation of an Agricultural Faculty at the Queen's University, whilst the value of the research work has secured general recognition through the Spahlinger bovine anti-tubercular tests. In an endeavour to improve the quality of live stock the Northern Ministry of Agriculture secured the passage of a Live Stock Breeding Act in 1922, which introduced the practice of licensing bulls. Thereby it was made possible to get rid of inferior sires. The interest of the reform lies in the fact that a similar practice was not introduced in Great Britain till ten years later, thereby suggesting that, in some instances at any rate, Devolution does enable desirable legislation to be enacted without the delays inherent in a highly centralized system. The financial assistance given to farming in Northern Ireland has followed the normal practice of the United Kingdom. The most valuable relief to the farming community was afforded by the derating of all agricultural land and buildings in 1929. This followed the precedent set in Great Britain. No independent enquiry as to the desirability of this reform in Northern Ireland had been completed, and it appears—quite apart from the merits of this individual action—that the Northern Government were at fault in not obtaining beforehand complete information upon this point. After all, it is partly to enable such local enquiries to be made that the subordinate Government exists.

So long as no differentiation was made in favour of home or Imperial, as opposed to foreign, agricultural produce, the Northern Ireland farmer had to compete on even terms with his rivals. In order to improve the reputation of his exports, legislation was passed in Northern Ireland with the object of introducing a system of grading. The first measure of this kind dealt with the marketing of eggs, and it came into operation at the beginning of 1925. It provided that all eggs sold in Northern Ireland should be graded in accordance with recognized standards. But there existed a distinct probability that legislation prescribing grading for the export market was, in fact, *ultra vires* under the provisions of the Constituent Act. This was clearly an inequitable restriction upon the powers of the subordinate Government, and it was removed by an Act of Imperial Parliament in 1928. Subsequent to this the Parliament of Northern Ireland regulated the standards to be observed in connection with the Marketing of Agricultural produce. They covered a wide field, and such legislation was applied to the Marketing of Eggs, of Fruit, of Potatoes, of Dairy Produce and of Meat. The principle of all these Acts was similar. They were intended to regulate the quality of all agricultural products exported to the British market. In this way very effective progress has been made in raising the reputation of agricultural produce from Northern Ireland, and thereby rendering it the more saleable.

The significance of this agricultural legislation lies in the fact that it would not have been enacted had not a local Parliament existed in Northern Ireland. Later the Imperial Parliament introduced a system of grading for certain agricultural products in Great Britain, but the scheme was voluntary. Consequently, it was not generally applied. The distinctive feature of the grading legislation in Northern Ireland is that it is compulsory in character and is enforced in the export as well as in the home market. This dual application is of supreme importance in Ulster since it is—unlike Great Britain—a surplus-producing area. The contribution of subordinate Government has proved therefore, within its constitutional limitations, of real value to agriculture in Northern Ireland.

The more recent developments in the agricultural policy of the United Kingdom as a whole provide an excellent illustration of the consequences of Devolution. The differences in agricultural conditions that prevail in Northern Ireland and Great Britain made it desirable that the local Parliament should exercise its powers to secure arrangements suitable to the Northern farmer. In so doing it has accepted the principle, but amended the details, of the later Agricultural Marketing Acts.

Since the report of the Linlithgow Commission in 1923, a series of Government enquiries were carried out in the United Kingdom respecting the methods of marketing agricultural produce. A separate enquiry took place in Northern

Ireland.[1] These enquiries revealed the need for rationalization of agriculture. This the Agricultural Marketing Act of 1931 was intended to achieve by co-ordinating the units of agricultural production under a central marketing board, in order that a common selling policy might be adopted. Similar legislation was not introduced in Northern Ireland on the ground, apparently, that unilateral action by home producers would be ineffective unless coupled with a restriction of foreign imports.[2] In this way it will be seen that the local Government is prepared to take an independent line when it feels the occasion demands.

The National Government, coming into power in 1931, at once indicated its willingness to abandon a policy of free trade in agricultural produce. The first of the Commissions appointed to enquire into particular aspects of the problem was that on pigs and pig products. Its report indicated the need of coupling reorganization with a quantitative control of overseas imports. This in fact was the general policy accepted by the National Government and inaugurated by the Import Duties Act of 1932. There can be no question whatever as to its value to the individual farmer in Northern Ireland. Not only was the market reorganized; not only was the price of certain commodities fixed; not only were subsidies paid on fat cattle and on wheat, but also the stress of foreign competition was removed. Farmers throughout the United Kingdom enjoyed these advantages; the farmer in Northern Ireland had in addition a particular cause of satisfaction. In 1932 penal tariffs were imposed on almost all agricultural produce coming from the Irish Free State. In the circumstances the surprise is not that the new agricultural policy has proved popular in Northern Ireland, but that it has not proved much more popular.

Legislation of the Imperial Parliament effected this revolution

[1] Cf. *The Marketing of Northern Ireland Agricultural Produce*, 1932.
[2] Vide a valuable article in the *Ulster Year Book*, 1935, entitled "The Evolution of Agricultural Policy."

in agricultural conditions. What then was the contribution of the Parliament of Northern Ireland? As one would expect, it is to be found in the *internal* aspect of Mr. Elliot's policy. That is to say the local Parliament has been concerned chiefly with the reorganization of agricultural marketing methods and not with the control of imports—a matter which is outside its authority. But it is worth observing that modification was made in the Import Duties Bill owing to the representations of the Northern Ireland Ministry of Agriculture. In the Bill as introduced imports of maize were subjected to the 10 per cent duty. This would mean a serious increase in expenditure for the many small farmers in Northern Ireland who use maize for feeding their stock—especially pigs. In consequence of the protest maize was placed on the Free List.

Two distinctive contributions of the Northern Government to the reorganization of agriculture may be used to illustrate the merits of local self-governing institutions in the adaptation of complicated measures of this kind. Under the Pig Marketing Scheme in the United Kingdom pig producers are required to contract for the supply of pigs to curers "since irregular production cannot be associated with regular prices."[1] In other words, the producer agrees to supply the curer with a stated number of pigs on a fixed date. In England the practical operation of these provisions frequently places the producer in an awkward quandary. In Northern Ireland it was decided not to adopt the contract system at all.[2] Since practically the entire output of pigs in Northern Ireland is sold for bacon there exists no alternative market—as for fresh pork—and consequently the output of bacon in Northern Ireland corresponds with the total supply of pigs available. In the absence of alternative outlet producers could not contract for the supply of pigs.[3] Secondly, the predominance of small farms in Northern

---

[1] *Report of Reorganization Commission for Pigs and Pig Products*, Ec. Series, No. 37.
[2] The special conditions prevalent in N.I. were recognized by the Commission.   [3] *Ulster Year Book*, ibid.

Ireland would in itself be sufficient to render the contract system unworkable.

The second illustration of the practical value of Devolution in the field of agricultural organization may be taken from the adaptation of the Milk Marketing Act.[1] In England and Wales 70 per cent of the milk produced was absorbed on the liquid milk market and 30 per cent manufactured, whilst in Northern Ireland the relative proportions were almost exactly reversed. Here then obviously existed a case for modifications to meet local needs. And such steps have been taken. They involve negatively the non-adoption of the pooling system as recommended by the Grigg Commission for England and Wales; and positively assistance to the creamery supplier not merely by means of a levy upon liquid milk sales but also by a direct subsidy of £200,000[2] from the Central Exchequer, to supplement the creamery price for milk.

The account we have given of the work of the Ministry of Agriculture of Northern Ireland in its relation to Imperial agricultural policy is not—needless to say—intended to be exhaustive, but merely to indicate the nature of its achievement. After all, in this particular field Northern Ireland does require a treatment different from that of the remainder of the United Kingdom inasmuch as her system of rural economy is in large measure different in type. Thus there is presented a peculiarly favourable sphere for the successful working of Devolution. And, on the whole, the farming community in Northern Ireland acknowledges the reality of its achievement. To a reader with no practical experience of farming a variation of 10 per cent in the price of feeding stuffs for pigs or the method adopted for the sale of milk may appear matters of the utmost triviality. But to farmers they mean a great deal, even though they are admittedly points of detail. In actual importance the independent action of the local Parliament

[1] See *Report of the Reorganization for Milk*, p. 140–41, on the need of co-operation between Great Britain and N.I.
[2] In 1934–35, 1935–36. Vide Milk Act, 1934.

does not bear comparison with that of the Central Government. But it does ensure the success of such legislation by adapting it to particular local needs.

The following figures illustrate the effect of the recent revolution in agricultural policy in Northern Ireland.

	Wheat—Area in Acres	Flax—Area in Acres	Cattle— Number	Pigs— Number	Poultry— Number
1922	6,400	27,500	800,000	118,000	—
1924	5,023	42,838	735,622	139,778	6,814,400
1927	5,952	26,334	697,334	236,285	7,897,500
1931	3,035	7,440	680,649	235,672	8,690,800
1932	3,260	6,093	714,757	219,767	9,370,600
1933	6,158	9,784	733,638	270,565	10,150,100
1934	8,676	15,676	768,536	380,348	10,291,900
1936	6,873	25,377	769,663	521,255	10,569,746

These figures throw an instructive sidelight on the fortunes of farmers in Northern Ireland since 1922, and in addition yield decisive evidence as to the effect of State intervention in agriculture. It will be noticed that an increase in the area under wheat is recorded, since the Wheat Act of 1932 entitled growers to a deficiency payment sufficient to raise the average price of wheat of millable quality, marketed in the United Kingdom, to 10s. per cwt. in respect of 27,000,000 cwts. In 1935 the area under wheat had increased to 9,067 acres—that is almost three times as much as it was in 1931. This constitutes a fitting tribute to the most successful, from the farmers' point of view, of all Mr. Elliot's schemes. On the other hand, the area under wheat is still very small indeed. As a consequence, Northern Ireland in 1935 contributed £191,000 more to the Wheat Fund than her farmers received in deficiency payments.[1] The farmers in Northern Ireland received subsidy payments for fat cattle from the United Kingdom Exchequer amounting in 1934–35 to £216,809. The increase in the number of pigs is most remarkable. In four years it has more than doubled itself. The supreme importance to the practical farmer of the agri-

[1] See Chapter x.

cultural reforms undertaken by the Parliament at Westminster is therefore clear beyond question. But it is also true to say that in Northern Ireland the ground had been well prepared previously by the local Government; and further that Mr. Elliot's reforms would not have secured a like measure of success had not the local Ministry adapted them in detail to suit the rural economy of Northern Ireland. Therefore, one may conclude that in this field Devolution has fulfilled its proper functions to the advantage of the farming community of Northern Ireland.

IN EDUCATION

Education provides an illustration of the work accomplished by the subordinate Government that is different in kind from that which we have examined in Agriculture. For Education, as a whole, is a "transferred" service. So far as Northern Ireland is concerned it is under the complete control of the Ministry of Education, subject only to the general constitutional limitations imposed upon the legislative power of the local Parliament. Consequently, in the field of education we shall find, not the dual legislation that characterized agricultural reform, but only legislation of the subordinate Parliament.

Already the words of Lord Craigavon as to the necessity of a reconstruction of the educational system in 1922 have been quoted. He said: "It is admitted on all sides that our educational system in the North is not one that can be even amended, but one that requires to be rooted out of the soil in order that we may begin to plant a new fabric."[1] Almost immediately a Committee was appointed under the chairmanship of Mr. (now Sir Robert) Lynn to enquire generally into the administration of education in Northern Ireland. Upon the Report of the Committee was framed the Education Act of 1923—perhaps the most significant single legislative achievement of the Northern Parliament. The need for reform was certainly pressing, but action was taken without a very full considera-

[1] *N.I., H. of C. Debates*, vol. i, cols. 173-4.

tion of all the more controversial problems involved. As a consequence, experience has already suggested no fewer than five amending Acts.[1] The general intentions of the original Act, which was introduced by the then Minister of Education—the Marquis of Londonderry—on March 14, 1923, are clear. They involved the delegation of a large measure of educational authority to the County and County Borough Councils, thereby establishing the principle of democratic control for the first time in Irish educational administration; a general supervision of educational services as a whole by the newly created Ministry; the provision of religious instruction in all public elementary schools; the strict enforcement of school attendance and increased facilities whereby promising children may continue their education after the age of fourteen. The decentralization of educational authority has resulted in an amalgamation of some of the smaller schools and the provision of large well-equipped modern schools in their place. In intention the provisions of the Act were commendable, and their application has done a great deal to improve the quality of education in Northern Ireland. There has been a much needed improvement in school attendance, a steady increase in the number of pupils attending secondary schools, and a general expansion of technical education.[2] On the other hand, the standard of education in Northern Ireland does not compare favourably with that in Great Britain. This is particularly true in rural districts. Many small isolated schools still survive and work is carried on frequently with quite inadequate staffs. An interesting sidelight on the position is thrown by the fact that, on an average, more than four-fifths of the State scholarships at the Queen's University are awarded each year to pupils from industrial areas.

The Act of 1923 aroused a storm of religious controversy.

---

[1] Passed in 1925, 1928, 1930, 1931, and 1935 respectively.
[2] The number of pupils attending technical schools has increased from 20,000 in 1925 to 23,000 in 1934. In secondary schools in the same period from 8,000 to 13,000.

A fortnight after the introduction of the Bill in 1923, the Catholic Bishops of Northern Ireland declared in a manifesto that "the proposed schools are impossible for our children." Their opposition was aroused by the nature of the provisions for "simple Bible teaching." At the same time, the leaders of the Presbyterians and of the Church of Ireland demanded that the appointment of teachers in transferred schools should be delegated to representatives of the parents or trustees acting with nominees of the Education Authority. For a considerable period the Act gave rise to keen controversy between the Ministry and the representatives of the two Protestant Churches. The grievances of the latter now appear to be satisfied, but the Roman Catholics remain acquiescent rather than content.

The need for educational reform in Northern Ireland in 1921 was unquestionable. But under centralized Government its enactment would certainly have been long deferred. The existence of subordinate self-government was therefore valuable in that it enabled a radical reform to be carried through with a minimum of delay. This gain was in small part counterbalanced by the loss of the impartiality customarily associated with Central Government in matters arousing strong local feeling.

IN LABOUR AND UNEMPLOYMENT RELIEF

The Ministry of Labour is the largest of the departments established in 1921. Its duties cover a wide field. It is responsible amongst other things for the administration of industrial regulations, of trade boards, of the factory and workshop code, of workmen's compensation, of the employment exchanges, of unemployment insurance, of old-age pensions, of widows' and orphans' pensions, and of various employment services in the nature of relief schemes. In addition the Ministry exercises a partial control over National Health Insurance. In normal times the administration of these duties would present a complicated task. In times of depression, such as Northern Ireland has experienced, these duties appear formidable indeed. The extent of unemployment in Northern Ireland is illustrated by the following table giving the percentage of persons unemployed within each trade group in recent years.[1]

Trade Group	Percentage of Persons Unemployed			
	1930	1931	1933	1934
Building	27·2	35·2	39·3	36·6
Distributive	17·4	19·5	19·1	18·8
Flax, Linen and Hemp ..	32·4	28·6	20·5	17·4
Food and Drink	17·5	16·5	16·0	15·8
Shipbuilding and Engineering	19·8	45·1	57·1	37·1
Tailoring and Dress	24·6	28·8	24·9	26·0

It will be seen that unemployment in the building trade has not improved; in the linen industry, although showing a steady diminution it is still serious, whilst in 1933 the percentage of unemployment in shipbuilding reached alarming proportions. In general the figures indicate the severity of the economic crisis in Northern Ireland.

The policy of the local Ministry of Labour has been uniform throughout the period of its existence. Its character is described in the following speech by Mr. Andrews, who has been Minister of Labour since 1921. In 1932 he defined the aims of his Department:[2]

"May I say that the general policy remains what it has always been, namely, that in connection with these four great social services which my Department is charged with the responsibility of dealing with, to remain in step or in parity with Great Britain. That was the policy which the Government decided upon when we took over our powers more than 10 years ago, and from that policy we have never varied either as regards administration or legislation."

[1] Taken from the *Ulster Year Book*, 1935.
[2] *N.I., H. of C. Debates*, vol. xiv, cols. 945–46.

This is a clear and accurate statement of the policy that has been pursued. The work of the Local Government in this field has been done in administration, not in the enactment of original legislation. It is a policy that has occasioned two main criticisms. On the one hand it is claimed that a comparatively poor province as Northern Ireland cannot afford social services on the scale adopted in Great Britain; and on the other that the Ministry is not doing sufficient to meet the necessities of the local situation .There was a certain amount of substance in both criticisms, though the first has been answered by the Unemployment Reinsurance Agreement, under which Great Britain covers expenditure, as a whole, on unemployment. The second criticism cannot be pressed home since the subordinate Government does not enjoy financial powers sufficient to support a new departure in social policy. Such discretion as the Ministry may exercise has been confined to relief schemes. Such schemes have been undertaken on a small scale by the majority of the County Councils from monies provided by the Local Parliament. A special grant of £300,000 was made by the Government of the United Kingdom to be used for relief schemes in Belfast. Further Government assistance has been authorized by the Local Parliament for the making of grants to enable sites for new industries to be acquired.[1] But in general, the Local Government is not in a position to effect, even if it so desired, a radical reform of labour and unemployment policy. State provision for the assistance of unemployed persons in Northern Ireland must remain identical in all essentials with that of Great Britain.

The distinctive contribution of the subordinate Government in Labour and in Unemployment policy is therefore administrative. Within this limited sphere the work of the Ministry in generally reckoned to have been valuable in securing prompt attention to local grievances and needs.

[1] Vide Industrial Development Act (N.I.), 1932.

THE VALUE OF DEVOLUTION

It is not possible in a study of this kind to analyse the effect of a grant of Devolution in every aspect of social and economic life in Northern Ireland. But a review of its consequences in Agriculture, in Education, and in Labour policy gives a clear conception of the nature of its distinctive contribution. In Agriculture it has been the principal function of the subordinate legislature to standardize the quality of agricultural products and to adapt legislation of the Imperial Parliament to suit the particular rural economy predominant in Northern Ireland; in Education the subordinate legislature has carried through a radical programme of reconstruction; in Unemployment it has accepted in its entirety the policy of the Imperial Government, thus confining itself to purely administrative work. These three instances bring into relief three different aspects of the work of the Local Government, namely, its adaptation in detail of the legislation of the Central Parliament, its legislation on matters of internal importance and its work in administration. These functions are stated in descending order of importance. It may appear paradoxical to claim that adaptation is more significant than initiation or administration, yet in this particular instance such is the case. Administrative functions can be executed by the Central Government without any notable loss in efficiency, radical reforms for special areas can be undertaken by the Central Parliament even though there is a prospect of delay, but the adaptation of legislation to suit local needs is a task for which only a local legislature is properly equipped. It is no mere chance that has marked out for notable success the agricultural policy of the Northern Government, for in that field it possessed an admirable opportunity for the exercise of its most characteristic asset.

If we are correct in supposing that the adaptation of legislative details constitutes the most valuable contribution of Devolution to government, then the affinity popularly believed to exist between Devolution and *laissez-faire* liberalism is groundless.

U

Devolution was advocated so strongly by various Liberal statesmen in the early years of the century that it has acquired by contact the slightly *démodè* air that clings to the relics of the Liberal Party. It is regarded as a reform, no doubt admirable in the days before State intervention attained its present dimensions, but one which would now prove but an additional bulwark to reactionary individualism in the Celtic fringe. But, in fact, local legislatures—unless given much wider powers than these delegated to Northern Ireland—would be quite unable to check the purpose of central legislation. They would not enjoy the opportunity of reclining in indolent inactivity while some local pundit

> Like Cato gives his little Senate laws
> And sits attentive to his own applause.

On this point the evidence of Northern Ireland is conclusive, for the Government there have always possessed strong *laissez-faire* sympathies, and yet have marched step by step with Great Britain in the application of the social and economic legislation of the last fifteen years. Indeed, the adaptation of the Agricultural Marketing Acts suggests that the existence of a subordinate Government facilitates the effective application of complex economic reforms. Therein, certainly, has lain the greatest contribution of the Local Government to the ordinary citizens of Northern Ireland. It may appear a small contribution by which to justify its existence. Perhaps it is. But on the other hand, the satisfaction of the ordinary needs of the ordinary citizen is the most important—Chesterton would have said the only important—task of government. Therefore in so far as the Government of Northern Ireland accomplishes this function then it does not lack a *raison d'être*.

CHAPTER XIV

CONCLUSION

THE INTERACTION OF POLITICS AND CONSTITUTIONAL THOUGHT

THE grant of Devolution to Northern Ireland was the product of two quite distinct motives—the one constitutional and the other political. Local self-government by the component parts of the United Kingdom had been advocated for many years previous to 1920 as constituting in itself a most desirable administrative reform. But it is highly improbable that a radical decentralization of government could have been effected under any guise had not its claims been reinforced by a practical issue of extreme urgency. In 1920 the political motive for Devolution was obviously predominant. But constitutional thought had not been entirely uninfluential. The Coalition Government had to find an escape from the Ulster predicament. They snatched at the opening offered by a grant of Devolution, simply because many years of discussion had familiarized statesmen with its constitutional implications. The reform was prompted by political considerations, but it was remembered that weighty constitutional reasons had been advanced in calmer moments to support the adoption of an identical measure. The immediate cause of action was political, but it was built upon a foundation that constitutional thought had planned.

This dual source of inspiration had always been latent in the demand for Devolution, but it is only within the last thirty years that the exact balance between them has become apparent. In the speech in which Mr. Asquith introduced the third Home Rule Bill in 1912, he described the Bill "as only the first step in a larger and more comprehensive policy" which would eventually give to the other component parts of the United Kingdom the same freedom to deal with their local affairs and thus release the Imperial Parliament to fulfil its duties to the whole country and to the Empire. Speaking of the existing parliamentary conditions he declared:

"I do not exaggerate when I say that if you were to sit continuously during the whole twelve months of the year, and worked through them with unremitting ardour and assiduity, you would find at the end not only that there are still large arrears of legislation which it had not even been attempted to overtake, not only enormous sums raised by taxation, whose appropriation had never been discussed[1], but that there were vast areas of Empire—I do not speak of the self-governing Dominions—for which we are still directly responsible as trustees, to whose concerns we had not been able to afford so much as one single night. . . . What we are doing now we should do with the distinct and direct purpose of the fuller and further applications of the principle. . . . Home Rule in this larger sense, in my opinion, rests upon necessities, is demanded by the responsibilities, and is indeed due to the honour of the Imperial Parliament."[2]

This speech is a very explicit statement of the intention of the Prime Minister to use the Home Rule Bill as a starting-point for a general scheme of Devolution. As we know now this policy was not fulfilled. In part the failure was due to unforeseen developments in the Irish Question. Home Rule for Ireland was still-born; so the possibility of extending it to other parts of the United Kingdom never arose in the particular form anticipated by Mr. Asquith. But had the proposals for Devolution contained in themselves a distinctive source of vitality then the climax of the Irish Question would have done no more than delay their adoption. Inasmuch as the character of the Irish settlement proved a death-blow to any prospect of immediate all-round Devolution, so it is clear that Mr. Asquith and his contemporaries failed to realize the extent to which their proposals for Devolution were inspired

---

[1] In 1910 £52,615,286 were voted without a single word of debate; in 1911 £67,046,752. Vide *Round Table*, vol. ii, 1911.

[2] Quoted in Spender and Asquith, op. cit., vol. ii, p. 16.

by an exclusively Irish problem. When the immediate issues of that problem were solved then Devolution was relegated to complete obscurity in day-to-day politics. In 1914 the measure of the dependence of proposals for Devolution upon the motive force of Irish politics was clearly underestimated. In retrospect, however, one is liable to reckon it complete. *Post hoc propter hoc* here provides an explanation that is the more tempting in that it is substantially accurate. But there did exist a distinct demand, quite untrammelled by Nationalist pretensions, for a decentralization of government. Its advocates claimed that it provided the natural check to the progressive concentration of political and administrative power. Its practical influence has been indirect. A decline in the vitality of this constitutional reform coincided with the decline in the fortunes of the Liberal Party. Certainly it was a policy peculiarly in accord with the Liberal outlook, and its practical realization under the ægis of a Conservative or Labour Government is not easy to imagine.[1]

DEVOLUTION AND THE CENTRAL GOVERNMENT

Mr. Asquith, in company with the large majority of the advocates of Devolution, was concerned almost entirely with the benefits likely to accrue to the Central Government from its adoption. The experiment in Northern Ireland, whose features we have analysed, is on too limited a scale to yield conclusive evidence on this point. But such evidence as it does afford suggests emphatically that Mr. Asquith was right in his supposition. The amount of time now spent in discussing the affairs of Northern Ireland at Westminster is negligible. This saving is apparent not only in the more formal business of the House but also at question time. In administration the relief afforded to the Central Government is equally clear. Only a small section of the Home Office is needed to cope

[1] Though Labour members have supported strongly the programme for Scottish Home Rule.

with the affairs of Northern Ireland, and the work to be accomplished by this special section has diminished steadily since 1925. In the event of a grant of Devolution to a larger area, as Scotland, a proportionately greater relief to the Central Government would be afforded. The existence of the Scottish Office might be terminated, the Cabinet reduced in size and the burden of work on the House of Commons materially lightened. On the whole, therefore, an analysis of government in Northern Ireland leads one to conclude that federal Devolution would be effective in diminishing the work of the Central Government.

So far as the House of Commons is concerned this advantage would be offset by non-attendance of members, unless the practice of dual membership were disallowed. Until 1929 it was customary for members of the Imperial House of Commons for Ulster constituencies to be, in addition, members of the House of Commons of Northern Ireland. As the sessions of the latter for the most part coincided with those at Westminster, non-attendance in one or the other House was rendered inevitable. Since 1929 it has been the declared policy of the Ulster Unionist Party that its candidates should not seek election for more than one House. This party normally returns 11 of the 13 Ulster members to Westminster, so its pronouncement has virtually settled the issue so far as Northern Ireland is concerned. One difficulty is thereby solved, but its solution creates another. For Northern Ireland now experiences a distinct scarcity of candidates suitable for election to the two Parliaments. In larger self-governing units this difficulty would tend to assume considerable proportions. It might be evaded either by the creation of a unicameral legislature or by holding the sessions of the local Parliament during the summer and winter recess. By the latter means relief is afforded to the parliamentary time-table, but not to members. They would have to, in Mr. Asquith's phrase, work "with unremitting ardour and assiduity" throughout the year.

THE OVERRIDING IMPORTANCE OF LOCAL SENTIMENT

If an analysis of self-government in Belfast, owing to its limited application, makes possible no final conclusion upon the consequences to the Imperial Parliament of a grant of federal Devolution, yet it is singularly revealing with regard to the probable effects in the self-governing areas. Since the latter constitute by far the more vital aspect of Devolution such evidence is extremely valuable.

The experience of half a century has shown that it is idle to contemplate a grant of Devolution under modern conditions unless it be demanded by the areas concerned. Speaking in the Scottish Home Rule Debate of 1889, Mr. Gladstone clearly implied that the initiative should lie with the component parts of the British Isles. He said:

"I cannot deny the title of Scotland to make such a claim (for Home Rule). Moreover . . . I have a perfectly sound conviction that if such a claim were made . . . as the clear and deliberate declaration of Scottish opinion, Parliament would accede to it . . . I hold that all judicious Devolution which hands over to subordinate bodies duties for which they are better qualified by local knowledge, and which at the same time sets free the hands of Parliament for its proper business, does not weaken it, but strengthens it, gives vitality to it . . ."

Mr. Gladstone recognized that a grant of Devolution to Scotland would possess the incidental advantage of facilitating the work of Parliament, but he did not contemplate a drastic decentralization of government when no local demand existed. This very proper perspective was destroyed in the interactions of Anglo-Irish politics. In order to assimilate the distinctive national claims of Ireland to a general demand for better government in the component parts of the United Kingdom, Mr. Joseph Chamberlain put forward proposals for Home-Rule-All-Round. His policy, though promoted by ephemeral considerations, was nevertheless accepted, perhaps without any profound conviction, by the majority of English statesmen for the next thirty years. The ultimate outcome was the Conference on Devolution, appointed in 1920, to consider the value of Devolution to the *Central* Government. Its report was indecisive, and it did not encourage the Government to act upon its recommendations. Mr. Speaker Lowther (later Lord Ullswater), who presided, has described the atmosphere that prevailed at the Conference: "The discussions," he wrote, "had been of great interest, as they raised recondite and sometimes difficult questions of constitutional lore and law, but all along I felt that they were academic rather than practical, and that the driving force of necessity, which had been so active a force in the Electoral Reform Conference, was absent."[1] At the time the Conference assembled the Government had decided on separate treatment for Ireland, so in fact there existed no strong local demand for any form of self-government. Such as there was in Scotland or Wales was excluded from the consideration of the Conference by the implication of their terms of reference. Thus the record of the Conference remains to guide any who would attempt such reform in the future. Its lesson is this—even if the principle of Devolution of government be accepted, its practical realization can be effected *only* at the wish of the localities.

Such demand as now exists for an extension of the principle of self-government comes from Scotland and Wales, and is founded partly on national sentiment and partly on a desire for improved local administration. The former is of sufficient strength as to render a scheme of regional Devolution totally unacceptable in Scotland. The publications of the Nationalist parties indeed are utterly contemptuous of "this form of political materialism that despises the spiritual and ideal elements of national life . . ."[2] and with some justification. For Devolution by economic regions implies an artificial division of the United Kingdom in accordance with a plan prepared and enforced

---

[1] *A Speaker's Commentaries*, vol. ii, p. 271.

[2] *Home Rule for Scotland*, a Publication of the Scottish Home Rule Association.

by the Central Government, and so involves once again an absence of local determination as to the desirability of such decentralization. At the present time the Scottish Standing Committee, consisting of all Scottish members and about fifteen others, exists for the purpose of giving special consideration to Scottish affairs. The practice was originated by the Liberal Government in 1894 and was placed on a permanent basis in 1907. All Scottish Public Bills are referred to this Committee, where a discussion on detail may take place amongst members possessing a specialized knowledge. Since its decisions are in no sense final it follows that, on the one hand the value of these discussions is not very great, and on the other that there is no saving in parliamentary time comparable to that achieved by Devolution on the Ulster model.[1] But the very existence of such a Committee is a tacit admission of the need for some form of Devolution for Scotland. The success of the Scottish Board of Agriculture confirms the existence of such a need in certain branches of administration.

The various sections of the Scottish Nationalist Party demand full legislative and fiscal independence for Scotland. For example, the Government of Scotland Bill introduced in the House of Commons in 1927[2] suggests "a single chamber Parliament dealing with Scottish affairs which shall have *sovereign* power to make laws for the peace, order, and good government of Scotland." It was proposed that representation at Westminster should cease. Such a form of government would approximate more closely to Dominion status than to Devolution. Elections in Scotland show that the main body of Scottish opinion does not support so radical a change in the structure of government. But it is probable that a more moderate measure of Devolution, in accordance with the principle of the Northern Ireland experiment, might secure very serious consideration both in Scotland and in Wales.

[1] Vide *Conference on Devolution Report*, pp. 28–9, for a detailed analysis of time spent in Parliament, Cmd. 692.
[2] Bill 172, 16 & 17 Geo. V.

At first sight it appears paradoxical to conclude upon the overriding importance of local sentiment in this question and then to recall that the Prime Minister of the one existing local legislature described the acceptance of Devolution as "the supreme sacrifice" made by Ulster in the interests of peace. But, in fact, the contradiction is not real, since the people of Northern Ireland confirmed this "sacrifice" by exercising their privilege of "opting out" of the all-Ireland Parliament under the terms of the Anglo-Irish Treaty. In this way the province decided to continue subordinate self-government within its area. It may be argued that the choice which confronted Northern Ireland in 1922 was not very real. That, of course, must be admitted. But Devolution in Northern Ireland is, none the less, quite unmistakably the consequence of local conditions and local politics. That it appeared unattractive as a form of government to Ulster Unionist party in 1920 does not alter the fact that it came into being on account of local sentiment.

THE DISTRIBUTION OF POWERS

The measure of authority to be delegated to the Parliament of Northern Ireland was not decided on constitutional grounds. The Act of 1920 was designed to formulate a scheme of government for Ireland as a whole. Its provisions therefore were dictated with a view to political pacification rather than administrative efficiency. When Southern Ireland broke away from British rule the Act was amended in form so as to be rendered applicable to Northern Ireland alone. But it was not amended in substance. As a consequence powers were delegated to Northern Ireland which had been drafted to meet a quite different situation. No regard was paid to the needs of the six counties as a political and economic unit. This lack of special consideration might well have proved a more serious handicap upon the success of the experiment than in fact it has. Its outcome is to be seen in the distinction drawn between "excepted" and "reserved" matters. The "reserved" matters, it will be remembered, were to be administered by the Imperial Parliament only until "the date of Irish Union." Since that date is unlikely to occur in the immediate future, the *status quo* has become the accepted system of government. "Reserved" matters, including the Supreme Court and the Post Office, are therefore administered from Whitehall as the result, not of a conscious endeavour to plan a rational distribution of powers as between central and local authority, but rather of a historical incident. The atmosphere in which the Act of 1920 was originally drafted, and in which it was later amended, was certainly most unfavourable to the inauguration of a complex constitutional experiment. In the event of any later decentralization in the government of the United Kingdom, the experience acquired in Northern Ireland would provide a valuable criterion by which to decide the measure of the authority that should properly be delegated to a subordinate Parliament. In general, the powers conferred upon the Government of Northern Ireland have proved insufficient to ensure an adequate measure of final responsibility in Belfast. This criticism is especially relevant in the realm of finance. Moreover, in a larger area possessing a more balanced economy than Northern Ireland there would exist an initial presumption in favour of a wider delegation of authority.

THE DISTINCTIVE CHARACTER OF THE ULSTER EXPERIMENT

In considering the desirability of a measure of federal Devolution for the United Kingdom in the light of the fifteen years' experience afforded by the Ulster experiment, one is struck at once by the individuality of the case. It is dangerous to deduce unqualified generalizations from a highly particularized experiment. It is frankly incredible that circumstances resembling those that have prevailed and now prevail in Ulster would be reproduced elsewhere. Yet the very functioning of self-government in Belfast has been conditioned by this historical and political background more than by any other influence. From the first the experiment was handicapped by a quite incidental distribution of executive and legislative power. That handicap would be unlikely to appear in any later grant of Devolution elsewhere. Its existence in the Constitution of Northern Ireland has demanded at times a large measure of co-operation and goodwill between the Imperial and local Government in order to prevent a collapse of the whole experiment. For these reasons it is essential to bear in mind the particular disadvantages, as opposed to the particular advantages, under which Devolution in Northern Ireland had functioned, before concluding on the desirability of a more general application of this form of decentralized government.

The disadvantages loom large. Northern Ireland is not in any sense a natural economic or administrative unit. It comprises, not an historic nation bounded by a traditional frontier as Scotland or Wales, but only the six north-eastern counties of a province of Ireland marked off from the remainder of the country by a straggling, entirely artificial land frontier. It is a political creation designed to answer the necessities of a pressing political problem. Administrative and economic convenience could not be taken into account since it would demand the incorporation of the six counties with the remainder of Ireland.

The virulence of sectarian feeling, especially in the larger towns of Northern Ireland, shows but few signs of abatement. The intensity with which it survives confronts the subordinate Government, responsible as it is for the maintenance of law and order, with a task of no little difficulty. The problem is rendered the more acute by the almost complete identification of political with sectarian divisions. The Government of the day is thereby tempted to discourage its extremist supporters, if at all, then only to the extent that respectability demands.

There is also a political problem. Parties in Ulster are well-nigh irreconcilable; and thus there is imposed upon the subordinate Government the most fatal burden that can encumber democratic institutions. The Ulster Unionist—quite apart from flag-waving politicians—feels a deep loyalty toward the Throne. He prizes the connection with England on sentimental quite as much as on material grounds. It may be that in the past the Union brought very real advantages to the Ulster industrialist; and certainly to-day the Unionist does not under-estimate the importance of the British market. But the benefits derived from a complete fiscal union were obviously greater in the high tide of *laissez-faire* expansion than in this age of economic nationalism. Yet a diminution of material prosperity does not lessen the measure of Unionist loyalty. So many Irish Unionists—drawn not merely from Ulster but from every corner of Ireland—have devoted their lives to the service of the Crown, have won distinction in the administration, in the political life, in the fighting services of the United King-dom, that now it were hard indeed to sever the link. So many illustrious names are inscribed on the Unionist roll of honour that a tradition has grown up which no mere decline in material fortune could overthrow. Then, on the other hand, there are the Nationalists. In 1919 their parties carried all but a tiny minority of constituencies in the whole of Ireland. Dáil Eireann assembled and proclaimed Irish independence. In the years that followed there were moments when it seemed as though the final ambitions of Nationalist Ireland were to be realized. But it was not to be. The South secured virtual independence. But the achievement was marred by Partition. The dream of Tone, of Davis, of Pearse, had been well-nigh fulfilled—save in one disastrous respect. Ireland might be free, but it was not united. Despite denunciations of the trickery of the British Government, the awkward fact remained. The South was conscious of the injustice but soon reconciled itself to a *modus vivendi*. But the Nationalists within the six counties, small in numbers, forming a permanent minority in an area determined by Unionist policy, were placed under the rule of their hereditary opponents. The position to them appeared desperate; and this led them into innumerable tactical errors. They refused to recognize the "Partition" Government. It was not till 1925 that Mr. Devlin and a few of his colleagues took their seats in the Legislature, and to this day the Republicans abstain. The edge of former bitterness may be blunted a little now, but Nationalists are not, nor ever will be, reconciled to a divided Ireland.

> Was it for this the wild geese spread
> The grey wing upon every tide;
> For this that all that blood was shed,
> For this Edward Fitzgerald died,
> And Robert Emmet and Wolfe Tone,
> And all that delirium of the brave?

As the Unionist is bound to Great Britain by links stronger "than bars of gold," so too the Nationalist is bound to Ireland by every tie of race and blood.

The aims of the respective parties are therefore irreconcilable. The gulf that divides is not made any the narrower by the memory of the innumerable political executions that took place in Ireland from 1916 onwards. Nor has the Unionist Government done anything to reassure the minority. Indeed, the abolition of Proportional Representation, commonly regarded as an integral feature of the settlement of 1920, revived the most profound distrust of its intentions. The existence of these political divisions constitutes a very severe handicap upon the experiment of Devolution in Belfast. When politics are viewed from the narrow window of an age-old conflict; when social and economic life is congealed by icy gusts of sectarian bitterness; when generosity of feeling must always give way to party interest, then a position is created in which men of first-class brains are not trusted and men of second-class brains have not the vision to see beyond the prejudices which history has formed around them. Should a similar decentralization of government be adopted either in Scotland or Wales it would have a far better chance of enduring success inasmuch as a measure of fundamental agreement as to the form of government would prevail between the various parties.

The particular disadvantages under which self-government operates in Northern Ireland are offset to some small degree by two particular advantages, the one incidental and the other general. The former is enjoyed by virtue of the political situation. The British Government, no matter what party be in office, is most unwilling to see the Irish Question once more in state of flux. Should self-government in Northern Ireland break down this will obviously occur. So the Government of the United Kingdom is anxious to do all in its power to establish the experiment upon a secure foundation. Its anxiety on this point has not escaped notice at Belfast. Thus the subordinate Government is in a position to exert a very real pressure at Westminster by judicious diplomacy. When Mr. Campbell, the Nationalist leader, congratulated Mr. Pollock, the Minister of Finance, upon securing an additional half a million from the British Exchequer for the Northern Ireland Unemployment Fund in February 1936, he said, "there is no Irishman North or South but desires to get as much British revenue as possible." The remark is unduly cynical, but it is reckoned very proper in Ulster that the Imperial Government should pay with some liberality for the convenience of a self-governing Ireland. The second advantage is to be found in the Ulster character. The people of that province lack neither a capacity for genuine hard work nor a determination to bring a difficult task to a successful conclusion. Hitherto a proper interest in the art of democratic self-government has not been aroused. But should their enthusiasm be awakened, then one could feel confident that an intelligent and practical solution would be found even for the more exceptional difficulties that confront constitutional government in Ulster.

THE ACHIEVEMENT OF DEVOLUTION

One may conclude, therefore, that whatever merits Devolution has displayed in Northern Ireland would be multiplied elsewhere. For the disadvantages under which it functions may reasonably be supposed to be greater than any it would encounter in other parts of the United Kingdom. The actual achievement of Devolution in Northern Ireland (which we summarized in the last chapter) is not dramatic or in any way sensational. But it has done something to improve administration, and it has secured the enactment of legislation which could not have passed the Imperial Parliament owing to lack of time. Her self-government is a government of local affairs, but this has proved of advantage in that local conditions can be appraised, local needs can be met more easily and more quickly than would be possible under centralized government. In addition, the recent revolution in the agricultural policy of the United Kingdom has shown that the existence of subordinate self-government facilitates the adaptation of a wide programme of radical reconstruction in order to suit it to a rural economy different in type from that of the larger political unit. This is a distinctive and important contribution to the solution of one of the fundamental problems of modern government.

GENERAL CONSIDERATIONS ON CERTAIN ASPECTS OF DEVOLUTION

Mr. Speaker Lowther was once described as the "ordinary man" possessing "ordinary qualities in an extraordinary degree." If this is so, then it is of particular interest to observe his objections to the proposal, put forward at the Conference on Devolution, for subordinate legislatures in England, Scotland, and Wales, similar in type to that now functioning in Northern Ireland. He wrote:[1]

"The more I considered the proposal of one supreme and four independent legislatures the less I liked it. The confusions that might arise, the multiplicity of elections, the novelty of five Prime Ministers and Cabinets of probably divergent political views, the enormous expense of building four new

[1] Op. cit., vol. ii, p. 269.

sets of Parliament Buildings and Government Offices and providing all the paraphernalia of administration frightened my economical soul. . . ."

The working of Devolution, with a subordinate legislature established in Belfast, reinforces the conclusion that is to be deduced from Canadian experience, in suggesting that Mr. Lowther was mistaken in his belief that the existence of independent Legislatures and Cabinets within the British Isles would lead necessarily either to conflict or to confusion. With good will and a determination to work the experiment, differences in political outlook may be quite easily adjusted. Since the Unionist Government of Northern Ireland has been in power at Belfast it has had relations with Coalition, Labour, Conservative, and National Governments. It was actually a Labour Government that engaged in the somewhat delicate preliminary negotiations regarding the Boundary in 1924; and it was a Labour Government that drafted the second Miscellaneous Provisions Act in 1931 at the wish of the Ulster Government. In both instances the final stages were transacted by a Conservative or National Government. But the incidents are instructive and go far to disprove Mr. Speaker Lowther's contention. Likewise the fear that Devolution would mean administrative or legislative confusion has been shown to be entirely groundless. Very considerable care has been taken at Stormont to ensure that the powers devolved shall not be exceeded; but for the rest the operation of two distinct legislatures and administrations within the same area has raised no problems insoluble by co-operation and good-will. A sidelight upon the harmony that has been attained in this field is thrown by the fact that only two cases involving the validity of orders or of legislation enacted by the Parliament of Northern Ireland have hitherto been brought before the Courts.

The spectacle of self-government in Belfast, however, does nothing whatever to reassure persons with "economical souls," likely to be frightened by expenditure on local institutions. Stormont, a gift of the British Government, is as elaborate in political conception as it is simple in architectural design. Then again the salaries paid to the higher executive officers of the local Government are not suggestive of strict economy. Cabinet Ministers, unlike the guards of the Caliph of Bagdad, have no reason to complain that:

> . . . our emoluments are infinitesimal.

But then it does not follow that heavy expenditure in Northern Ireland means heavy expenditure in Scotland or in Wales. In matters of this kind much is bound to depend on the outlook of those who control the subordinate Government.

AN ESTIMATE OF ITS VALUE

A decentralization of government undertaken at the expressed wish of the people in the area concerned has obvious attractions. Experience in Northern Ireland has proved that Devolution is a practical form of government under modern conditions. In addition it has suggested that such a reform in government both enlarges the scope for local initiative and achieves a more prompt satisfaction of local needs. All the problems that arise in the modern State are obviously not central problems, and experience in Northern Ireland has shown that a very proper decision on issues of local incidence may be made by a subordinate legislature enjoying reasonably wide powers. Further, it has proved that neither confusion in administration, nor conflict between central and local Parliament, even though they be of differing political complexions, is a necessary consequence of Devolution. Local self-government in Northern Ireland has been somewhat extravagant, but that extravagance does appear incidental to, rather than inherent in, the particular form of government. On the other hand, a satisfactory financial relationship, capable of general application, has not yet been established as between the central and local Parliament. Nor is it possible to refute the objection[1] frequently raised—that

---

[1] E.g. Laski, *Grammar of Politics*, p. 413.

local institutions of this type tend to encourage a retrograde outlook and to foster the growth of vested interests; for on neither of these points has experience in Northern Ireland proved reassuring.

It is idle to expect dramatic results from any grant of Devolution. But an analysis of government in Northern Ireland encourages the belief that under reasonably favourable political and economic conditions it would prove a most valuable constitutional reform. The experiment in Northern Ireland has involved extra expenditure in the work of government. But it were narrow indeed to condemn it on that ground alone. For the existence of a local Parliament has brought the realities of constitutional government very close to the people of Northern Ireland. Thereby it is awakening a new interest in the art of government and a sense of public obligation that did not exist before. The first practical trial of Devolution in the United Kingdom has taken place under conditions that weighted the scales against its success. Yet its achievements are by no means insignificant. In an age when Democracy itself is passing through the gravest crisis in its history, Devolution has shown that it has a most welcome contribution to make, by nourishing in a large and populous State that superabundant vitality which Democracy displayed in the heyday of its triumph.

APPENDIX

LIST OF AUTHORITIES

No book has been published in the British Isles dealing with the question of Devolution either in its theoretical or its practical aspect, though reference to the issues involved by a grant of Devolution are to be found in various works on government in the United Kingdom. The names of the books in which such references—usually of a rather summary character—do appear are noted below in so far as they shed any real light upon the question. A study entitled *Devolution in Great Britain*, by Wan-Hauan Chiao, was published in the U.S.A. in 1925. The experiment in Northern Ireland is specifically excluded from the scope of the author's enquiry. He analyses in some detail the probable consequences of Devolution upon the Central Government. The Conference on Devolution provides the most valuable evidence, even though the Report as a whole does not carry conviction.

In respect of government in Northern Ireland we find again that no book has been published dealing with the functioning of any aspect of this experiment in Devolution. Consequently, the evidence I have collected is derived largely either from personal information or from various official and parliamentary publications. Of the latter, the more important are listed either under General Authorities or under the chapters to whose contents they are especially relevant. It is to be observed that the *Ulster Year Books*, which are published by H.M. Stationery Office at intervals of about four years, contain much valuable information in respect of the work of the subordinate Government at Belfast in a readily accessible form. Attention should also be drawn to another publication of the Stationery Office, namely, the *Constitution of Northern Ireland* (2 vols.) by Sir Arthur Quekett, who is Parliamentary Draftsman to the Government of Northern Ireland. The first volume of this work traces the legal development of the Constitution of Northern Ireland. The second volume, which is much longer, sets forth with valuable annotations the actual text of the constitutional enactments.

GENERAL AUTHORITIES

Public General Acts.
Parliamentary Debates—Official Reports.
The Annual Register—from 1885.

CHAPTER II

C. K. Allen. Bureaucracy Triumphant. Oxford, 1927.
W. Bagehot. The English Constitution. London, 1878.
The Works of Jeremy Bentham, edited by Bowring.
L. Curtis. Civitas Dei. London, 1934.
A. V. Dicey. The Law of the Constitution. London 1908.
R. von Gneist. Student's History of the English Parliament. London, 1889.
E. Halevé. The Growth of Philosophic Radicalism. London, 1934.
H. Macmillan. Reconstruction. London, 1934.
F. W. Maitland. A Constitutional History of England. Cambridge, 1909.
    Introduction to Gierke; Political Theory of the Middle Ages. Cambridge, 1900.
J. S. Mill. Autobiography, Utilitarianism and Representative Government. London, 1873 and 1865.
J. Redlich. The Procedure of the House of Commons, 3 vols. London, 1908.
    Local Government in England, 2 vols. London, 1902.
Bertrand Russell. Freedom and Organization, 1814–1914. London, George Allen & Unwin Ltd., 1934.
G. M. Young. Early Victorian England, 2 vols. Oxford, 1934.
Report of the Committee on Finance and Industry. Cmd. 3897, 1931.

CHAPTER III

Lady G. Cecil. Lord Salisbury, 4 vols. London, 1921–32.
W. S. Churchill. Lord Randolph Churchill, 2 vols. London, 1906.
R. C. K. Ensor. England 1870–1914. Oxford, 1936.
St. J. Ervine. Parnell. London, 1925.
J. L. Garvin. The Life of Joseph Chamberlain, vols. i–iii. London, 1933 and 1934.
D. R. Gwynn. The Life of John Redmond. London, 1932.
John Morley. Life of Gladstone, 3 vols. London, 1908.
Report of the Committee on National Finance. 1912.
Report of the Proceedings of the Irish Convention. Cmd. 9019.

CHAPTER IV

I. Jennings. Parliamentary Reform. London, 1935.
H. Laski. A Grammar of Politics. London, George Allen & Unwin Ltd., 1931.
R. Muir. How Britain is Governed. London, 1933.
    National Self-Government. London, 1918.
Report of the Conference on Devolution. Cmd. 692.
Lord Ullswater. A Speaker's Commentaries, 2 vols. London, 1925.

CHAPTER V

H. H. Asquith. Fifty Years of Parliament. London, 1926.
Lord Birkenhead. The Earl of Birkenhead, 2 vols. London, 1934.
W. S. Churchill. The World Crisis, 4 vols. London, 1931.
Archbishop D'Arcy. Adventures of a Bishop. London, 1935.
J. W. Good. Ulster and the Irish Question. Dublin, 1920.
D. R. Gwynn. Life of John Redmond. London, 1932.
R. M. Henry. The Evolution of Sinn Fein. Dublin, 1920.
R. McNeill. Ulster's Stand for Union. London, 1923.
E. Majoribanks and I. Colvin. Life of Lord Carson, 2 vols, 1934.
Lord Midleton. Ireland Dupe or Heroine? London, 1932.
Lord Morley. Recollections, 2 vols. London, 1917.
Sir J. O'Connor. History of Ireland, 1798–1924. London, 1926.
J. A. Spender and Cyril Asquith. Life of Lord Oxford and Asquith,
   2 vols. London, 1932.
J. A. Spender. Through Fifty Years. London, 1931.
Report of the Proceedings of the Irish Convention. Cmd. 9019.

General Authorities on the Government in Northern Ireland

(i) *Its Constitution*

   Government of Ireland Act, 1920. 10 & 11 Geo. V. ch. 7.
   Irish Free State (Consequential Provisions) Act, 1922. 13 Geo. V.
      ch. 2.
   Irish Free State (Constitution) Act, 1922. 13 Geo. V. ch. 1.
   Government of Northern Ireland (Miscellaneous Provisions) Act,
      1928. Geo. V.
   Government of Northern Ireland (Miscellaneous Provisions) Act,
      1932.

(ii) *Its Operation.*

   Acts of the Parliament of Northern Ireland.
   Bills of the Senate and of the House of Commons.
   Journals of the Senate.
   Minutes, Proceedings and Records of the Senate. Published in
      annual volumes.
   Journals of the House of Commons.
   Votes and Proceedings and Records of the House of Commons.
      Published in annual volumes.
   Debates of the Senate—Official Reports.
   Debates of the House of Commons. Official Reports.
   House of Commons Papers and Command Papers.
   Statutory Rules and Orders of Northern Ireland. Published by
      authority.
   The Ulster Year Books. Issued in 1926, 1929, 1932, and 1935.
   The Belfast Gazette.

CHAPTER VI

W. S. Churchill.   The World Crisis, The Aftermath. London, 1931.
J. L. Hammond.   Life of C. P. Scott. London, 1934.
F. Pakenham.   Peace by Ordeal. London, 1935.
Sir A. Quekett.   The Constitution of Northern Ireland, vol. i.
　　Belfast, 1928. vol. ii, 1931.
Articles of Agreement for a Treaty between Great Britain and Ireland
　　scheduled to 13 Geo. V. ch. 1.
Correspondence between the Irish Free State and Northern Ireland.
　　Cmd. 1560.
Proposals of H.M. Government for an Irish Settlement, 1921. Cmd.
　　1470.
Correspondence between H.M. Government and the Prime Minister
　　of Northern Ireland. Cmd. 1561.

CHAPTER VII

Local Government (Elections and Constitution) Act [N.I.]. 12 & 13
　　Geo. V. ch. 22.
Representation of the People Act [N.I.]. 18 & 19 Geo. V. ch. 24.
Pamphlets of the Proportional Representation Society.

CHAPTER VIII

Standing Orders of the House of Commons. H.C. 195.
Standing Orders of the Senate.
Standing Order relative to Local Bills. H.C. 198.
Northern Ireland Special Arbitration Committee, 1924. Cmd. 2072.

CHAPTER IX

A. B. Keith.   Governments of the British Empire. London, 1934.
Report of the Inter-Imperial Relations Committee. Imperial Confer-
　　ence, 1926.
Report of Select Committee on Ministerial Salaries, 1921.
Ministries of Northern Ireland Act. 12 Geo. V. ch. 6.
Salaries of Ministerial Officers [N.I.]. 12 Geo. V. ch. 9.
Rules Publication Act [N.I.]. 15 & 16 Geo. V. ch. 6.
Civil Authorities (Special Powers) Act [N.I.]. 12 & 13 Geo. V. ch. 5.
Agricultural Produce Act [N.I.]. 20 & 21 Geo. V. ch. 23.
Agricultural Marketing Act [N.I.]. 22 & 23 Geo. V. ch. 22.
Housing Act [N.I.]. 22 & 23 Geo. V. ch. 32.
National Health Insurance Act [N.I.]. 20 & 21 Geo. V. ch. 13.
Report of the Committee on a Minister's Powers. Cmd. 4060.
Report of the Machinery of Government Committee, 1918. Cmd. 9230.

CHAPTER X

Outline of Financial Provisions (Govt. of Ireland Bill), 1920. Cmd. 645.
Further Memorandum. Cmd. 707.
Appropriation Accounts. Annual, 1922.
Financial Statement of Revenue and Expenditure. Annually.
Report of the Ministry of Finance. Annually.
Finance Accounts. Annually.
Report of the Committee on Financial Relations between the State
    and Local Authorities, 1931. Cmd. 131.
National Health Insurance Fund. Annual Accounts.
Unemployment Fund. Account for 1933–34. H.C. 312.
Unemployment Insurance (Northern Ireland Agreement) Act, 1926.
    Geo. V. ch. 4.
Memorandum explaining this Act. Cmd. 2588.
Unemployment (Agreement) Act (Northern Ireland), 1936. 26 Geo. V.
    & 1 Ed. VIII. ch. 3.
Memorandum explaining this Act. Cmd. 5081.
Northern Ireland. Special Arbitration Committee—
    First Report, 1924. Cmd. 2072.
    Final Report, 1925. Cmd. 2389.
Reports of the Public Accounts Committee. 1922.

CHAPTER XI

W. S. Armour. Armour of Ballmoney. London, 1933.
J. W. Good. Ulster Unionism. Dublin, 1920.
D. Ireland. Ulster To-day and To-morrow, a pamphlet. London,
    1931.

CHAPTER XII

Annual Reports of the Ministry of Home Affairs.
Jury System—Report of Committee, 1924. Cmd. 25.
Jury Laws Amendment Act [N.I.]. 16 & 17 Geo. V. ch. 15.
Civil Authorities (Special Powers) Act [N.I.]. 12 & 13 Geo. V. ch. 5.
Report of a Commission of Enquiry appointed to Examine the
    Purpose and Effect of the Civil Authorities Acts. London,
    1936.
Emergency Powers Act [N.I.]. 16 & 17 Geo. V. ch. 6.
Education Act, 1923 [N.I.]. 13 & 14 Geo. V. ch. 21.
Local Authorities (Elections and Constitution) Act [N.I.]. 12 & 13
    Geo. V. ch. 22.
Annual Reports of the Ministry of Education. 1923.
Report of the Committee on the Financial Relations between the State
    and Local Authorities, 1932. Cmd. 131.

CHAPTERS XIII AND XIV

Annual Reports of the Ministry of Agriculture.
Agricultural Research. Annual Journal.
Agricultural Statistics. Report of the Ministry.
Report on the Marketing of Northern Ireland—
    Agricultural Produce. 1932.
Agricultural Marketing Act [N.I.], 1933. 23 & 24 Geo. V. ch. 22.
Census of Production, 1930.
Trade—Annual Statements of the Trade of the United Kingdom.
Reports of the Ministry of Education.
Unemployment Fund 1933-34. H.C. 312.

SUBJECT INDEX

NAME INDEX

Abercorn, Duke of, 155, 171 ff., n.
Anderson, Sir John, 288 n.
Andrews, J. M., 112, 186, 234, 258, 303
Archdale, Sir Edward, 112, 175, 185, 234
Armour, Rev. J. B., 95, 232
Armour, W. S., 112, 245
Asquith, H. (Earl of Oxford and Asquith), 91 f., 98 ff., 116, 197, 307 ff.

Babington, A. B. (Attorney-General), 267
Bagehot, Walter, 27, 165 ff.
Balfour, A. J., 46, 54, 57, 92
Barbour, J. M., 175, 235 ff.
Bates, Sir R. D., 112, 234
Bentham, Jeremy, 31, 39
Birrell, A., 51, 54
Bottomley, Horatio, 242
Brand, Speaker, 46
Bright, John, 44, 86
Brooke, Sir Basil, 234, 240
Burke, Edmund, 27, 31 f.

Campbell-Bannerman, Sir Henry, 57
Campbell, T. J., K.C., 158, 319
Carson, Lord, 91 ff., 98 f., 103, 115, 231 ff., 245
Cecil, Lord Hugh, 99
Chamberlain, Joseph, 44 f., 47 ff., 311
Charlemont, Lord, 158, 176, 234, 278 f.
Chesterton, G. K., 306
Chichester, Lord Deputy, 80
Churchill, Lord Randolph, 44, 47, 84 ff., 94
Churchill, W. S., 101, 115, 120

Craigavon, Lord (formerly Sir James Craig), character and policy of, 233 ff., 17, 105, 111 f., 118, 133 ff., 166, 180, 187, 245 ff., 300
Crewe, Lord, 105
Curtis, Mr. Lionel, 23 f.

D'Arcy, Dr. (Primate of all Ireland), 97
Davis, Thomas, 317
De Valera, Eamon, 117
Devlin, Joseph, 98, 134, 138, 250, 253, 318
Dickens, Charles, 33
Dillon, John, 56, 115 f.
Dixon, Captain, 166
Donnelly, E., 241
Dunraven, Lord, 54

Elliot, Walter, 167, 297 ff.
Evans, Sir L. Worthington, 126

Feetham, Justice, 120 f.
FitzAlan, Lord, 107

Garvin, J. L., 49
George, Lloyd, 90, 103, 112 117 f.
Gladstone, W. E., 42 ff., 47 ff., 83 f., 104, 230, 244, 311
Gneist, Professor R. von, 28
Godwin, W., 32
Good, J. W., 241
Goschen, Sir Edward, 46
Grattan, Henry, 80 f.
Green, T. H., 40
Gregg, Dr. (Archbishop of Dublin), 261
Griffith, Arthur, 56

Halèvy, E., 30 ff., 40
Hammond, J. L., 114
Harcourt, Sir William, 51

For Product Safety Concerns and Information please contact our EU
representative GPSR@taylorandfrancis.com
Taylor & Francis Verlag GmbH, Kaufingerstraße 24, 80331 München, Germany

www.ingramcontent.com/pod-product-compliance
Lightning Source LLC
Chambersburg PA
CBHW070552270326
41926CB00013B/2292